For the Missouri Center for the
Book Collection, on the
Collection's inaugural

September 1993   Tom Weil

LAST AT THE FAIR

LAST AT THE FAIR

A Book of Travel

Tom Weil

HIPPOCRENE BOOKS
New York 1986

Elsewhere is a negative mirror. The traveler recognizes the little that is his, discovering the much he has not had and will never have.

—Italo Calvino

This book is for Edith, who has roamed with me,
and is also dedicated
To the memory of my father, Paul Kalter Weil, who
believed travel was an education, and
To professional travelers everywhere

My thanks to George Blagowidow of Hippocrene Books
for his help and encouragement and, as before,
to Ruby and Mike Stern
for their continuing interest.

For information, address: Hippocrene Books, Inc.
171 Madison Avenue, New York, NY 10016.

ISBN 0-87052-242-6

Printed in the United States of America.

Contents

1
Introduction

THERE COMES A TIME IN THE WORLD OF TRAVEL AND adventure when everything has been seen and said and done. After that, discovery gives way to tourism and repetition succeeds novelty. No age wants to believe that such a time has arrived, but it's possible we've now reached the point when virtually nothing new remains to be discovered and nothing original remains to be said about familiar places and sights.

Already nearly a century ago Lewis Carroll worried in *Sylvie and Bruno Concluded*, a work less known than *Alice in Wonderland* but one hardly less charming or fantastic, about the "the necessary exhaustion of all subjects of human interest." Carroll recognized that "the day must come—if the world lasts long enough—when every possible tune will have been composed—every possible pun perpetrated—and, worse than that, every possible book written!" If, in fact, today is that day, this then, is the last possible book—finished, fortunately (for me, if not for the reader) just in time.

Two generations before Lewis Carroll, even the great Goethe lamented in a conversation with Eckermann in 1828 that "the world is now so old, and so many eminent

9

men have lived and thought for thousands of years, that there is very little to find and say that is new. Even my theory of colors," he added remorsefully, "is not entirely new."

An Italian saying suggests that what's new is not true and that which is true is not new. That aphorism is certainly not new. Is it true? Perhaps so, as applied to the world of travel. Gone are the days when great blank spaces stretched temptingly across large portions of maps—empty areas waiting for intrepid adventurers to fill in the details. Imagine the excitement and challenge facing Richard Burton, the great nineteenth-century English explorer and Orientalist, when, in the autumn of 1852, he offered his services to the Royal Geographical Society of London "for the purpose of removing that opprobrium to modern adventure, the huge white blot which in our maps still notes the Eastern and Central regions of Arabia." Sir James Hogg, the society's chairman, duly commissioned Burton to learn Arabic, and by the next year the explorer had reached Mecca and Medina. New information he supplied soon inked in part of the "huge white blot."

Even later—as late as our century—some maps continued to intrigue travelers with the blank spaces of the unknown, emptinesses which seemed especially mysterious when juxtaposed with the exquisite detail of well-surveyed areas. A. C. Jewett, an American engineer in charge of a project to install a hydroelectric plant for Kabul, capital of Afghanistan, wrote on May 31, 1911, in regard to his passage through the Khyber Pass that "when one goes to Afghanistan he is generally spoken of as having 'gone off the map.'" What a striking destination that—"off the map." It reeks with mystery and possibility: it seems medieval, or perhaps even pre-biblical, in its sense of the unknown, its suggestion of *terra incognita*.

It wasn't only in the obscure regions of the East, or other remote places, where unmapped lands remained to be explored and explained. As recently as the mid-nineteenth century in the United States the territory of Nevada appeared on maps of the time as the "Great American Desert" or the "Unexplored Region." But in less than a quarter of a century, shortly before *Roughing It* appeared in 1872, Mark Twain was already worried that its subject matter, the West, was too "hackneyed." How fast the "Unexplored Region" must have been explored and exploited: yet another space on the map filled in, the land tamed and settled, the inhabitants and folklore written about to the point of being "hackneyed." Perhaps Twain's work was the "last possible book" about the West—or so he feared a century ago.

Unexplored regions these days lie beyond the reach of most men. Such provinces are either microscopic or subatomic, or they are celestial. The scope for discovery has now, on the one hand, been narrowed to the confines of narrow tubes of magnification: arcane scientific progress takes place in a miniworld observed through a microscope, or even in areas unseen and only imagined and theorized into existence. Or, on the other hand, such progress occurs in the remote heavenly regions espied through the telescope or by a lens lofted in a spacecraft. Few, if any, birds or insects, flowers, or places remain to be named by or after their discoverers. Now, if a man is lucky, a chunk of dead ore rattling around the firmament may bear his name. I suppose it's not beyond the realm of possibility—or the realm within our powers of observation—that somewhere out in the far reaches a heavenly body, or a celestial tribe, will one day be discovered that will prompt some earth-bound mortal to muse original thoughts and to offer new perspectives on the find in a way similar to how Montaigne, at the end of the sixteenth century, wrote his essay "On Cannibals" after encountering a man from recently discovered Brazil. But it's more likely that no such discovery will occur. Nor, perhaps, will any other more mundane findings surface: we may well have reached the end of the age of discoveries of the type which can be accomplished or understood by men unaided by microscope or telescope, by computer or spacecraft, not to mention by foundation grant or government funding.

It is not only science which has pre-empted the search for new frontiers. Technology, science's offspring, has also diminished the power of individuals to search out and discover for themselves new places, original ideas, previously unseen perspectives. One example—hardly an original idea—is the effect the modern airplane has had on travelers' perceptions. Travel by jet eliminates the texture of space and distance. So easily are they conquered, one often fails to appreciate the remoteness and strangeness of far, isolated places that, once upon a time, were visited only by the most hardy adventurers. Those days, a man gave a good part of his life, and often even his life itself, to reach a distant land; these days, we simply give our American Express card—a plastic juju—and within hours we land at our destination, be it Kent or Tashkent, Ouagadougou or Brazil. The latter was so remote and exotic to Montaigne that it occasioned noteworthy reflections—"The discovery of so vast a country seems to me worth reflecting on," he wrote—but is so accessible to us that the only reflections it occasions are in the lens of a camara as we click our way through the country, pressing on to our next stop.

This isn't to say that the supreme accessibility afforded by air travel is somehow tainted because it's so easy. But that sort of facile mobility is new and different, and it can't help but color—or, more accurately, dull—our perceptions, so effortless and so voluminous do they become, thanks to the seemingly ubiquitous jet. Flight attendants based in Kansas City will tell you how they fly off to Athens for a weekend. If the Parthenon is that easy to reach, and the decision to travel to it that casual, is not the experience somehow devalued? One element which lacks is that great delectation of travel—anticipation. So short is the lead time and so minimal the effort and preparation that the delicious preliminaries—that foretaste of coming hard-won experiences which earlier overland or seafaring travelers had time to savor—are missing. Then, too, easy access proliferates experiences too quickly to be artfully absorbed. This weekend Athens, next weekend Rome, and in another week or two Cairo— and soon all the great stone piles, the Parthenon, the Colisseum, the Pyramids, are lumped together in the mind until, finally, the peripatetic traveler requires an ever more striking or novel sight in order for his imagination to be stimulated.

Of course, it's not only personal, experienced impressions which multiply so rapidly these days. We're also bombarded with printed impressions. There is some sort of perverse symmetry in the fact that, as science has managed to develop the means to control human reproduction, technology has at the same time created ever more effective ways to improve mechanical reproduction. While the number of people is being limited, the quantity of images to which people are exposed is virtually unlimited. That proliferation of paper has no doubt contributed to the devaluation of individual perception.

Even more than the plane, the press has changed the way we see. In fact, the output of the press has been so bountiful that, in a way, it's caused us to stop seeing, so numerous are the repeated images which spin before our eyes. Overexposure diminishes the freshness and spontaneity of the exotic—or what used to be exotic. Alan Moorehead, in *The Blue Nile,* noted how "a certain staleness overtakes great monuments that have been too much excavated and restored and then photographed, painted and walked over by millions of tourist feet." Time was, of course, back before the time- and space-defying feats of the jet and the press, when images of the original were rare. "In our time," Moorehead writes, "a thousand travelers' books and spate of illustrated magazines and moving pictures have made a cliché of the East, but in 1798 nothing in Egypt was familiar to the Europeans. Travelers marveled at everything they saw."

Never again will Egypt be so fresh as that country was during the early nineteenth century, its age of discovery by Europe. When François Jomard published, between 1809 and 1813, the twenty-four volumes of his *Description de l'Égypte*, which contained a number of engravings, many in color, people read about and saw reproductions of an ancient civilization quite new to Europe. But by now, how old that civilization has become to us. "In this age of the rotary press," C. W. Ceram wrote in *Gods, Graves and Scholars*, "it is not easy to appreciate the significance of Jomard's choice and comprehensive compilation." Ceram goes on:

> Today, when every scientific discovery of importance is almost immediately disseminated all over the globe, multiplied a millionfold by its being chronicled in pictures, film, word, and sound, the excitement of great discoveries has been very much diluted. One publication follows on the heels of the next, always competing for attention, contributing to a process whereby everybody knows a little about something but nothing in particular.

With its awesome powers of reproduction, the press copies originals to the point where they are attentuated by their images.

Thanks to the picture, the cliché—the word means "photo" in French—has to a large extent been substituted for the original. The photograph affords a vicarious way of seeing, a way that, after a time—after a certain number of images seen—dilutes the direct perception that once comprised the principal means of observation. Of course, a preview—one in the literal sense: a pre-view—can enhance a subsequent view of the sight seen *in situ*. In *Tom Sawyer Abroad*—the story of Tom's and Huck Finn's balloon trip to Africa—Huck's first view of the Pyramids from the air excites him into commenting: "It made my heart fairly jumpy. You see, I had seen a many and a many picture of them," and now, he went on, he was awed to discover that "they was *real*, 'stead of imaginations." Arnold Toynbee expressed in more elegant Oxford English a thought similar to the one young Huck voiced in his Pike County dialect: "It is always an extraordinary sensation," wrote Toynbee of his visit to Bamian in the Afghanistan mountains, "to see, in the life, some famous building or landscape with which one has long been familiar from photographs, maps and plans."

There is, I think, something especially enchanting about reaching a far destination whose image you have long carried in your imagination. Like Huck, your reaction is, so that's how it really looks. William Rothenstein, the early twentieth-century English art figure, spoke in his memoirs *Men and Memories* of visiting the Tuscan landscape he'd so often seen depicted in paintings. Sight of the source afforded him "the satisfaction of mere *recognition*; to see with our own eyes that which we have seen depicted, or of which we have read, is an unfailing pleasure."

On occasion, a printed or painted image can even serve to stimulate the reader or observer to seek out the scene depicted. Perhaps such an activist response was more common in bygone days before reproduced images flooded people's perceptions. Back in 1877, E. G. Squier, an American journalist and sometime archeologist (he became famous for his work on the Mississippi Valley Indian mounds), published *Peru, Land of the Incas,* which contained a dramatic woodcut of the so-called Bridge of San Luis Rey, a fourteenth-century suspension bridge made of maguey plant fibre ropes and cables, which spanned the Apurimac River on the Inca Royal Road between Cuzco and Lima. The woodcut came to the attention of Hiram Bingham, a young Yale history professor, who later stated that the illustration "was one of the reasons why I decided to go to Peru." It was a fateful encounter—that between Bingham and the bridge picture—for during his trip to Peru Bingham discovered, in

1911, the long-lost Inca ruins of Machu Picchu. (The picture also impelled Prosper Mérimée, the French writer, to use the bridge in a story set in Peru, and that, in turn, inspired Thornton Wilder's novel, *The Bridge of San Luis Rey.*)

But these days the reproductive powers of the press are so fecund, one's imagination is more likely to be dulled rather than stimulated by the sight of yet another picture of some remote scene. It would be overstating the case to say of press-created images what Jorge Luis Borges, the Argentine fabulist and poet, said about mirrors and copulation—that they "are abominable, because they increase the number of men." But surely there is a point beyond which the benefits of a preview's familiarization or the satisfaction of recognizing a scene previously seen on the printed page are outweighed by the surfeit of images which not only prepare us but also precondition us and even, to a certain extent, pre-empt the reality. After you have seen a certain number of bare-breasted native women in the richly hued pages of *National Geographic* or in the Sunday magazine supplements or on the lastest television special, then a glimpse of a real-life nipple during an African excursion may hardly elicit a response. The actual sight doesn't create a new reality; it simply confirms a pre-existing conception, planted in our mind by the pictures we've already seen.

In addition to the jet plane and the rotary press, television—a kind of "insta-press" that imprints, rather than prints, before your very eyes—is the third and last technological development which has served to alter our way of looking at and experiencing events and places. Television distances you even farther from the original than does the fixed image or the written word. Unlike the printed page or still photo—which can be touched, examined, reviewed, referred to, studied—the screen picture flickers away to leave only a residue of an image, if that. Even at a place like Disneyland—the kingdom of vicarious experiences—you can "climb the Matterhorn" or "raft down an animal-infested jungle river" or "submerge into the dangerous depths in a submarine." Television, however, offers only one tactile experience—pushing the off/on button. For the rest, you're pelted with a series of ghostly images—phantoms as insubstantial as a very vaguely remembered dream.

The jet, the page, and the screen not only offer us too much—in the form of a speed that banishes space, and of a multiplicity of images—but also give us too little, for they fail to furnish one important dimension—the element of time. Omitted from the modern ways of experiencing, visiting, seeing is any connection with the past: history has been banished. The accumulation of days and months and events which form the context—an almost tangible texture—in which places and cultures exist has been diminished by the techniques resulting from innovation and progress. It is ever rarer these days to experience that "feeling of tense excitement occasioned by the realisation that this ship was carrying me back across ten centuries." So felt Cecil Stewart (as he wrote in *Byzantine Legacy*) in December 1936 on a boat taking him from Salonika to Mt. Athos, the remote, isolated thousand-year-old monastic community nestling on the tip of a peninsula in northern Greece.

After leaving Mt. Athos, Stewart quickly regained those ten centuries, for when he returned to civilization he caught up with the current events that had occurred during his trip in time: Edward VIII had abdicated, the Crystal Palace in London had burned, and Basil Zaharoff, the international arms "merchant of death," had died. To this day, Athos remains one of those rare jet- and press-free places: the only way to reach the religious settlement is by sea, and once there you find virtually no copies of current periodicals. The monks live out of time and out of touch with the news of the day. When Stewart visited Athos in 1936, even the camera was something new: "The camera on Athos," he wrote, "is still a comparative novelty and a source of considerable interest to the younger monks who, cut off from the outside world, insist on being photographed, and with surprising vanity take infinite pains to look their best."

Travel by definition involves transcending space, but how much richer the journey becomes when you can also introduce the historical dimension. In *Discourse on Method*, Descartes said, "To live with men of an earlier age is like traveling in foreign lands." Conversely, traveling in ancient foreign countries can—if you are aware of the historical background—be like visiting the past at the same time you are present at the past's remnants. With all the emphasis today on the visual—television, movies, photographs, slick reproductions—the invisible is largely ignored, but that which is not seen often adds to a place the depth of an additional dimension—time. Jonathan Russell wrote in his *Letters from a Young Painter Abroad to His Friends in England*, published in London in 1750, that he'd observed sightseers who

> ... stand upon the same spot of ground for a good while, as it were in deep contemplation, where there was no appearance of anything very remarkable or uncommon. Tho' such a one might be thought *non-compos*, he might probably, from his knowledge in history, be then calling to mind some brave action, performed upon that very spot.

Failing a knowledge of history, the traveler is imprisoned in a kind of "now-ism." This affords only a superficial perception of the place being visited: lacking is the resonance of time's echo.

Perhaps it's inevitable that the modern means of information dissemination, and the concomitant new modes of perception, have made it increasingly difficult to transcend the immediate and, as did Cecil Stewart at Mt. Athos, to experience the sensation of visiting another era.

One remote corner of the world where that sort of

experience is possible, however, is the tiny village of Maloula, tucked away in a valley where small houses cluster by and on a steep cliff of the Anti-Lebanon range some thirty-five miles north of Damascus. Like Mt. Athos, the village is a relic: it is virtually the last place in the world where Aramaic, the language used in biblical times—by Christ, by his disciples, and by most of the people of the Middle East—is still spoken as an everyday language. (Maloula, which has four thousand inhabitants, also boasts the Mar-Sarkis monastery church, claimed to be the oldest Christian church in the world.)

The villagers at Maloula are perhaps by now accustomed to visitors asking them to speak Aramaic. I induced a cheerful old man wearing a bedouin-style headdress to say a few words to me. The language sounds guttural and throaty, similar to Hebrew in the same sort of way that Dutch is to German. Possibly the dialect that Aramaic most resembles is Swiss German, a memorable concatenation of sounds in its own right. When John Louis Burckhardt, the nineteenth-century Swiss adventurer and explorer whose career is discussed in the chapter on Petra, spoke Arabic, which he learned for use on his Middle Eastern travels, people in the area occasionally questioned him about his curious accent. Burckhardt would reply that his mother tongue was Hindustani, and if his inquisitor pressed him for a sample of that language he'd speak Swiss German, the growls of which would forstall further inquiries. Charles Darwin wrote that the language of the Fuegians of Good Success Bay on Tierra del Fuego "scarcely deserves to be called articulate. Captain Cook has compared it to a man clearing his throat; but certainly no European ever cleared his throat with so many hoarse, guttural and clicking sounds." Well, Darwin must never have visited Switzerland. "Schweizer-deutsch" is perhaps the only set of meaningful human sounds that are more guttural and throaty than Aramaic. But what you're hearing when you listen to Aramaic is more than just a virtually obsolete series of rough sounds: it is a language which has probably been spoken longer than any other tongue on earth.

The Aramaeans consisted of barberic tribes of bedouins who, about 1030 B.C., attacked Israel and were defeated by King David. During the next few hundred years, other cultures gradually absorbed the Aramaeans, but their language remained a living force. One reason the language survived was because of its convenient written form. Instead of cumbersome cuneiform writing, it employed in a modified version the simpler and more practical Phoenician alphabet. Another reason was its adoption by the dominant culture that existed about 500 B.C. when the Achaemenian rulers (centered in what today is Iran) chose Aramaic as the *lingua franca* of their far-flung empire, so the language became the official vernacular of the Persian Empire, and people from Egypt to India spoke it. By the end of the pre-Christian era, Sumerian and Hebrew were dead languages—Josephus' *Concerning the Jewish War*, for example, was written not in Hebrew but in Aramaic, as were the Babylonian and Jerusalem Talmuds. Aramaic had become the common tongue of all peoples of the Middle East, so remaining for nearly a millenium until Syria fell to the Arabs in A. D. 635.

Jesus spoke Galilean Aramaic, a dialect. The name "Jesus" is the Greek form of the Aramaic word "Jeshua," a form which appears in Ezra 3:2 and 4:3. The word "Christ" is Greek for the Aramaic "Meshiah"—"anointed"—from which derives the English word "messiah." A few transliterated Aramaic phrases appear in the Gospel of Mark—the only place in the Bible where one can pronounce the same sounds spoken by Jesus. Among these phrases is that in Mark 15:34: "Eloi, Eloi, lama sabachthani? which is, being interpreted, My God, my God, why hast thou forsaken me?"

After the rise of the Arabs in the seventh century, Arabic replaced Aramaic, which survived only among Christians who escaped from the Mohammedans and secluded themselves in isolated settlements such as Maloula, where thirty-two hundred Christians now co-exist with eight hundred Muslims. For some fourteen hundred years Aramaic has been handed down through the generations. Perhaps soon its final living syllables will be uttered: Aramaic will have its last word. Arabic has been encroaching on the village—it is the language used in the schools—and a mosque has been built in Maloula, next to the police station so the Christians won't vandalize the Mohammedan house of worship.

It is curious—and is it not poignant?—to realize that what was once the dominant language for much of the then civilized world has now almost disappeared. The written form of Aramaic has, in fact, long been extinct: for years it has been a language of the tongue but not of the pen. Aramaic, then—that biblical-era language now anachronistic in this secular age, that tenuous link to the remote yet vivid and well-documented past—is one of the few phenomena in the world of travel that defies the modern techniques of reproduction. You can't screen the archaic Aramaic or photograph it and, now analphabetic, the language can't be set onto the printed page. Yes, I realize you can tape it, but that would be a mere plastic or electronic copy of the tongue's living reality—too far removed from context, I think, to afford even the suggestion of the sensation of experiencing the original. Unlike many other aspects of the modern age, Aramaic can't be experienced very satisfactorily in a vicarious way—to hear the language of the ancients spoken as the living remnant which it remains, you have to undertake the long journey to Maloula, for only there do the long echoes from the distant past come alive.

I mention Aramaic because the language exemplifies, I think, the added dimensions of actuality and of time which modern techniques of reproduction omit. Unlike the insubstantial derivative images of television, Aramaic, I suggest, exists both in the density of reality, a reality which can't be pictured, and in history, two elements which our times sometimes slight. Add the dimension of history and travel is enriched. In fact, are not the two—the past and the exotic—different aspects of a similar experience? Thomas Babington Macauley went so far as to claim that awareness of the past and travel abroad were virtually the same. In his essay "History," which appeared in 1828 in the *Edinburg Review,* he wrote: "The effect of historical reading is analagous, in many respects, to that produced by foreign travel. The student, like the tourist, is transported into a new state of society. He sees new fashions. He hears new modes of expression. His mind is enlarged by contemplating the wide diversities of laws, of morals, and of manners." Macauley goes on to caution, however, that the traveler "must not confine his observations . . . . He must see," failing which "men may travel far, and return with minds as contracted as if they had never stirred from their own market-town."

A sense of history combined with a sensibility—knowing and seeing—are, then, the two elements required for a full appreciation of travel to exotic places. The interweaving of what is seen with what has been creates a rich texture of experience. *Last at the Fair,* is, hopefully, not simply a book of travel but also a book about seeing— seeing rather than just looking—and about placing what's seen into a context that transcends the object or the experience itself. It is a plea to remember that everything has its place in time as well as in space.

Writing in 1923, Joseph Conrad lamented the passing of travel writers such as Marco Polo—"his meticulous descriptive gift, his cautious credulity, his eye for splendor and his historian's rather than a traveler's temperment." That sort of tradition—one which pays tribute as much to the history and background of places as to the immediacy of their appeal—is now old-fashioned, but perhaps it is one to which a book of travel can still aspire.

But aspiration doesn't necessarily comprehend inspiration. And at this point in time, there is the nagging question—what still remains to be said? After all the television specials and *National Geographic* spreads, not to mention the accounts of travelers through the ages, what new observations can a latter-day traveler offer? One is faced with the difficulty of seeing or saying anything novel. After all, if Goethe could complain a century and a half ago "that there is very little to find and say that is new," then far lesser mortals, writing after the accretions of the intervening one hundred and fifty years, are confronted with even greater difficulties in finding fresh perspectives and ideas. Perhaps the only justification for such an effort is to rummage about a bit in the past and, in the present, to try to cast a fresh eye on the travel scene in an attempt to discern a few leavings that previous observers have somehow not seen fit to highlight.

Even the great Leonardo, in his *Notebooks*, wrote about himself nearly five hundred years ago:

> Seeing that I cannot find any subject of great utility or pleasure, because the men who have come before me have taken for their own all useful and necessary themes, I will do like one who, because of his poverty, is the last to arrive at the fair, and not being able otherwise to provide for himself, takes all the things which others have already seen and not taken but refused as being of little value.*

For a man who "discovered everything," as Eugene Delacroix, the French nineteenth-century painter, not inaccurately described Leonardo, that is a strangely self-deprecating statement. If, five centuries ago, the archetypical Renaissance man felt he was "last at the fair," then are not all of us who come after him very late indeed? Or can we believe, as did Walt Whitman, that "the powerful play goes on, and you may contribute a verse"?

Selections from the Notebooks of Leonardo da Vinci, edited with commentaries by Irma A. Richter (London: Oxford University Press, 1966).

—2—

Via the printed page or the photographic image, the armchair traveler vicariously visits nearly every place in the world. Even back in 1908—long before the advent of the speed and fertility of the most modern reproduction techniques—Winston Churchill noted in *My African Journey:* "So much has been written, so many facts are upon record about every country, even the most remote, that a judicious and persevering study of existing materials would no doubt enable a reader to fill himself with knowledge almost to repletion without leaving his chair."

But with it all—articles, photographs, planes moving speedily from place to place, moving pictures flashed on large or small screens—the traveler who's chair-bound rather than destination bound, and receptive rather than perceptive, misses those extra dimensions available only by being there and seeing—wherever the "there" might be. Those dimensions, which modern methods have to an extent robbed us of, are a sense of space and, hopefully, a feel for time. Churchill continues: "But for the formation of opinion, for the stirring and enlivenment of thought, and for the discernment of colour and proportion, the gifts of travel, especially of travel on foot, are priceless."

We travel, then—or, ideally, should do so—to discern color and proportion: color in many of its senses—local color, contrast, tone, hues, shadows—and proportion in at least two of its meanings—dimensions in place in space and the relationship of the object or site to history. But, alas, seldom does the pressed traveler in fact see the range of colors and proportions that are present. What are the barriers to such perceptions? One, discussed in the previous section, is the dulling of the senses by the flow of images that reaches us before we ever reach the real object or locale. These reproductions—preproductions, they might be called, for they precede our live view—tend to take the edge off the sharpness of our eye, thereby diminishing our ability to see with a fresh perspective what lies before us. Furthermore, the speed and compression of visits, thanks to the jet, make the series of destinations attained less distinct. Haste levels what might be intaglio experiences, cut in sharp relief into our memories, to ones that lack dimension and become flattened.

But apart from those modern barriers to depth perception, there exist other intrinsic and perennial obstacles that tend to prevent travelers who look from really seeing. For one thing, our vision is often too narrowly focused by the lenses of nationality and personal background through which we view the world. What might strike us as strange is to others normal. It was a fact unremarked and unremarkable in India, for example, that the diet of one of that nation's modern prime ministers (Morarji Desai, who held office in the late 1970s) consisted only of raw mashed vegetables washed down with his own urine. To the Western mind, this is somehow odd. But then to non-Americans our national habit of guzzling the colored sugar water of colas perhaps seems bizarre. What if it became known that the president of the United States drank his urine? Would that be a new genre of Washington scandal? Possibly to Indians it's curious that the American president doesn't drink his urine.

Cultural background, that matrix of customs and understandings that comforts and guides us so effectively when we remain home-based, blinds us to the richness of the outside world that's not ours. "We all call barbarous anything that is contrary to our own habits," wrote Montaigne in his Brazil-inspired essay, "On Cannibals." He went on: "Indeed we seem to have no other criterion of truth and reason than the type and kind of opinions and customs current in the land where we live."

Why do we cling so tightly to practices which elsewhere are unknown—conventions which attain ends that in other places are accomplished by different and often even better means? So many of any particular culture's usages are arbitrary. In the Greek monastic community of Mt. Athos, Iviron monastery uses the old Georgian system of time which sets 12 o'clock as the hour of sunrise; Vatopedi employs the time system of the outside world; all the other monasteries follow the Byzantine method, which makes sunset 12 o'clock. Among those other monasteries is Dionysious, whose courtyard tower clock face bears Turkish rather than "Western" (Arabic) numbers. But all these systems accomplish the purpose of measuring time: our sun-high-in-the-sky-high-noon is not the only way to look at time. But, then, why look at time at all? The most provocative clock I have seen anywhere is the one over the door of Rangoon Museum: the timepiece lacks hands.

Cultural provincialism becomes most apparent when exchanges and changes occur. In the tenth century Maria Argyra, cousin of the Byzantine princess who married the German Emperor Otto II, shocked the Italians by introducing the use of forks to Venice. Two centuries later the direction of influence was reversed when, in the twelfth century, the Venetians puzzled and vexea the Byzantines by introducing to the Christian East the bell tower, erecting in Constantinople a campanile as a gift to the Byzantine Empire. This became a new way to call the faithful to services. Up to then, the "semanton," a wooden board beaten with a stick—the method used to this day in many Mt. Athos monasteries—summoned the devout to prayer.

Nationality raises a barrier to internationality. To each country or culture the people of other lands represent an aberration from the norm. When visiting Tahiti in September 1773 on his second voyage, Captain Cook recorded in his journal that the Tahitians called veneral disease "apa no Pretane"—the English disease. More recently it's become commonplace for Europeans to taunt Americans for, among other quirks, being overly wary of foreign plumbing: "Can you drink the water?" "The toilets don't flush." Europeans, of course, deride each other for a variety of supposed eccentricities.

Churchill, in *My African Journey*, mocks the legendary pedantic German research professor: "It is a pity that Herr

Diogenes Teufelsdröckh, of the University of Weissnichtwo, did not meet them [a tribe that wears no clothes] in his rugged wanderings, for they would surely have enabled him to add another page to his monumental work on the functions of the tailor." Lord Chesterfield, writing to his son in Italy, cautioned the boy that "you will meet swarms of Germans wherever you go." But it was Eugene Delacroix, however, who expressed what is probably the ultimate chauvinistic comment when he observed in his *Journal* that Germans "make the mistake of not being Frenchmen." French travelers, in turn, make their own mistakes: they see everything in reference to their homeland. Sacheverell Sitwell, the great English travel writer, commented tartly about "Frenchmen, who infer a compliment when something abroad recalls a scene in France." Sitwell cites as an example El Deir, a large churchlike structure hewn from the rock at Petra, the Nabatean city in southern Jordan, a construction which, Sitwell says, often reminds Frenchmen of Saint-Sulpice church in Paris.

So spins the kaleidoscope of national perceptions. If the traveler can somehow transcend his background and, for a time at least, stop viewing foreigners or foreign scenes through the narrow scope of nationality, then he will see more—more than simply a German as a non-Frenchman or Saint-Sulpice in every largish classical church. After all, the derivation of the Old French word "foreign" comes from a word that means simply out of doors, abroad, at large. The original term doesn't imply difference or strangeness or, for that matter, inferiority. Admittedly, contemporary French is harsher and more judgmental: "foreigner" (étranger) is a verson of "strange" (étrange). But not only is the old form more gracious, it's also more accurate—at least when travel is performed to its best advantage. Insofar as possible, we should be innocents abroad—innocent of all the preconceptions and free of the "preproductions" that have preceded our trip. Mark Twain, in *Following the Equator*, offered what I think is a well-nigh perfect definition of the ideal tourist: the "unbiased traveler seeking information."

A purist would no doubt add one further condition for clear seeing—namely, that a traveler who really wants to see should roam alone, free of a traveling companion who might distract him. But that may be going too far. To ask that one should travel solo in order to concentrate his entire attention on the journey, rather than diluting it on a partner, smacks of barrenness. But it must be admitted that in some ways the solitary traveler is at an advantage. Alone, one is thrown completely into the travel experience. Undistracted by the need to exchange impressions with someone else, the visit itself becomes more intense.

Proust suggested that "the need to speak prevents one not merely from listening but from seeing things." Articulating in a conversational way to a bystander thoughts on what you observe might sharpen your perception but it can also detract from the act of observation: the ensuing dialogue replaces the previous concentration. But (perhaps paradoxically) summarizing to yourself—in the form of a thoughtful review of what you've viewed or, better, by means of a travel diary—forces you carefully to observe what you're seeing, which sharpens your impressions. Knowledge that in the evening you'll be recording your day's experiences heightens your sensitivity to your experiences. For the pure traveler, one possessed by the compulsion to visit and to see as much as possible, the journal—mute but always awaiting your words—is perhaps the best companion.

Costals, the novelist in Henry de Montherlant's *The Girls*, once considered taking a trip with one of his mistresses, but then he decided to travel alone, realizing that of all the interesting places he'd seen twice—once alone and once with someone he loved—"it was always the time he had traveled alone that came to his mind most vividly." Vincent Nolte, a nineteenth-century international business adventurer, tells in his reminiscences *Fifty Years in Both Hemispheres* of a remarkable lone traveler, an

English naval lieutenant named James Holman. Speaking only English, Holman wandered the world alone for twenty-seven years—a most challenging activity, for Holman was blind.

Solitude on the road is not on all counts the most desirable state, but aloneness does breed awareness. Like a forming crystal left undisturbed to complete itself, unarticulated observations somehow seem to be nurtured and enriched by remaining unspoken while you muse upon them, until finally they're perceived sharp and clear in the mind's eye.

So it is that, if the traveler somehow manages to transcend the confines of his own culture and national perceptions, if he can dismiss the pre-trip images, gleaned from the printed page or the flickering screen, that tend to inhabit and inhibit his imagination, and—a last factor, though one not as telling as the others—if he is willing to experience his travel adventures alone, he can, hopefully, not only visit but also experience, not simply look but also see.

To see is a great challenge. At best we see only a small fraction of what passes before our eyes, whether traveling or otherwise. The world's richness is overwhelming. The sensory stimuli that bombard us, the ceaseless flow of impressions and ideas, are so numerous that it's all we can do to isolate from the unending flow a few specifics on which to concentrate. Bergson's theory of the brain—a most appealing theory but one which somehow has been little noted or discussed—suggests that the tremendous flow of outside impressions is not so much gathered by the brain as it is reduced by it to manageable proportions. The brain, he claims, is less a collector than a transformer. The brain's function is not to originate consciousness; rather, it channels consciousness by reducing the overwhelming magnitude of the life flow to a lower number of impressions, a quantity with which we're able to cope. Without that reductive device locked in our skulls, sensory data would swamp our being and prevent us from sorting out in a reasonably orderly way the individual sensations that enable us to cogitate, to react, to function. The creative impulse, it might be noted, releases a similar sort of flow but in an opposite direction. People who feel the need to create have within them an excess of raw material—impressions that cry to become expressions. In time, those inchoate impulses burst the confines of the brain and litter the world without with books, paintings, sculpture, and other debris of the creative mind. From where and why this storehouse originates, I do not pretend to know.

Jorge Luis Borges has sketched a character whose brain somehow fails to perform the reductive function described by Bergson. Thrown by a horse and left paralyzed, Ireneo Funes—"the Memorious," so Borges calls him—lives for nineteen years as if in a dream: "he looked without seeing." Finally returning to life, Funes found it "intolerable in its richness"—an overwhelming richness. He sees and remembers everything, literally everything, including, for example, the shape of southern clouds at dawn on April 30, 1882, a pattern he compares with the mottled binding of a book he'd seen only once. By way of contrast, Hamlet points out a cloud formation to Polonius and suggests it looks like a camel, then a weasel, then a whale. The difference between Hamlet and Funes is the difference—at times fine—between the artist and the madman. As with Funes, uncontrolled perception is insanity, as it was with Balzac's Louis Lambert, who "had every form of memory—for places, for names, for words, things and faces. He not only recalled any object at will, but he saw them in his mind, situated, lighted and colored as he had originally seen them." Perhaps insanity—one form, at least—is but a failure of the brain to reduce the flood of impressions to manageable proportions.

Those of us not cursed with Funes' or Lambert's incredible collecting machine, which takes in all of the intolerable richness of the world, can no doubt sharpen our ability to see by practice. One sort of exercise in seeing might, for example, involve close observation of a specific field of random, even meaningless, patterns, such as, say, a wall. Even that kind of humble, nondescript patch of matter can illustrate what lies before us for the seeing. In the section of his *Notebooks* on "The Artist's Course of Study," da Vinci refers to the advantages to the painter of a close observation of walls—"a new device for study," he calls the technique. "When you look at a wall spotted with stains or with a mixture of stones. . . ," he writes, "you will be able to see in it a resemblance to various landscapes adorned with mountains, rivers, rocks, trees, plains, wide valleys and various groups of hills; or again you may see battles and figures in action; or strange faces and costumes." Leonardo gives the same advice—"look at walls"—in the passage on "How to increase your talent and stimulate various inventions." And in another section of the *Notebooks* he refers to Botticelli, who claimed that "by merely throwing a sponge soaked with different colours at a wall a stain is formed wherein a lovely landscape might be discerned."*

The wall reveals to us not only that which it holds but also what we ourselves contain. In *Philosopher or Dog,* a charmingly sardonic novel, the great Brazilian writer Machado de Assis links the seen with the seer: "He who knows the soil and subsoil of life knows well that a fragment of a wall. . . [is] rich in thoughts or feelings when we, ourselves, are, and the association of inanimate objects with men and their reflection of them is one of the most interesting of terrestial phenomena." Because what we bring to the act of seeing affects what we're able to see, it's useful to clear the mind of those preconceptions and "preproductions" discussed earlier, to keep in mind historical connotations, and to maintain an open mind receptive to the new.

The play of the imagination over an evocative wall can read into the surface a meaning richer and deeper than a

---

*Richter, ed., *Selections from the Notebooks of Leonardo da Vinci.*

passing glance might reveal. Refined sight coupled with acute insight enables the viewer to transcend the surface—the superficial. From the inner wall of a partly demolished house, Rilke, in *The Notebooks of Malte Laurids Brigge*, reconstructs an entire domestic scene. On this surface, now naked to casual passersby on the street, he sees the old wallpaper with its blisters and ripped shreds, the wormlike rusty toilet pipe that runs along the base of the wall, the faded paint, the cleared rectangles where mirrors and pictures once hung, the dust and spider webs; and from all of these patterns that he so acutely notes, Rilke (or Brigge: they are one and the same) envisions "the stubborn life of these rooms [that] had not let itself be trampled out." He speaks of the sicknesses that transpired there, the sweat of armpits that perspired there; he smells the tang of urine, smouldering soot, potatoes cooking, and grease mouldering. For Rilke, even an empty wall brimmed with meaning.

Those of us with artistic or poetic imaginations less fine than Leonardo's or Rilke's can't emulate them, but we can, in our own small way, try to imitate them. Even if we are unable to discern in a fairly bare wall everything those sharp eyes and keen minds could perceive, perhaps other views richer and more evocative than mere blank surfaces—paintings, landscapes, ruins—can, with effort on our part, reveal to us more meanings than we've previously managed to see in them.

How much in life we let flash by without realizing it was ever there to be seen. Even the most insubstantial and fleeting phenomenon—a human shadow that momentarily darkens a wall before passing from view—can, and at least occasionally probably should, be noticed and pondered upon. What better emblem is there than your own shadow to give you an inkling of your essentially insubstantial and impermanent being? That recognition is an antidote to the hubris of believing that the sixty or seventy years of our particular existence is of any ultimate importance. View your shadow upon the solid stone blocks of the Pyramids, for example, and you can feel the very texture of time weaving its way over you like a mummy's shroud. At least for a few moments—standing there looking at your shadowy self on the ancient stones—you become aware of your location in time. You escape the time-trap of one locked in the present and oblivious to the past. You realize that the contemporary is but temporary. And you find yourself in an added dimension—a temporal context reached by juxtaposing your short existence against the long sweep of history.

But how seldom do we pause to look at our shadow on the wall—metaphorically, if not actually? Slade, an American artist in Malraux's *Hope*, argues that there is a touch of the poet in every man, but the touch is seldom felt. "That wall over there. . . . All those saps go trotting their shadows over it, and never give it a look." Eugenio Montale, the Italian poet, writes more poetically of the man who "never gives a thought to that shadow of his/the dog-days brand upon a flaking wall!"* So it is that we drift onward through the days, largely oblivious to our shadowy existence. A man's shadow momentarily smudges the wall—that most insubstantial of visions affords ephemeral evidence of an ephemeral being.

It only remains to be considered whether we can change our habitual unseeing tendencies and become capable of seeing, so that even we who are "last at the fair" can enjoy some of its wares. "Every man will speak of the fair as his own market has gone in it," wrote Laurence Sterne in *Tristram Shandy*. What, then, can we latecomers make of our market? To speak well of our fair we must see well. In light of all the shadows that darken our vision, is it possible to enlighten our minds to see?

Professional seers—adventurers, writers, artists, statesmen—claim that people can cultivate the ability to see. Richard Burton, the great English nineteenth-century ad-

---

*"Bones of the Cuttlefish" in *Selected Poems*, translated by George Kay (Baltimore: Penguin Books, 1969).

venturer and explorer, referred in the preface to *Ultima Thule*, his book on Iceland, to "that 'sixth sense' developed by the life-long habit of observation." And in a 1955 letter to his brother Julian, Aldous Huxley mentions "methods for training people to pass at will from conceptualized perception to direct virgin perception." This is the sort of training that involves divesting the preconceptions instilled by one's nationality and culture in order to bring a fresh eye to unfamiliar scenes. Jack London referred to this kind of exercise in a travel context when he wrote, "When a man journeys into a far country, he must be prepared to forget many of the things he has learned, and to acquire such customs as are inherent with existence in the new land; he must abandon the old ideals and the old gods, and oftentimes he must reverse the very codes by which his conduct has hitherto been shaped."

Once a person becomes aware of the pleasures of seeing, he can most likely train himself to see. The process is not unlike learning a foreign language, except that the grammer, syntax, and vocabulary of seeing involve not words but tone and tint, shape, depth, and a good dose of knowledge coupled with imagination. Hopefully we will learn to see with the euphony of, say, Italian rather than with the cacophony of Swiss German. After the language of seeing is learned, even a blank wall becomes expressive. It is a case of exploiting what Delacroix referred to in his *Journal* as "that delicacy of the organs that makes one see what others not see, and which makes one see in a different way."

By training, by habit, and by effort, each of us can, in time, become seers. "The art of observing," Winston Churchill wrote to his brother Jack, "is one which can be cultivated—and it is an excellent thing to try and see the odd, queer and unnoticed side of things." And what sort of things can you see when you observe the unnoticed side? One example is what Alan Moorehead, that most practiced travel observer, saw at a camp near Lake Randolph in Kenya, where he noticed (as described in *No*

Room in the Ark) near the water "an intricate network of footprints made by many different birds. These, with the droppings, and the fallen feathers and the bones of fish, made a series of abstract patterns on the beach, and they were not unlike paintings in prehistoric caves." If primitive art can be seen in the pattern of bird waste, then surely the acute observer can see in the more substantial sights the world has to offer much that is normally overlooked.

To see is all that can be hoped for: to understand what we've seen is perhaps too much to ask. The travel essays that follow are based on the seen, and that is coupled with due tribute paid to the past. They are based on observation and—in the spirit of the Chinese word "pai," which means both "to explain" and "in vain"—explanation is for the most part omitted. I have simply tried to see the various places discussed—the evocative islands, Devil's and Easter; the ruin-rich relics, Pagan and Petra; the remote enclaves, Benjamin Constant and Mt. Athos—in the two dimensions of their foreground (how they now appear) and their background (how they relate to the past).

My intention is that what follows can in a certain sense be read as an extended interpretation of Laurence Sterne's observation in *A Sentimental Journey:* "What a large volume of adventures may be grasped within this little span of life, by him who interests his heart in every thing, and who, having eyes to see what time and chance are perpetually holding out to him as he journeyeth on his way, misses nothing he can fairly lay his hands on."

Whether I have managed to fulfill that intention is for the reader, to whom time and chance have brought these pages, perhaps long after I have gone, to judge. Dear and gentle reader, read my words and then pray tell—before you, too, have gone—whether you believe that I have come too late to the fair.

2
Devil's Island

—1—

THE "DRY GUILLOTINE," AS THE PENAL COLONY IN FRENCH Guiana on the northeast coast of South America was called, was a death machine of fiendish efficiency. Even now, long after the release by death or by law of the last prisoners, Devil's Island remains a tribute to its namesake.

Of the seventy thousand convicts sent to French Guiana during the century the devilish penal colony functioned, fifty thousand died there. The punishing climate killed many of them, while disease—including leprosy, which first appeared in 1885, and frequent epidemics of yellow fever—claimed others. To the natural hazards were added the depravity of the guards, undernourishment, and overwork in the form of forced labor. In French "la guillotine séche" means not only the dry guillotine but also one that is harsh and unfeeling. Though terse, the French phrase is a rich description of French Guiana's great prison colony, which, in any language, meant death.

The great death machine in the jungle of the New World improved on the best that European minds could imagine. Even the real guillotine was made more efficient in the penal colony. In the early 1930s a French Guiana excutioner named Chaumié invented a device to prevent the victim from squirming before his death. Just prior to the descent of the guillotine's blade a one-pound weight would drop on the condemned man's head and stun him. The knife could then fall on a fixed target and make a clean cut. Chaumié must have been an especially able man: he was the only executioner in French Guiana who managed to escape death by murder. He eventually died, so the story goes, when the blood of a guillotined leper splattered on him at an execution, transmitting the disease to him.

Nature itself in French Guiana surpassed the most morbid imaginings of even the ultra-gloomy Franz Kafka. Kafka's fictional penal colony in his famous short story greatly resembles, by design or by coincidence, Devil's Island. Like Devil's Island, Kafka's prison colony is an island, and one where guards speak French. The authorities there use a wondrous machine to carry out sentences—literally: the device sports a set of needles which carve a sentence on the naked body of the bound and gagged prisoner. Kafka's fiction has its analogue in the real penal settlement, where small vampire bats would attack sleeping convicts at night, the parasites sucking blood while injecting a noncoagulating agent so that the victim would bleed to death or to the morning, depending on which arrived first.

French Guiana wasn't always a death machine. At the beginning, the Europeans hoped it would turn out to be a money machine, for they traveled there in search of gold. The long, low range of hills called Tumac-Humac, inland on the border with Brazil, was reputed to be the El Dorado. Sir Walter Raleigh, an early soldier of fortune in the area, wrote in *The Rich and Beautiful Empire of Guiana*, the first book about the Guianas, published in 1596, that "every pebble one touches is warm with the promise of silver or gold."

Raleigh's expedition was long remembered. After killing two monkeys which had been lovers of some young girls, Candide—Voltaire relates—decides with his companion Cacambo to go to Cayenne, capital of French Guiana, where they hoped to find some Frenchmen who could help them. The way through the jungle was difficult, and soon they found themselves in Inca country called El Dorado, which, a 172-year-old resident informs them, an Englishman named Raleigh almost reached. Candide never got to Cayenne, and the gold nuggets he collected in El Dorado were lost. He ended up in Suriname—Dutch Guiana, adjacent to French Guiana.

Other early adventurers gravitated to the area to seek their fortunes. Aubrey, in *Brief Lives*, gives a picture of the early days of Guiana exploration in his chapter on Captain Thomas Stump:

He had too much Spirit to be a Scholar, and about at 16 went in a Voyage with his Uncle (since Sir Thomas) Ivy to Guyana in Anno 1633, or 1632. When the Ship put in somewhere there 4 or 5 of them straggled into the Countrey too far: and in the interim the wind served, and the Sailes were hoist, and the Stragglers left behind.

It was not long before the wild People seized on them, and stript them: and those that had beards, they knocked their braines out: And (as I remember) did eat them: but the Queen saved T. Stump and the other boy. T. Stump threw himself into the River (Oronoque) to have drowned himself, but could not sinke; he is very full chested. . . . He sayes there is incomparable Fruits there; and that it may be termed the Paradise of the World.

Stump may have called the area "Paradise of the World," but, in fact, the jungle country was hostile to men's dreams, though more than hospitable for their nightmares; the rich and beautiful empire that promised gold in the end delivered death.

The penal colony has long since been abandoned and the great death machine there dismantled, but the former prison empire, which Devil's Island epitomized, continues to exert a macabre and even mysterious attraction. A recent booklet on the Guianas warns that French Guiana is "only for the adventurous," and as late as 1971—the year I visited the country—there appeared a book which contained a map with the legend "Unexplored" written across the otherwise blank space of the jungle area between the Comte and the Mana rivers. These days, few places on earth offer the possibility of discovery which the word "unexplored" suggests.

French Guiana has always been a remote and unfriendly land. A convict there once described it as "a lost country. The only country in the world to which nobody ever came for pleasure." But there I found myself, early one steaming November morning, on a small boat fighting its way across the rough shark-infested waters off the coast of French Guiana, heading toward Devil's Island.

—2—

To endure the daily nightmare of the dry guillotine, the convicts in French Guiana dreamed of escape, which they called "La Belle"—the Beautiful. The prisoners would have given anything to flee the lost country I was so eager to visit, and many of them did give everything, for they died trying to escape from the great death machine.

One escape route crossed the Marowijne River, which marks the frontier between French and Dutch Guiana. The river teems with piranha fish, which in less than a minute can reduce a man, even a hefty one, to bones. Some prisoners tried to escape another way—by sea in a small dugout canoe called a "corial." This route took them, so they hoped, up the coast to British Guiana, but frequently the strong current carried the men beyond to Venezuela and the mouth of the Orinoco River, which became known as "the grave of the Frenchmen." Joseph Conrad tells in a short story of an escape by boat from French Guiana by three anarchists, one of whom shoots the other two. This sort of hazard was, in fact, a real one. In 1932, Jean-Arnaud Spilers, known as "the king of escape," left the penal colony with five fellow prisoners but only "the king" and one other convict reached Venezuela two weeks later. Those two had managed to survive by killing and eating one of the others.

My trip into the country from which so many had tried to escape began in Paramaribo, capital of Dutch Guiana. I'd reached Paramaribo by air—the easy way to conquer the jungle. In fact, you don't really conquer the jungle by flying, you simply avoid it. But somewhere along the way I wanted to get the feel of the dry guillotine—nothing cutting, just a slight touch—so I decided to continue on to Cayenne, capital of French Guiana, by land.

My introduction to French Guiana was a needle in the arm in Paramaribo. The tourist office there informed me that all travelers to the French colony required a yellow fever shot. That news made me begin to wonder what I was getting into, or what might get into me. I asked the nurse at the Institute of Tropical Hygiene in Paramaribo if yellow fever was a real danger in French Guiana. Her answer was a jab in my arm. Then she entered in my health card—its yellow color mimicking what I imagined the color of my skin might be if I caught the disease—a circular stamp in purply ink which, properly tropical, showed a palm tree and two loin-clothed figures holding long bows and which bore the legend, "Bureau of Public Health Suriname." It all looked very important and quite official, that stamp, but would the mosquitoes respect it?

That afternoon I left Paramaribo in a car—of sorts—for the seventy-five mile trip through the jungle to the Marowijne River, the border between Dutch and French Guiana. The antique vehicle broke down a couple of times, but the driver managed to repair the engine with a few pieces of wire, shifting them around from place to place to where they were most needed. We passed through Moreng, a company town where Alcoa Aluminum, which mines bauxite there, owns everything except the cats and dogs, so the driver informed his passengers. We continued on past thatched houses of bushnegroes and moved deeper into the jungle until arriving at Albina, a village on the Marowijne River across from the French Guiana town of St. Laurent du Maroni, and there I spent the night in a so-called hotel only one step removed from a jungle hut and from the jungle itself.

The evening's entertainment was to listen to news of the outside world transmitted on shortwave from Holland via Bonaire, a Dutch island in the Caribbean. The world news seemed very remote. A hard tropical rain fell, then suddenly stopped. The lights kept going out, so it took me the rest of the evening to write my travel diary for the day, and then I went to bed. Moments later, mosquitoes arrived in force to sniff the new blood, and every whine around the net draped over my bed threatened a fatal bite. I lay awake wondering if the yellow fever serum was effective yet.

Early the next morning I took the ferry across the piranha-filled Marowijne River from Albina to St. Laurent du Maroni, formerly the administrative center of the French Guiana penal colony. At one time the hospital at St. Laurent had on display a collection of mummified heads guillotined in the prisons around the turn of the century. But I didn't linger in St. Laurent to see the local sights—the heads, if they were still there; the nearby leper colony on St. Louis Island, to which authorities sent prisoners not to be cured but to disintegrate to death; a portable guillotine specially built for ease in transporting it around the penal settlement—because I wanted to reach Cayenne, the French Guiana capital some one hundred and sixty miles away, by nightfall.

You travel through the jungle of French Guiana by the rule of chance, not schedules. I made my way through St. Laurent to the far side of town and stopped by the cemetery to hitchhike. The activity on the road was hardly more alive than that inside the graveyard. A vehicle or two would pass every half hour or so, but they were all going only a mile or two farther. The sun—"the monster of the tropics," a convict once called it—climbed up into the flawless sky and soon started to cut into me. Finally, after about two hours, a pickup truck stopped and, thankfully, true to its name, picked me up. I jumped into the back and was at last on the road to Cayenne.

We charged down the rough dirt road that slashed through the jungle, bouncing our way along at sixty or sixty-five miles an hour. Occasionally we'd hit a short stretch of welcome pavement, then again pass onto an unimproved part where the truck, and I, shook violently. That primitive road we were hurtling over, and tossing on, had cost the lives of thousands of convicts. Begun around 1916 to connect St. Laurent with Cayenne, the road was known officially as Colonial Highway Number One, but the prisoners who worked on the project called it Route Zero: for them, the highway led only to death. Convicts assigned to the road would often mutilate themselves to escape the forced labor gangs. The death rate was about sixty or seventy per month; in all, some seventeen thousand men died to build the rough road known as Colonial Highway Number One.

André Gide gives an idea of the sort of roads the French were fond of building, using low-cost labor, through difficult areas of their colonies. In *Travels in the Congo* he describes a road (located near Bambio in the Middle Congo, which the French writer visited in the mid-1920s) that evokes to me memories of "Route Zero." "Every twenty yards or so," Gide writes, "there were huge pits by the side of the road, generally about ten feet deep; it was out of there that the poor wretches had dug the sandy earth with which to bank the road. . . . It has happened more than once that the loose earth has given way and buried the women and children who were working at the bottom of the pit." In a footnote Gide adds "that this murderous road, which was particularly difficult to lay, owing to the nature of the soil, serves exclusively for the car which once a month takes the Forestry agent" to a nearby market.

The construction of Route Zero through the jungle swamps of French Guiana was only one of the many deadly episodes that comprise the history of the penal colony. The story of the dry guillotine started in the eighteenth century when it became the fashion among European countries to send undesirables abroad to populate the colonies. The English sent such supposed riffraff to Maryland and then, after the American Revolution, out to Australia. In France, Talleyrand argued that the best rather than the worst should be sent to establish the colonies, but the French followed the English practice and used their overseas possessions as dumping grounds for what was considered human refuse. The opening chapter of Abbé Prévost's 1731 novel *Manon Lescaut* depicts a typical deportation procedure—Manon and a dozen other "women of pleasure" are being taken to Le Havre for shipment to Louisiana.

Later, in the 1760s, the French tried to populate Guiana with voluntary settlers, attempting to tempt them by promises of land and wealth; but of the eleven thousand people who emigrated to the colony, seven thousand of them died. It was that disaster which gave the country its reputation as a "green hell." So it was that in 1793, after the Legislative Assembly passed a provision for deportation of priests who failed to uphold "la liberté et l'égalité" of the Revolution (there was no complaint about the lack of "fraternité"), the authorities chose the punishing precincts of Guiana as the place of exile. The Assembly's delegate from Cayenne, Pomme, nicknamed "the American," was asked to advise French officials on deportation procedures.

But the political situation in Paris changed before any priests were deported to the green hell, and the first men sent out to Guiana were themselves revolutionaries, Collot d'Herbois and Billand-Varenne, both members of the notorious Committee of Public Safety that reigned under the Terror. Collot arrived in Cayenne in July 1795 and on June 8, 1796, he died there, apparently of yellow fever. The natives had only half-buried his body when they abandoned it, and the corpse was quickly bitten to shreds by pigs and birds scavenging for food. Collot was the first person deported to Guiana to die there. Many others were to come—and go—after him.

During the first part of the nineteenth century, the French government ordered various studies of the domestic penal system, which a handful of people claimed was repressive and in need of reform. Penitentiaries were then located at Marseilles, Brest, and Toulon. Victor Hugo's description of Jean Valjean, a "miserable" imprisoned at Toulon, portrays how prisoners were treated in those days: the "bolt of his iron collar was. . . riveted with heavy hammer blows behind his head," he was dressed in a red jacket, given a number (24,601), and at the penitentiary, an "irremediable misery," Valjean would laugh "that mournful convict laugh, which is, as it were, the echo of fiendish laughter." Hugo also describes an execution by guillotine, "not a lifeless mechanism" but "a species of monster" that "eats flesh and drinks blood." It was such conditions that encouraged the reform movement; de Tocqueville, in fact, was sent in 1831 to the United States not to observe "democracy in America," but on behalf of the reform movement to study the American penal system, which he discussed in his book *Penitentiary System in the United States* written with Gustave de Beaumont, his traveling companion in the States.

The mini-revolution of 1848 in France produced an upsurge in the number of prisoners. The penitentiaries became overcrowded and expensive to run, and so Louis Napoleon, the president of the Republic, decided that deportation would be better than incarceration; on May 30, 1854, the Assembly passed the law which, in effect, created the penal colony at French Guiana. Among the law's provisions were: Article 2, which required convicts to perform "les plus penibles"—the most punishing—forced labors; Article 3, which provided that prisoners could be chained together or made to drag an iron ball; and Article 6, which created the hated "doublage," a requirement that a convict had to remain in Guiana after release from prison as a "libéré" (a freed ex-prisoner) for a period of time equal to his sentence.

The "doublage" clause reflected the high hopes the French still entertained for their tropical colony. It was a persistent dream in Paris that Cayenne would become an outpost of French civilization. A half century before the penal colony was established, Napoleon himself had said, "For a long time I have dreamed about Cayenne. It is the most attractive country on earth for establishing a colony." Needless to say, Napoleon hadn't seen the place with his own eyes or felt the scorching tropical sun on his own skin. In a French book published in 1854, the year Guiana was made a prison state, hope was expressed that "with the help of time and luck, Guiana will become the Australia of France." Australia, of course, was where the English had sent their incorrigibles. But, unlike Guiana, Australia had subsequently shown progress and development.

Hopes for adding to the fifty-five thousand people who now populate the colony have persisted to this day. General de Gaulle, dreaming, like Napoleon, of creating an important French presence in the New World, said in 1960 that Guiana could become "a showplace of what France can achieve." In August 1975 the French Minister for Overseas Territories announced a comprehensive plan for the development of Guiana by settlers to be sent there from France. Within about a month after the announcement the office responsible for processing applications for emigration to Guiana received five thousand visits and over fifteen thousand letters from people interested in settling there. Eventually, over thirty thousand Frenchmen applied for government sponsorship to live in Guiana. The spirit of adventure and of enterprise which the French are known for is still intact, the newspaper *Le Monde* in Paris claimed. But beginnings in the colony have never been easy. Back in the 1850s, when the penal settlement was opened, some four thousand of the eight thousand men sent out to the prisons in Guiana died in the first five years, mainly of yellow fever.

Apparently, however, the old terrors of the jungle had been forgotten in modern-day France. The French government now seemingly viewed what had been the "dry guillotine" as a kind of latter-day El Dorado for Frenchmen wishing to escape Europe and start a new life in the New World. The plan of colonization was to develop 20 percent of Guiana's thirty-five thousand square miles, nine-tenths of which is jungle, with fruit farms and with timber to feed paper factories to be built in the colony. In the end, however, the French spirit of adventure became dispirited and little came of the latest effort to develop the Gallic outpost in America. The plan called for two hundred and fifty new farms, but only sixteen were established; as of August 1977, two years after the colonization program had been announced, out of the thirty thousand people who had applied to move to French Guiana only thirty had settled there. Perhaps the dry guillotine has not yet lost its edge.

About a hundred years earlier, when fully half the prisoners sent out to the then new penal colony died of yellow fever, the French government mounted one of its rare efforts to save men from the ravages of the dry guillotine. Embarrassed by the high death toll, Paris authorities for a time sent prisoners to New Caledonia, called "the Eden of convicts," rather than to the green hell of Guiana. But procedures soon reverted to normal, and in 1887 a new group of victims arrived at Cayenne—three hundred and twenty-four "recividists," or habitual criminals. During the next half century nearly sixteen thousand such prisoners were sent to Guiana. Some ninety-eight hundred died there.

As a result of articles by the journalist Albert Londres

printed in *Le Petit Parisien* and his September 1924 open letter to the Minister of Colonies in which Londres argued that the penal system in Guiana needed to be completely disbanded—not simply reformed—the authorities appointed a commission to study the problem. The panel decided to retain the system but to institute a few reforms, among them the abolition of dungeons and the reduction of solitary confinement to a period of fifteen days. In 1933 a Salvation Army unit was established in Cayenne, and the organization began to campaign with publicity and pressure for the penal colony to be closed. After the French elections of June 1936 the Popular Front Government decided to stop sending new convicts out to Guiana, but only after World War II was the system finally abolished and the existing prisoners in Guiana returned to France. The repatriation was finally completed in 1954— an even one hundred years and fifty thousand deaths after the penal colony had been established.

All that history, so it seems, has now been forgotten in the colony, France's oldest, settled by that country in 1604. Guiana is hardly the Australia of France these days, but it is a municipal department of the mother country and its inhabitants are French citizens who elect a delegate to the Chamber of Deputies in Paris. Cayenne—perhaps best known for the burning pepper, hot as the tropical sun, which carries its name—is a forlorn settlement of thirty thousand people and a pale imitation of a French provincial town: pale because the equatorial sun and climate have ashed the faces of the residents and faded the facades of the once freshly painted wooden buildings. In Cayenne appear the usual evidences of French civilization: an Avenue du Général de Gaulle and an Avenue de la République, as well as other streets named after Voltaire and Pasteur, and a top-heavy civil service—eleven thousand of the eighteen thousand members of the colony's work force are employed by the government.

A twenty-eight-page booklet published in Cayenne listing local events and attractions contains ads for, of course, restaurants (Joyce, in *Finnegan's Wake*, puns "Homard Kayenne")—La Rotisserie on Place Grenoble offers a "Menu Gastronomique"—and for other goods and services ranging from start to finish: the local Prisunic store advertised a sale on toys while Léonard Pauillac at 64 Avenue de Gaulle offered a "complete" funeral service, including preparation of the corpse and its shipment to any destination desired.

But nowhere in the booklet was there mention of what French Guiana is best known for—Devil's Island. It is as if the people condemned by chance to live in that lost land want to forget its past and their predecessors who were sentenced by law to live and die there.

—3—

As I write these words with my right hand I hold in my left a small nail I salvaged from a prison cell as a souvenir of my visit to the penal colony. Once sharp, strong, and shiny, the nail is now well warped and crumbly with rust, tangible evidence of the effect the dry guillotine that is French Guiana had on iron. But what the effect of the guillotine was on that less substantial substance—human flesh—can only be vaguely imagined by a latter-day casual visitor to Devil's Island.

As a tourist in the penal colony—a transient visitor who'd arrived and who could depart at any time of his own free will—I could scarcely put myself in the shoes or skins of the convicts who'd arrived on the islands that loomed ahead as the boat I'd caught at Kourou put out to sea. The scene which to the condemned men used to represent what would be endless years of misery ending, perhaps, in death now appeared to me—as the boat I was on approached the three prison islands—as an exotic tourist attraction. Filled with what Graham Greene has described as "that feeling of exhilaration which a measure of danger brings to the visitor with a return ticket," I could only pretend to be entering the great death machine. As I savored the rewards of my long trip to South America and through the French Guiana jungle on the convict-built Highway Number One to reach the area, my attitude was almost festive, much as how Joseph Wechsberg in *Looking for a Bluebird* described passengers on another boat, that one a transatlantic ocean liner, who, attending an elegant costume dinner, "simply got a piece of burnt cork and painted black stripes and a serial number on their bare torso, impersonating convicts from Devil's Island."

There is, after all, a certain romance about Devil's Island and French Guiana—as long as you don't have to live there. The place has come to symbolize adventure and the exotic. The hallucinating Latin American dictator in Gabriel Garcí Márquez's novel *The Autumn of the Patriarch* imagines a celebration attended by a general escorted by "escaped French prisoners in civilian clothes and loaded down with goodies from Cayenne." And in the movie version of Hemingway's *To Have and Have Not*, Harry Morgan, converted to the Free French cause in World War II, agrees to embark for Devil's Island to free a French prisoner being held there by the Gestapo.

But those examples are fiction: the reality was ahead of me in the guise of that trio of tiny, inhospitable-looking islands in the near distance and above me in the form of a harsh sun whose rays, even early in the morning, had begun to cut into my skin.

I tried my best to imagine myself as a convict approaching for the first time his home-to-be for the next ten or twenty years. Attempting to see a place through the eyes of another person, those of the real party in interest—in this case, a prisoner—can enrich a travel experience, and sometimes it's interesting to try such an approach. In *Which Tribe Do You Belong To?* the Italian writer Alberto Moravia tells of his attempt to view "beautiful" Bagamoy—a coastal town in Africa where slaves were loaded on ships to be transported to Zanzibar for sale by auction—as the captives saw the site. So entranced was Moravia by the "dazzling sunlight sparkling on the leaves at the top of palm trees, at the moment when the wind turns them back" that "for a moment I forgot to look at the landscape through the eyes of the slave." Moravia then pauses to see the scene as they did—to the slaves the sea, normally a symbol of freedom, represented an avenue to servitude, while the palm trees' feathery leaves meant not happiness but "anguish" and "anticipated home-sickness."

I remember once visiting Parris Island, the Marine basic training camp in South Carolina, and trying to imagine how a recruit might feel approaching the fearsome site. Gradually—so I imagined—the tension would build as the rookie drove by a mile-long row of stunted palm trees, which, as at Bagamoy, would represent "anticipated homesickness," if not "anguish." Then he would cross the R. C. Berkeley bridge (named after a Marine Corps officer) and come to Horse Island, which afforded one last view over the marshes to the mainland—a land being left behind for the terrors of basic training. Then, finally, just beyond the Iwo Jima statue, with its inspiring inscription, "Uncommon Valor Was a Common Virtue," would appear a more mundane sign with an arrow pointing off to the right—"Recruit Receiving": the victim has arrived.

Of course, even U. S. Marine Corps basic training at Parris Island is nothing compared to the rigors faced by prisoners consigned to the Paris-controlled islands of French Guiana. That trio of prison islands, which lie seven miles off the coast, bear a deceptively benign name. They're called the Iles du Salut—the islands of salvation, not an ironic name but one given to them after a group of nuns from a convent in Cayenne escaped a yellow fever epidemic by fleeing from the mainland to the islands.

The expression "prison island" is, in a certain way, redundant. All islands are, in a way, prisons, for one is confined to them. As Richard Burton, the nineteenth-century English explorer, said, "Little islands are all large prisons: one cannot look at the sea without wishing for the wings of a swallow." That feeling of insular confinement is quickly apparent if you stand on the large rock that is Alcatraz and gaze across at the nearby, yet inaccessible, attractions of San Francisco lying a few hundred feet across the water.

Islands make perfect prisons, and they have occasionally been used for that purpose. There is even a Devil's Island in the United States—Mark Twain refers to it in Chapter XXVIII of *Life on the Mississippi*—but not used for the same purposes as its namesake. Haiti's Gonave Island, however, was employed as a prison during the time of the French presence in that country. Sakhalin Island, off the coast of Siberia, was used by the czars as a prison in the late nineteenth and early twentieth centuries; in the same era, Maria Madre, one of four islands in the Pacific Ocean off the coast of Mexico near Tepic, northwest of Guadalajara, housed some two thousand prisoners (mostly pickpockets and thieves) guarded by one hundred soldiers who supervised the convicts as they toiled in the salt pits on the tiny, twenty-square-mile island. The Italian prison island of Asinara, just off the east coast of Sardinia, is still used as Italy's top security prison. In August 1979 two of the prison's four hundred inmates managed to escape; one was later found drowned but the other never turned up—apparently the first successful escape in Asinara's history.

In Table Bay, seven miles from Cape Town on the tip of South Africa, is Robben Island, which houses about five hundred inmates. Jan van Riebeeck, founder of the Dutch settlement at Cape Town in 1652, used the three-square-mile island to exile dissidents, and after 1850 it became a leper colony and mental asylum. The South African Navy took control of the island in 1931 and for thirty years used it to guard the sea-lanes leading to and from Cape Town. Robben subsequently reverted to its original use, again becoming a place of detention. The last known escape attempt occurred in 1963 when two prisoners made a raft out of gasoline drums and planks. One man drowned; the other was captured and returned to the island. Some of the prisoners on Robben are assigned to work in the limestone quarries, an activity that became the subject of the 1975 Broadway play *The Island.*

But of all the prison islands that the world has known, the trio which forms the Iles du Salut in French Guiana is perhaps the most famous. As my ship approached them I saw off to the right St. Joseph's Island, site of the solitary confinement cells; to the left Royale Island, where prison headquarters were located; and between and slightly beyond those two specks of land, the smallest of the group—Devil's Island.

The ship put in at the well-built Royale Island quay, constructed of neatly cut stone blocks which had no doubt cost a lot of sweat and death to build. At the port stands a two-story yellow building with a tin roof and bars over the windows where arriving prisoners were received and processed. I passed the reception center and started up a path, then climbed a steep flight of stone stairs which led to a deserted, dilapidated house, once the residence of the penal colony's commandant. Now the place had collapsed into a chaos of boards and other debris overgrown with tropical vegetation. The jungle foliage was more efficient than a wrecking crew. I continued on to the top of the island, a small plateau some six hundred feet above the sea, and there found a well-maintained stone block barracks building that now serves as a snack shop. Already panting with thirst, I gulped a drink before resuming my walk. Moments later I again grew thirsty.

Scattered about Ile Royale were other buildings, most of them nearly lost in the thick vegetation and all crumbling. The one-time hospital somehow seemed still filled with echoes of pain and suffering emitted by the then dying, now all dead. A nearby makeshift church with a tin roof was decorated with crude paintings, while not far away elaborate arabesques of vines and plants were engaged in reducing a few vacant structures to dust. But the most interesting relics were the cell blocks. How easily I passed through the rusty iron doors, now ajar and askew, that once barred the way of hundreds of prisoners. Inside—at least what used to be inside: most of the roofs had by then collapsed beneath the encroaching jungle—are iron rings to which convicts used to be chained and the remnants of cubicles which confined them.

After making my way through the jungle of ruined prison buildings and tropical overgrowth I returned to the quay to inquire about hiring a boat to get to the other two islands. On the path I met an engineer from Paris stationed at the French rocket launching center at Kourou on the coast just across from the Iles du Salut. Kourou is used these days by the European Space Agency (ESA) to launch communications satellites. Located not far from the equator, the launch site takes maximum advantage of the earth's rotation, thus permitting larger payloads to be lifted into orbit there. In July 1985 ESA sent from Kourou an Ariane 2 rocket to rendezvous with Halley's Comet when it passed close to earth in March 1986. (That project was artfully named Mission Giotto after the Florentine Renaissance painter who, in a Padua fresco, depicted Halley's Comet guiding the Magi to Jesus' birthplace.) The French engineer I met worked for the old European Launcher Development Organization which, in November 1971, shortly after my visit launched a three-stage Europe 2 missile from Kourou—or tried to, that is, for the rocket broke up when the guidance computer malfunctioned. Had the dry guillotine worked its deathly ways on modern technology?

The Frenchman and I tried to arrange transportation to Ile St. Joseph. The island lay only a few hundred yards from Royale, but the currents that swirl through the sea there are often so powerful small boats can't get across. Devil's Island, in fact, gained its name because of the turbulence of the water around it. Formerly, a rope device stretched from Royale to Devil's so prison personnel could supply the latter island with provisions when the sea was too rough to cross, as it often was.

At first the boatman we'd approached refused to carry us across to St. Joseph, claiming that the water that day was too dangerous. The French engineer and I decided to offer him extra money—hazard pay—for the trip. The boatman gazed across the narrow channel, perhaps scanning the weather or the currents or maybe counting his profit in advance. But we soon learned there was another reason for his caution: sharks. The boatman told us that the killers prowled those rough waters searching for snacks. The engineer and I looked at each other: he might know how to shoot rockets high into the sky, and I, more mundane, managed to exercise a profession or two, but did we want to risk ending our careers in the sea in a shark's stomach?

Ancestors of the present-day sharks had frequently dined on men. During the years the prison colony existed, convicts who died there were buried at sea because the tiny islands were too small to allow the amenity of a cemetery for prisoners. The cadavers were put in a casket open at the side and the box taken by boat a few yards into the water where guards would ring a bell. Moments later sharks appeared, previously alerted and attracted to the area by the chapel bell rung for the funeral service. In *The Compleat Angler* Izaak Walton expresses doubt about Francis Bacon's claim that "carps come to a certain place in a pond, to be fed, at the ringing of a bell"; Walton counsels silence if one wants to attract fish, but the sharks around the Iles du Salut had apparently never heard of Walton. After the bell sounded, the corpse was ejected from the coffin and within minutes the flesh devoured. Convicts on the islands developed a macabre little sideline of selling shark jaws on which they'd carved the legend "Prisoner's Tomb." An inmate once managed to escape the island in a coffin he'd stolen to use as a makeshift ship. A group of sharks patiently waiting for him to capsize soon companioned the man, but prison guards eventually captured him at sea. He was supposedly the only escaped convict in the history of Devil's Island happy to be returned to the safety of his cell.

The French engineer and I now joined the reluctant boatman in his meditation. We all three stood silently gazing at the sea. Creases of water roughed the surface and swells shaped crevices in it. There might've been sharks out there as well, but as far as I could see the sea was finless. Our pilot again objected that the water was too rough. It certainly wasn't difficult to visualize the unruly waves capsizing the little boat, and I even managed vaguely to imagine the slash of shark's teeth as they guillotined an arm or leg. But in spite of the very visible hazards of the turbulent water and whatever hidden dangers might be lurking below the surface, we finally persuaded the boatman to attempt the crossing to Ile St. Joseph, and we climbed into the small motorboat and ventured into the churning sea.

About a hundred yards separated Ile Royale and Ile St. Joseph; I think we covered a similar distance in vertical and lateral directions. Large swells rolled under the boat, twisting and lifting it for a few moments, then the water rolled on, suddenly plunging us into the trough that trailed the swell. The boat buckled and half-turned as the current fought to force us out to sea. The motor sputtered protests at being overworked. We bobbed and dipped, advanced and then lost ground—or water—when the turbulence knocked us off course. St. Joseph isn't exactly what one would call the promised land—and hardly "the Paradise of the World," as Aubrey's Thomas Stump had described Guiana—but, under the circumstances, we were extremely happy to reach the island.

St. Joseph is even wilder than Royale and much more desolate. Few people visit the island. Virtually every visitor to the penal colony remains on Royale. The boatman dropped us off and departed for Royale, leaving me and the French engineer alone on St. Joseph. We began our visit by walking along the overgrown seaside path to the far side of the island, where we found a small cemetery used for the burial of prison officials and their families, many of whom, according to the inscriptions on the gravestones, had died of yellow fever. We then started back along the trail but the dry guillotine soon began to cut into us: on the Iles du Salut even a short walk enervates you. Exhausted by the humidity—and perhaps also by the residual effects of crossing the treacherous waters—we sweated profusely and dragged ourselves along, finally stopping to rest and managing to muster just enough energy to crack open a coconut whose milk and meat, along with the pause, helped to revive us, at least for a time.

We continued on, now leaving the path and cutting through thick vegetation to find the cell blocks where the prisoners sentenced to St. Joseph had been caged. They were the so-called "mauvaises têtes" ("bad heads"), who included hardened killers or men who'd assaulted guards or tried to escape. Such problem prisoners were given the most feared and hated punishment in the penal colony—solitary confinement on St. Joseph.

We finally found the building where those solitary cells were located. Each windowless cubicle is about eight- by twelve-feet square and nine feet high. Instead of a ceiling there is a web of bars through which the prisoner could be constantly observed by guards who paced a catwalk running the length of the long building, which the convicts called "le château." Most of the inmates would do anything to get out of the cages and return to the relative comforts of Royale. Some rubbed powdered quinine into their eyes to give themselves the look of insanity, while others in solitary confinement really did become insane. Another trick was to insert under the skin a castor-oil seed which would cause pus to form. That gained the convict a trip to the hospital on Ile Royale, but it also often lost him a limb which had to be amputated if the induced infection spread out of control.

At the top of St. Joseph stands a cavernous building, one of the few in the penal colony whose roof is still in place. The tin sheets blocked off the light of day, shadowing the interior, but the sun's heat transcended the metal roof and penetrated inside, turning the cell block into a furnace which seared us as we passed through. The other buildings on St. Joseph all lie in ruins. Dense foliage has ripped away walls and clawed open bars, and rust has eaten into once impervious iron shackles, turning them into crumbling remnants of the fearful cages that awaited men condemned to solitary on St. Joseph.

In contrast to the brutal conditions on Ile St. Joseph, life for the prisoners on Devil's Island was relatively more pleasant, even though Devil's enjoyed a more sinister reputation, due, no doubt, to its suggestive name. The island wasn't used for the ordinary run-of-the-mill murderer or thief but was reserved for political offenders (as that term was variously defined at different points in time). Devil's is hardly spacious—some twelve hundred yards in circumference and one-third that in diameter—but within those narrow limits the captives were at least allowed to roam free. In addition, the political prisoners were furnished a daily ration of "vin ordinaire."

Inmates were also allowed to receive books and letters. An early political exile in the Iles du Salut—Laffon-Ladebat, president of the "Council of Ancients," who was deported from France in the 1790s—kept a journal during his stay in which he tells of receiving news and rumors of events in Europe. He also mentions studying chemistry and natural history texts, as well as reading books by Condorcet, by Montesquieu (*The Spirit of the Laws*), and by Goldsmith (*The Vicar of Wakefield*), which, the prisoner notes with a certain professional interest, contains "an excellent chapter. . .on penal laws."

But it was only a century later when the Iles du Salut, and Devil's Island in particular, became world famous—or notorious—with the arrival there of a young political exile named Captain Alfred Dreyfus.

—4—

Alfred Dreyfus was not only the most famous figure ever confined on Devil's Island but also the first person deported there under the provisions of an 1895 law which specified the Iles du Salut as a detention site for political prisoners. Dreyfus arrived at Ile Royale in March 1895— just one hundred years after the arrival in French Guiana of Collot d'Herbois, the first man deported to the colony to die there.

The names Dreyfus and Devil's Island are permanently linked in the convoluted turnings of the infamous affair which began in 1894 when the French General Staff's Intelligence Bureau intercepted an unsigned communication addressed to the German military attache in Paris. Because Dreyfus's handwriting resembled that in the note, suspicion fell on him, a captain attached to the General Staff; in due course he was court-martialed for treason and sentenced to exile on Devil's Island. On January 5, 1895, after being drummed out of the army in the courtyard of the École Militaire, Dreyfus was taken to the Central Prison of Paris in a van from which—agonizingly—he glimpsed for a few passing moments the house where shortly before he'd dwelled in domestic tranquillity with his wife and two young children.

Dreyfus languished in the Paris prison nearly two weeks until, in the middle of the night of January 17, officials woke the prisoner and took him to a cell in a train comprised of cars built especially to transport convicts on their way to the Guiana penal colony. The next day the convict train arrived at La Rochelle in southern France, where a hostile crowd quickly gathered to intimidate Dreyfus. The now notorious traitor remained in his train cell until nightfall when guards managed to maneuver him through the threatening throng to a carriage which took him to La Palice, a port from where a boat carried him to Ile de Ré, a prison island. There Dreyfus stayed until February 21 when he was suddenly put in a cell aboard

the convict ship *Saint-Nazaire* which set sail the following day for the Iles du Salut. The ship arrived at the penal
colony on March 12, but Dreyfus was kept confined to his
cell in sweltering heat for four days while preparations
were made for his arrival. It was necessary to burn the
fifteen huts on Devil's Island, which until then had been
used as a leper colony for prisoners, and to construct a
cabin for the new arrival. Dreyfus was temporarily imprisoned on Ile Royale until, finally, on April 13 the
authorities moved him to the tiny, rocky speck of land
that for over four years, until June 9, 1899, was to be his
home, if "home" is the proper term.

Dreyfus's shelter on Devil's Island was a small stone
hut—"more attractive than the cabin of Uncle Tom,"
wrote a later French visitor—complete with an anteroom
where one of the five guards detailed to watch the prisoner was always on duty. By day, wherever Dreyfus went
on the island, less than half an acre in size, a guard
followed him. At night, insects tormented him, making
sleep nearly impossible. The isolated convict yearned for
his distant family. One of his few tenuous contacts with
home was a photograph of his wife Lucie and his children
Pierre and Jeanne which in time became flecked with
dark spots—his tear stains.

All the prisoner's correspondence was censored. Hun-
gry for word from home, Dreyfus's heart fairly burst with
anticipation every time he saw the mail steamer from
France sail by. But even letters didn't ease the terrible
boredom and the eternal silence. "Where are the beautiful
dreams of my youth and the aspirations of my manhood?"
lamented Dreyfus in his Devil's Island *Diary*.

Dreyfus started to study English to pass the days, and
after a time he was permitted to receive some books,
among them works by Balzac, Montaigne, and Shakespeare. But soon insects laid eggs in the books, and they
quickly disintegrated. Ants also plagued him. They invaded his hut in such quantities that he was forced to
protect his table by putting its legs in old tin cans filled

with oil. Water had failed to deter the insects, which, Dreyfus relates in his *Diary*, had simply formed a pontoon with their bodies, allowing other ants to pass across the makeshift bridge to reach the table.

Finally, in November 1898, Dreyfus received word from his wife that a petition for commutation of his sentence had been presented to the French government, and on November 16 a telegram informed him that the court had granted a hearing on the matter. At 7 A. M. on Friday, June 9, 1899, Dreyfus suddenly found himself aboard the *Sfax* for transport back to France, where he arrived on June 30. His seemingly endless days on Devil's Island had finally come to an end.

By then, of course, the Dreyfus Affair had become a "cause célèbre" which had fractured the very structure of French society. Paris was split from top to bottom into pro- and anti-Dreyfus factions. Proust observed that the controvery about "the Case," as it was called, had even descended from the chic circles of the salons into "the subsoil of popular opinion," where butlers would argue about "the detention on the Devil's Isle of an innocent man." The case had continued to unfold during the exile of its principal figure on the remote prison island in French Guiana. Not long after Dreyfus had been banished to Devil's Island, Lieutenant Colonel Georges Picquart, new chief of Military Intelligence, came to realize that the handwriting on the fateful memorandum addressed to the German Embassy in 1894 had been written not by Dreyfus but by Major Count Walsin-Esterhazy, whom Dreyfus's brother Mathieu denounced for high treason on November 14, 1897. The enemies of Dreyfus claimed that Picquart had forged the new handwriting sample which incriminated Major Esterhazy. Esterhazy insisted on being tried—and was acquitted. Meanwhile, Émile Zola was tried for libel for his famous article "J'Accuse," which appeared in *L'Aurore*, Georges Clemenceau's newspaper, on January 13, 1898. After Zola's first lawyer, Labori, was shot, Clemenceau was retained to defend the writer, but to no avail—Zola was found guilty and sentenced to one year in prison.

After further charges and countercharges involving "l'affaire Dreyfus," the Supreme Court finally ordered a retrial of the case on June 3, 1899, and it was then that Dreyfus was repatriated. That trial took place at Rennes, where the soldiers who lined the walkway by the entrance to the building where the proceedings were held would turn their backs, to form a guard of dishonor, whenever the defendant appeared. It is not generally remembered that Dreyfus was, in fact, reconvicted of treason—"with extenuating circumstances" this time, as the court put it—and it was only seven years later, in 1906, when he was finally rehabilitated by a Supreme Court declaration of his innocence. Then, in July of that year, a ceremony was held in the École Militaire courtyard—the same place where Dreyfus had been drummed out of the army over eleven years before—to initiate the former Devil's Island convict into the French Legion of Honor. "L'affaire Dreyfus" was at an end.

The penal colony at the Iles du Salut, however, continued on. Well into the twentieth century, other prisoners succeeded Dreyfus on Devil's Island, which has come to stand for the entire penal colony that existed for a hundred years in French Guiana—the dry guillotine.

There were those who suggested it might have been more humane to use the real guillotine in the colony in place of the agonizingly slow death machine that was French Guiana. *The Century of Light*, Cuban writer Alexandro Carpentier's novel based on the life of Victor Hugues, a follower of the French Revolution, tells how Hugues introduced into the Caribbean the guillotine, which soon began to "centralize" life and form a part of people's "habitual and daily" existence. Children built small guillotines to behead cats, and vendors hawked miniature versions used to adorn living rooms. Hugues learns in Cayenne, however, that the guillotine hasn't yet reached French Guiana, his informant musing, "But perhaps the way we do it is worse because it's better to fall by a single gash than to die in installments."

Death on the Installment Plan—such was Louis-Ferdinand Céline's capsule description of life. Life itself is the greatest death machine of all, and yet men subject other men to the guillotine: the dry guillotine of French Guiana and Dr. Guillotine's wetter, quicker verson, or, to be more precise, Herr Schultz's version, for he invented the beheading machine which Dr. Joseph Guillotine saw when traveling in Germany. Since the doctor, an egalitarian, resented peasants being executed by hanging while nobles were eliminated by the sword, his level-headed solution was the introduction of the guillotine to France. The machine intrigued Louis XVI, who improved the device by slanting the blade at an angle. A few years later, in 1793, Louis saw how the improved death machine worked at close range—it beheaded him.*

Until capital punishment was abolished in France in 1981, it was the only country in western Europe that still applied the death penalty by guillotine, which had been a part of the French Penal Code since 1810. In recent years the guillotine has been sparingly used. Between January 1968 and October 1978, when the French National Assembly voted against eliminating an appropriation equivalent to $44,000 for the upkeep of the guillotine and the salary of the executioner who operates it, there were eight executions, the last in Douai in September 1977 when a North African immigrant laborer was decapitated for murdering a child. (In Spain, it might be noted in passing, the "garrote vil"—an iron collar twisted to snap the victim's neck after a minute or two of gradual strangulation—was

*Perhaps the only example of a tangible benefit stemming from the practice of execution by guillotine appears in the 1935 MGM film *Mad Love* (the English title—more descriptive—was *Hands of Orlac*): Dr. Gogol, played by Peter Lorre, resurrects the career of the great pianist Orlac, who'd lost his hands in a train accident, by grafting onto his smashed stumps the hands of a guillotined murderer.

used until recently, the last such execution having taken place in March 1974.) Prior to the October 1978 Assembly action, the last parliamentary debate on the guillotine question took place in 1908.

Time was when attending executions was a popular spectator sport. Over a century ago, in March 1857, Tolstoy watched the public execution by guillotine of one François Richeux, sentenced to die for robbery and homicide. Tolstoy was sickened by the operation of the "perfected, elegant machine," and the spectacle made a lifelong impression on him. Even twenty-five years later he recalled (in *Confession*) the gory separation of the head from the body and the thudding fall of the severed part into a box. Similarly, a hanging which Boswell happened to see while driving through the streets of Turin in the 1760s nauseated him (the executioner had to stand on the victim's head so the rope would be sure to choke him), and he dashed to a nearby church where he knelt before an altar.

Writing in 1925, Will Rogers chastised the large crowds that had recently gathered to see a hanging and the more than two thousand people who'd requested permission to attend three Sing Sing prison electrocutions. "Sometime they ought to turn around and turn the electricity on every one of the spectators," he said, pained by the "pleasure of watching somebody else die" which the curosity-seekers sought. Sir Richard Burton tells how his schoolmaster in France took some pupils as a treat "to see the execution of a woman who had killed her small family by poisoning, on condition that they would look away when the knife descended, but of course that was just the time (with such an injunction) when every small neck was craned and eyes strained to look, and the result was that the whole school played at guillotine for a week, happily without serious accidents."

That childhood excursion was a seemingly harmless activity for Burton, but in some men there lurks a more sinister and perverse interest in being voyeurs of death.

Vladimir Nabokov speaks in his autobiography *Speak Memory* of a German university student whose hobby was executions. The young man told of traveling to the Balkans to view a few hangings, visiting Paris to see a guillotining, and watching a beheading by axe in Regensburg, the latter spectacle disappointing because the drugged victim had failed to react to his execution. An even more extreme case was chronicled by the Goncourt brothers, who wrote in their *Journal* about a visit in the spring of 1862 to Fred Hankey, an Englishman living in Paris. Hankey, they related, enjoyed watching from a rented room a murderess being hanged while at the same time performing perversions on two prostitutes.

What dark recesses of the human pysche so interest men in observing death being inflicted? What even darker recess impels men to take such pains to organize and mechanize death—a death which, in time, will in any event slice us from life? Somehow, it seems, a part of what is Devil's Island possesses a part of every man's heart. In his "Reflections on the Guillotine," Camus suggests that we should attempt "to add to the sum of our actions a little of the good that will make up for the evil we have added to the world," a sentiment personified by Camus' character Tarrou who, his life changed by witnessing a guillotine execution, says "that there are on this earth plagues and victims, and it is necessary, in so far as possible, to refuse to be on the side of the plagues."

A visit to Devil's Island makes you realize that only in that modest way can we in the end in some small measure foil the great death machine and salvage from the nothing that is our life at least a decent death.

3

Easter Island

—1—

IT IS A MYSTERY WHY SO MANY VISITORS TO EASTER IS-land have found it a mysterious place. Easter—that speck of lonely land in the remote reaches of the Pacific Ocean—seemed to me one of the most open and leasι mysterious spots in the world. When the Dutch sea commander Jacob Roggeveen discovered the island on Easter Sunday in 1722, one of his officers, Captain Bouman, brought a native onto the ship. The islander "showed the greatest wonder at the built (sic) of our ship," Roggeveen's account goes, but the native was especially taken by his own reflection in a mirror, which he turned over in an attempt to discover the source of the apparition. So Easter Island struck me, for I found it as transparent as that seemingly see-through mirror the native imagined he was looking through. Those who have viewed Easter as mysterious have perhaps seen there a reflection of their own desire to find mysteries—and then to try to solve them.

Many books about Easter bear titles that suggest detective stories rather than travel tales (*Island of Enigmas* and *The Riddle of the Pacific*). After spending seventeen months there in 1914 and 1915, Mrs. Scoresby Routledge still felt puzzled enough by the tiny land to call her book *The Mystery of Easter Island*. Easter also baffled Stephen-Chauvet, a French doctor who never even visited the island; he called his book, written in the 1930s, *Easter Island and Its Mysteries*. Another writer, one who did visit, described the place as "a region, this, of evil mystery" that casts a "weird spell." The French novelist Pierre Loti, who spent a few days on Easter in January 1872 began his account like the opening lines of a Gothic romance: "There exists in the midst of the great ocean, in a region where nobody goes, a mysterious and isolated island."

Why have all these observers—and many others as well—seen Easter Island as a place of mystery? One answer might be that in a scientific age people are attracted to places and problems that have not yet become demystified. Then, too, the posing of a mystery permits the finding of a solution. Easter is a kind of archeological and anthropological Everest: just as Mallory climbed the mountain because "it was there," so people can solve—or try to solve—the riddles of Easter Island which the visitors themselves pose. But many of the "mysteries" are more apparent than real. Father Sebastian Englert, a Capuchine missionary who lived on Easter Island for nearly thirty-five years, complained that "authors who knew little about what they wrote have created all sorts of mysteries where none really exist" and have made "incomprehensible much that has a reasonable and moderate explanation."

One writer Father Sebastian viewed with approval, however, was Alfred Metraux, whose work *Ethnology of Easter Island* the missionary considered "the most complete book on the subject." Metraux, who spent the last half of 1934 on Easter as part of a French-Belgian research expedition, commented on the "halo of mystery and strangeness" which had surrounded the island ever since Roggeveen discovered it, but he went on to note his "fear that it has now become almost impossible to obtain any fresh information concerning the island's past." Maybe that furnishes a clue to the reason why so many visitors view Easter Island as a place of mystery: since little new remains to be discovered, the only original contributions possible are new solutions invented to fit old puzzles. So, true to its name, Easter Island induces people to resurrect moribund mysteries—Where did the islanders originate? What do the great stone figures mean? How were the effigies transported and raised? Why were the statues in process suddenly abandoned and left unfinished?—to solve and then lay them to rest, at least until the next visitor raises and answers the same "mysterious" questions.

The best known recent attempt to solve an Easter Island "mystery" was Thor Heyerdahl's 1955 Aku-Aku expedition, undertaken to investigate the theory that people who originated in South America settled the island. The earliest visitors had always assumed the opposite—namely, that the islanders were of Polynesian origin. Captain Cook, who visited Easter in 1774 on his second voyage, observed that "in colour, figures and language, they bear such affinity to the people of the more western isles, that none will doubt that they have had the same origin." Twelve years later La Pérouse, commander of a French expedition, affirmed that "there can be no doubt, as Captain Cook observes, of the identity of this people with that of the other islands of the South Sea: they have the same language, and the same cast of features." And a century later Pierre Loti flatly asserted: "As for the inhabitants of Easter Island, they came from the west from the Polynesian archipelagos; there is no doubt of that."

Sir Peter Buck, in *Vikings of the Sunset*, published in 1938, tried to trace the origins of the islanders even farther to the east and earlier in time, theorizing that migrants from India and, later, Indonesia combined with Oceanic Negroes (the same race as the Australian Bushmen of today) and Mongoloids to become a seafaring race who sailed to various Pacific islands, including Easter.

Buck's theory may have been suggested to him by his own mixed origins, for he himself was an amalgam of East and West. Born in New Zealand in 1880 to a Maori mother and an Irish father, Buck always included his native name, Te Rangi Hiroa, along with his European one on his publications. At the time of his death in 1951 Buck was director of the Bishop Museum in Honolulu, having previously practiced medicine and served as a member of parliament in New Zealand.

Between these two approaches—the early one that looked west to Polynesia and Heyerdahl's, which looked eastward to South America—there appeared other theories which attempted to solve the mystery of the origin of Easter Islanders. In 1924, Professor J. Macmillan Brown proposed as one of his solutions to *The Riddle of the Pacific*, as he called his book, the idea that Easter was the remnant of a once far-flung Pacific civilization that had sunk into the sea. "All the indications point to an empire in the east Central Pacific having gone down," he claimed, comparing the island to how Europe might be if the continent were entirely submerged except for a part of Westminster with its Abbey—"an Easter Island of the Atlantic." Brown, it must be added, is one of the most imaginative of the Easter Island mystery writers: one of his many ingenious theories is the notion that natives transported the stone statues on sledges of banana tree stems and by an aerial tramway lubricated with yams.

Mrs. Routledge, writing five years before Professor Brown, quickly dismisses the idea that Easter Island is the remnant of a large sunken land mass, but she does take pains to deal with the claims of theosophists who asserted that occult revelations disclosed that the island is all that remains of a continent called Lemuria which existed during the Lemurian epoch, a time when the world was populated by beings on the fourth trip around the planets and who were the same size as the stone statues—some are thirty feet tall—which they carved on Easter Island.

Such are some of the explanations proposed to solve

one of the island's mysteries, the origin of the people. The answers sometimes seem much more mysterious than the riddles. It's only relatively recently that the people, statues, and other aspects of Easter Island culture have been considered mysteries worthy of investigation. Those of us who today view the island as a great archeological treasure no doubt find it difficult to realize that Easter wasn't always appreciated as such, but in fact the place was, with rare exceptions, viewed for years in principally economic terms. Not until 1935 did Chile finally designate the site a national park; and only in 1938 did Easter become an historic monument. And even as late as 1975, it was seriously proposed that Easter be used as the site of a three-day Rolling Stones concert and festival to which 100,000 rock fans would be airlifted. Chile's director of tourism considered the project, then decided against it, concluding that "in a quest for momentary notoriety, the whole future of the island was going to be damaged."

Most early expeditions to the island saw in it not mystery but opportunity. From the very beginning, when Roggeveen discovered Easter, outsiders sought to exploit its commercial possibilities rather than to investigate its culture, much of which was destroyed or distorted or had disappeared by the time Mrs. Routledge arrived in 1914 on the first expedition which systematically studied in detail the island's archeology and ethnology.

Roggeveen's 1722 expedition was sponsored by the Dutch West India Company, the same organization that had established Dutch colonies in the Hudson Valley. The directors of the company, along with many other Europeans, were excited over reports of the discovery of a supposedly new continent off the South American coast. There is something delightful in the idea that as late as the early eighteenth century serious men still believed that an unknown and unexplored continent remained to be conquered. In 1687 the crew of *The Batchelor's Delight*, commanded by Edward Davis, a Dutch sea captain, spotted off the west coast of South America a mysterious island—one much more mysterious than Easter, for in fact it was never seen again. Wafer, the ship's officer, wrote that "we fell in with a low sandy island. . . . To the westward about twelve leagues [48 miles] by judgment we saw a range of high land which we took to be islands. . . . This land seemed to reach about fourteen or fifteen leagues in a range, and there came thence great flocks of fowls."

The news of the discovery of Davis Land, as the island came to be known, caused a stir in a Europe ripe for new lands to conquer. There had been no discoveries in the South Pacific since Tasman had come upon Tasmania in 1642 while sailing along the Australian coast. Excited by the report, sea captains in port taverns all over Europe—Cadiz, Bristol, Amsterdam—gossiped about the news and dreamed of finding a large South Sea continent which would turn out to be an El Dorado. It was to find that hoped-for treasure-land that the Dutch West India Company organized the three-ship expedition commanded by Jacob Roggeveen. Europe's great gold hunger had for years been one of the most powerful forces behind the great voyages of discovery.

Cruising the Pacific waters, Roggeveen noted in his log on Tuesday, April 2, 1722, that they had "yet not come in sight of the unknown Southland (according to existing accounts of it), for the discovery of which our Expedition and Voyage is specially undertaken." After holding a council, the ship's officers decided to continue sailing in a westward direction, and a few days later they found a speck of land: "About the 10th glass in the afternoon watch The African Galley, which was sailing ahead of us, lay to wait for us, making the signal of land in sight; when we came up with her, after four glasses had run out, for the breeze was light, we asked what they had seen. On this we were answered that they had all very distinctly seen a low and flattish island lying away to starboard, about 5½ miles off, to the nor'ard and west'ard."

In a practice often followed by explorers, it was decided to give the place "the name of Paasch Eyland, because it was discovered by us on Easter Day." Naming an area for the day Europeans found it was a common custom. The Spanish explorers were especially fond of the practice. According to Herrera, historian to the king of Spain, in 1513 Ponce de Leon "nam'd it *Florida*, because it appear'd very delightful, having many pleasant groves, and it was all level; as also because they discovered it at Easter, which as has been said, the Spaniards call *Pasqua de Flores*, or *Florida*." Similarly, in November 1602 Sebastian Vizcaina, a Spanish explorer, named the Pacific coast area (claimed sixty years earlier for Spain by Juan Rodriguez Cabrillo) San Diego, noting in the ship's journal, "On the 12th of the said month, which was the day of the glorious San Diego [Saint James, one of the 12 Apostles, believed to be the person who brought Christianity to Spain], . . . almost all the men went ashore. A hut was built and mass was said in celebration of the feast of Señor San Diego." In November 1493 on his second voyage, Columbus happened one Sunday on an island he named Dominica after the day he found it, and on Amerigo Vespucci's third trip he called the estuary area on South America's east coast, reached January 1502, Rio de Janeiro. One of the most descriptive place names was bestowed on some South Pacific islands discovered by Magellan in the spring of 1521; the natives there stole the explorer's skiff, thus prompting him to name the place Ladrone ("Thief") Islands. (The Ladrone are now known as the Mariana Islands.) Perhaps the most evocative place name in the world is Australia's Daydream Island.

As for that other Pacific Ocean island, Roggeveen's "Paasch Eyland," the explorer wondered if it was the promising Davis Land the expedition had been sent out to find. Roggeveen at first hoped so: "There was great rejoicing among the people and everyone hoped that this low land might prove to be a foretoken of the coastline of the unknown Southern continent." But the explorer quickly realized that his discovery was no El Dorado, which the West India Company could exploit, but only an out-of-the-way island with some "remarkably tall stone figures" and a bunch of thieving natives. Disappointed in the lack of commercial possibilities, Roggeveen remarked that what was first thought to be silver and mother of pearl objects turned out on closer examination to be made of some vegetable root, "as one might say in Holland, of good stout parsnips or carrots."

Both the tone and content of Roggeveen's log suggest that Easter Island was simply a mistake, an interruption in the search for the fabulous South Sea continent. He wrote about his visit in a matter-of-fact manner quite lacking any sense of wonder. After a brief shore visit, it was decided—with Dutch persistence and a strong sense of mission—to continue the voyage to "see whether we could discover the Low and Sandy Island." So the ships sailed on, still in the "hope that a good discovery of a high and wide-stretching tract of land should result after a little while."

They never found the mysterious continent or the elusive Davis Land, and no one else ever did either. Perhaps Wafer had incorrectly described the location of Davis Island in his journal, or maybe "the low sandy island" had sunk back into the waters of the Pacific and disappeared after he'd spotted the place. But South Seas sailors continued to search for the island. George Robertson, master of HMS *Dolphin*, commanded by Captain Wallis, who discovered Tahiti in June 1767, noted in his journal on May 4 his "hopes of falling in with Davis Land," but by May 14 he "now gave over all hopes of seeing Davis Land and Concluded that there was no such place." Seven years later, when Captain Cook was cruising the same waters on his second voyage, he also entertained hopes of finding the lost land: "We expected to have seen the low sandy isle that Davis fell in with. . . [but] in this we were disappointed."

Cook did reach Easter, however, and his practical eye focused as sharply as had Roggeveen's on the island's commercial possibilities—or lack of them. Cook noted that "no nation need contend for the honour of the discovery of this island, as there cannot be places which afford less convenience for shipping than it does. Here is no safe anchorage, no wood for fuel, nor any fresh water worth taking on board." But over a century later Policarpo Toro, a young Chilean naval officer, convinced his country to take possession of Easter for exactly that reason—to use the island as a supply port for ships sailing between the Panama Canal and Australia and New Zealand. It was the island's supposedly strategic location, rather than the mysteries of its history and culture, which interested Chile and induced that country to annex Easter on September 9, 1888.

It is a mystery, however, why Chile supposed the island would make a logical supply point for transpacific crossings. Pierre Loti, who visited Easter in January 1872, tells how his boat *La Flore*, a French training ship, had to make a long detour from the normal marine routes across the Pacific to reach the island which, he noted, lies on the path to nowhere Loti's judgment, however, is not completely accurate. If you happen to be sailing from North America's west coast toward the South Pole, then Easter Island does lie on your route. It's not generally remembered that Admiral Byrd stopped briefly at Easter on his second expedition in 1933. His visit was not altogether successful. After he and ten other men reached shore a storm blew up and forced their ship, the *Jacob Ruppert*, to put out to sea for safety. Marooned, the shore party spent the night on the beach in the rain with nothing to eat except two chickens obtained by barter for a shirt. Byrd was afraid that headlines around the world would announce that the famous explorer had gotten stranded on a remote island.

But if Easter was never appropriate as a way station for ships, it did offer other commercial possibilities. In the nineteenth century the island was used as a source of man (and woman) power by ship captains who raided the population to obtain slaves. The first such raid occurred in 1805 when the New London schooner *Nancy*, operating out of Mas Afuera Island near Juan Fernandez—the "Robinson Crusoe" island off Chile's coast—abducted twelve men and ten women to work in gangs hunting for sea lions. For the first three days at sea the prisoners were kept bound. After their release, the men immediately jumped overboard (the women failed to escape). A small boat put out from the *Nancy* to chase the swimmers, but they all managed to avoid recapture, one of them supposedly making it all the way back home to Easter.

Later, in December 1862, six Peruvian ships commanded by Captain Aiguire arrived and the shore party displayed on the ground a glittering collection of trinkets which attracted the islanders and distracted them sufficiently to enable a troop of eighty crew members armed with rifles to seize about a thousand of the natives. The prisoners were carried away to toil in the guano deposits on the Chincha Islands off the coast of Peru. Most of the slaves died there, and of the hundred survivors who were finally released, only fifteen lived long enough to reach home; but those few carried smallpox with them, which quickly killed over half of Easter's population, reducing it to less than six hundred inhabitants.

Apart from the traffic in human flesh, outsiders found Easter suitable for other sorts of business activities. For many years the island was nothing more than an oversized sheep ranch in the middle of the Pacific. During his visit in 1786, La Pérouse left on Easter some pigs, sheep, and goats, the island's first quadrupeds. "I do not flatter myself that the pigs I present them with will flourish," La Pérouse wrote—and he was right, not only about the pigs but also the other animals, for they were eaten or otherwise vanished without leaving descendants. But, later, Europeans successfully introduced sheep, which eventually increased to a population of some forty thousand—forty times the number of people—and the export of Merino wool became the island's mainstay. In 1871 the Catholic mission on Easter joined with two local European residents to form an association to raise sheep for wool and for a supply of fresh meat to sell to passing ships. One of those residents was a former French merchant marine captain named Jean Onezine Dutrou-Bornier.

Dutrou-Bornier is one of the most colorful characters in the history of Easter Island. A veteran of the Crimean war, he abandoned the military to become a soldier of fortune. He managed to obtain a trade commission from Alexander Salmon, a Tahitian businessman, and during a South Sea island tour to search for commercial deals, Dutrou-Bornier reached Easter, where he proceeded in 1867 to acquire title to some three-quarters of the island, mainly in exchange for red calico and other such goods. The following year he married Koreta Paukurunga, queen of the island, and then convoked a council of state and assumed the office of president and prince consort.

Dutrou-Bornier continued to consolidate his hold on Easter. On a hill above Hanga Roa, the island's village, he set up two ship's cannons, and from time to time he'd lob a few shots onto the town to evidence his power. Dutrou-Bornier also established his own church to compete with the one run by the missionaries, and he offered special services to the islanders. One ceremony unmarried couples who wanted to void vows given previously to the priest who'd married them; another procedure released from service native nuns whom Dutrou-Bornier would then induct into his harem. This sort of activity, as one might suppose, made Dutrou-Bornier rather unpopular with the missionaries, who decided to leave the island in 1871. When the boat arrived for Father Roussel and his associates, almost all the natives boarded to leave with them; but Dutrou-Bornier bribed the ship's captain to refuse to sail until the islanders returned to shore, and about one hundred and seventy-five of them were forced to remain on Easter. Six years later, on Easter Day, 1877, the French warship *Seignelay* arrived to find one hundred and eleven natives but no Europeans. Dutrou-Bornier, the

French visitors were informed, had died a few months before when he'd fallen off a horse while drunk. It was a good story but not a true one: the ruler of Easter Island had in fact been murdered by some of his unhappy subjects.

Sheep farming remained the island's most important source of income until the late 1960s when regular jet service to Easter was introduced by LAN-Chile. In the mid-sixties about half the island's 45.5 square miles was given over to grazing and pastureland which supported about 48,000 sheep—the human population then was 1,070—and yearly revenue from the sale of wool and meat amounted to the equivalent of some $50,000. By February 1972, the year of my visit to Easter—by which time there were 1,050 inhabitants, all at Hanga Roa, 47,000 sheep, 1,000 horses, about 1,000 head of cattle, and a scattering of pigs and chickens—the tourist industry had replaced sheep farming as the island's principal income producer, and that development gave a boost to a traditional local business which had existed for years—the manufacture of legends, ancient objects, and mysteries.

—2—

Easter Island tempts investigation. Compact and self-contained, remote, well statued and historied, the island is as neat as a rat maze and not all that much larger. So Easter attracts investigators, outsiders who require fables and artifacts to use in solving the island's mysteries. The natives are only too happy to supply the demand for raw material: that's a kind of business with them, and a challenging one. It's no mean feat to fabricate stories or objects to satisfy visitors searching for solutions to Easter's puzzles: the imagination necessary to invent tall tales is no less than that required to raise tall statues.

The local manufacture of information or tangibles for consumption by inquisitive outsiders is an important business—a kind of cottage industry—in the world of travel. As with all industries, it exists to fill a demand: travelers, and especially professional investigators, want to get to the bottom of a place, and so they dig and probe and question. The danger for the outsider, however, is that what he learns or finds may convince him—wrongly—that he truly understands the place. The Irish writer and diplomat Conor Cruise O'Brien once observed in regard to outsiders who study an alien culture (one of his examples is, like Easter, insular: the Aran Islands) that among the locals being investigated "there seems to be a curious delight in the feeling that the stranger knows far more than oneself and yet—being a stranger—understands nothing." One reason for this possession of knowledge without understanding is that often much of what the stranger "knows" has been tailor-made for him to conform to the kind of mystery he's come to solve.

This sort of made-to-order product is a common commodity, especially in remote or exotic places. One of the most remarkable factories of the past and its artifacts is housed in the Church of Maria Auxiliadora in Cuenca, a beguiling town in southern Ecuador, which I visited some six weeks after Easter Island. In *The Gold of the Gods*, Erich von Däniken has already told about Father Crespi, the grizzled, bearded keeper of a large, unwieldly assortment of disparate objects which he claims are from Babylonia, Egypt, and other ancient civilizations. Däniken wrote in 1972 that Father Crespi "has been living in Cuenca for forty-five years. He is accepted as a trustworthy friend of the Indians, who during past decades fetched the most valuable gold and silver objects from their hiding-places piece by piece and gave them to him." After describing some of the supposedly precious pieces, von Däniken concludes, "Take my word for it, when you catch sight of the treasures in the back patio of Maria Auxiliadora, you have to be very strong-willed not to get 'gold-drunk.' "

Father Crespi proudly conducted me through his "museum." It was less a display than a disorganized storeroom of possessions seemingly acquired at random by an eccentric scavenger. The old man pointed out an array of "ancient" pottery; "rare" metal, stone, and ivory (or perhaps "ivory") objects; stuffed birds, spiders, and butterflies mounted (separately) on boards; and lots of "gold" items, all the while supplying a running commentary on all sorts of original ideas about history. To my eye, many of the pieces looked like fabrications—bad modern copies of what someone imagined antiques might look like if they were made to order to prove theories about the past. To any question or hint of objection, Father Crespi would respond by producing an item which supplied the missing artifact that, to his mind, conclusively overcame any possible doubt about his eccentric theories. But Father Crespi's tales—like his displays—were also for the most part fabrications.

Less gullible than von Däniken, John Lloyd Stephens, the nineteenth-century American explorer of the Middle East and Central America, tells of his 1836 visit to a priest in Samaria, in the Holy Land, to see "the oldest manuscript in the world." The priest demanded payment, and after Stephens had delivered the fee the man "brought down an old manuscript, which, very much to his astonishment, I told him was not the genuine record, giving him very plainly to understand that I was not to be bamboozled in the matter." Stephens was considerably more sober than the "gold-drunk" von Däniken at Father Crespi's. Casanova in his Memoirs refers to a museum in Mantua which uncannily resembled Father Crespi's "museum." Casanova writes that Don Antonio Capitani, the museum proprietor, was "an extraordinary eccentric. The treasures of his museum consisted of the genealogy of his family, books on magic relics of saints, coins supposedly dating from before the flood, a model of Noah's ark copied from the original and a badly-rusted old knife, which he claimed to be the one with which St. Peter cut off the ear of Malchus."

The same sort of dubious antiquities as those in Father Crespi's Cuenca museum and Don Antonio Capitani's Mantua museum have been produced on Easter Island. From the very first expedition mounted especially to investigate Easter—that of Mrs. Routledge in 1914—the natives were prepared to give the customer what she (or he) wanted. Mrs. Routledge tells of buying an "old" wooden figure she happened to have seen being carved the week before. When informed by Mrs. Routledge that she realized the object was new, the seller responded by insisting it was ancient, adding that, in any case, if she didn't want the figure he'd keep the piece for later sale to some ship captain in search of antiquities.

By the time the next major expedition arrived, a Belgian-French team of anthropologists and archeologists in 1934, the natives had learned aggressive marketing techniques. Alfred Metraux tells how they rowed out to meet the arriving ships sporting feather headdresses—not relics but cheap, modern imitations worn to arouse the interest of the sailors in buying the wooden carvings on offer. After these "shady hucksters" with their "grotesque" and "repulsive" wares, as Metraux describes them, arrived on board, one enterprising youth, told that the visitors had come to study the island and look for ancient objects, informed the investigators that few such items remained but, he advised, the natives would be glad to make whatever objects the expedition needed and that no one back in Europe would know the difference. Metraux declined the offer.

After establishing himself on the island, Metraux finally decided to rely on a man named Juan Tepano for information about Easter. He was apparently the star purveyor of stories about Easter's history and traditions. Twenty years earlier Mrs. Routledge had utilized Tepano's services, but only after she'd passed through a learning curve. He was, she wrote, a man of intelligence who spoke a little pidgin English. At the beginning he seemed to have indulged in the habit of inventing much of his mate-

rial, for Mrs. Routledge notes "how his perceptions gradually grew of what truth and accuracy meant." Metraux
later discovered that Juan Tepano was for the most part
only relating tales that his mother told him. On being
introduced to the old lady, Metraux found a "living
mummy," a tattooed and living "monster" with clawlike
hands. By—and even of—such sources are legends made.

World travelers who have heard quaint local tales—and
had their fill of them—will envy Robert Gibbings, the
English writer, who actually once managed to find someone whose yarns never reached the consumer. In *Blue
Angels and Whales*, Gibbings tells of meeting an old har-
pooner who "stood outside his cottage with one foot on a
monstrous bone and told me stories of the past." So far so
usual, but Gibbings then adds: "but he spoke in a dialect I
could not understand, and for all that I can do his legends
must die with him."

Many tales or objects are no doubt manufactured for
inquisitive outsiders because they arrive at a place with
an overly prepared mind and are too eager to find what
they've previously read or heard about. When J. Macmillan Brown went to Easter Island in the 1920s, between
the expeditions of Mrs. Routledge and Alfred Metraux, he
asked to see an "ahu"—a seaside rock temple—that
Thomson, paymaster of the *Mohican*, a ship which had
visited for eleven days in 1886, called the "kino-kino." A
"flickering smile" passed across the face of Brown's guide,
the son of the man who'd guided Thomson, and the visitor was then taken to a weathered natural volcanic formation shaped like a manmade ahu. "Kino-kino," Brown
soon found out, means "gone to ruin." And when Pierre
Loti examined a "reimiro"—a quarter-moon-shaped pec-
toral decoration worn by women on Easter—he thought it
was a boomerang, an object that to his too-imaginative
mind evidenced the migration of people from Australia
all the way across the South Pacific to Easter Island.

The great dream of virtually all professional visitors to
Easter has been to solve the great "rongo-rongo" mystery,

and for years the natives have capitalized on this market. A rongo-rongo is a "talking board"—a wooden tablet filled with little pictures, cut with rats' or sharks' teeth, that supposedly represent writing. No one has yet been able to decipher that script, the first and only native writing found anywhere in the South Seas, and its meaning is the only true mystery about Easter Island. It will probably remain a mystery, but not for lack of attempts to find the solution. Missionary Eugène Eyraud discovered the tablets in 1864. In a letter to the superior of his order in Valparaiso, Chile, Eyraud reported that "the characters are relics of a primitive writing and that they are preserved without any inquiry into the sense of them." But the islanders soon learned to become interested in the rongo-rongos. Like news of the discovery of Davis Land two centuries before, discovery of the ancient talking boards piqued the curiosity of Europeans and challenged them to make the tablets talk again, and the natives were always glad to help the outsiders.

The first attempt was made by Tepano Jaussen, bishop of Tahiti, who came into possession of some tablets when they were by chance used to hold handmade cord wrapped around them for presentation to the bishop as a gift from the islanders. In 1868 Jaussen found a man named Metoro Tauaure, who claimed to be able to read the script. Metoro duly performed: he took a board and began chanting as he looked at the writing. Father Jaussen excitedly copied down the translation; but when it turned out that Metoro had apparently been reciting a chant he knew rather than reading the one on the board, the bishop abandoned his attempt to decipher the script, concluding, "We must give it up; there is nothing in it." That is probably the most accurate statement ever made about the rongo-rongo, but it failed to discourage subsequent efforts to find the solution. Although few genuine tablets were found, there were always many islanders available who volunteered to "read" the boards.

In 1874 an American named Croft, a resident of Tahiti,

obtained photos of Bishop Jaussen's tablets and one Sunday an Easter Islander came to interpret a rongo-rongo for Croft. As the native read the script fluently, Croft recorded the translation. Croft later misplaced his notes, and so he summoned the man back the following Sunday to reread the tablet. The native repeated the reading, and Croft copied down the man's words. A few days later the American found his notes from the first session, and comparing them with those from the second, he immediately saw they were different, so he asked the native to return a third time. The man invented yet another interpretation, and Croft, finally disillusioned, refused to believe that the same tablet could have three different meanings on three successive Sundays.

The next attempt—and the first one on Easter Island itself—was in 1886 by Paymaster Thomson of the *Mohican*. Carrying with him photos of Bishop Jaussen's tablets, Thomson was anxious to obtain an interpretation of the writing. The paymaster located a native named Ure Vaeiko, an island patriarch who'd been a cook for Easter's King Ngaara, who'd died just before the Peruvian slave raids some twenty-five years earlier, at which time the raiders had supposedly carried off the last man able to read the rongo-rongos. Thomson tried to induce Ure to read the script; but the old man, afraid that if he revealed the secret of the writing he'd ruin his chances for salvation in the next world, refused all offers of money and gifts.

Ure escaped from the foreigners and tried to hide until the *Mohican* sailed, but Thomson and some of his colleagues set out across the island one rainy day and found the fugitive in a stone house in the hills. At first Ure refused even to look at the script, but he did agree to relate some of Easter's ancient traditions. While he told his tales the foreigners furnished him with "certain stimulants," as Thompson described them in his account. The old man's euphoria soon banished his fears about his place in the hereafter. A picture of a rongo-rongo was then produced, and it caused a rather unexpected reaction: never having seen a photograph before, Ure was surprised how accurately it reproduced the original object. The islander apparently had no objection to a piece of paper—even if it pictured secret, sacred writing—so he proceeded to offer a "fluent interpretation" of the photo. But, Thomson relates, it soon "became evident that he was not actually reading the characters," for "when the photograph of another tablet was substituted, the same story was continued without the change being discovered." Thomson added: "The old fellow was quite discomposed when charged with fraud at the close of an all-night session."

Later, the redoubtable Mrs. Routledge had a try at deciphering the mysterious script. During her visit in 1914, she—of course—found various islanders eager to read for her; but she quickly concluded that there was no relationship between the written signs and the spoken words uttered by her experts: "The natives were like children pretending to read and only reciting." But then she located an old man—"the last man acquainted with the script": investigators, it goes without saying, almost invariably tend to find the very last person who can solve the mystery at hand. As the native began to read, Mrs. Routledge listened attentively. But when he interpreted some of the signs as relating to Jesus she lost interest, concluding, "The outlook was not promising."

When Alfred Metraux arrived at the island in 1934 he caused something of a sensation by offering a large reward to anyone who could produce a genuine rongo-rongo, with a further payment to be made for the purchase of the object. The locals hastened to rummage in secret caves—Easter's equivalent of attics—but nothing salable was produced, either by the searchers or by skillful wood carvers. By then, in fact, no rongo-rongos remained on Easter Island, for earlier visitors had removed all of them. The tablets are scarcer than Vermeers: only some twenty-one exist, and to this day the script has never been definitively interpreted. In the mid-1950s Thomas Barthel, a German ethnologist, claimed to have deciphered the writing, but other experts have rather convincingly disputed the validity of his interpretations. The quest to solve the mystery will no doubt continue—as will efforts by Easter Islanders to produce information to meet the demand.

The more challenging the mystery, or the more original a proposed theory, the greater the demand for facts or artifacts to support results. Barthel noted that "the fascinating job of deciphering the early writings of mankind is beginning to run short of material." To solve the riddle of the "talking boards" that no longer talk—one of Easter Island's few true mysteries and one of the world's few remaining undeciphered languages—would represent a great feat of detection.

Similarly, what if Thor Heyerdahl could have proved conclusively that it was South Americans rather than Polynesians who settled Easter Island? Jokingly asked by a member of his expedition if he wanted someone to dig up a South American pot to prove his theory, Heyerdahl replied that whatever turned up would be of interest; but, he added, he'd be especially pleased if his workers found an object which suggested contact with American Indians. (Heyerdahl would no doubt have enjoyed the type of discovery made by Paymaster Thomson in 1886—a rock drawing of a bird-man which "bore a striking resemblance to the decoration on a piece of pottery which I once dug up in Peru, while making excavations among the graves of the Incas.")

It is not generally realized that Heyerdahl's expedition was a private one, organized and paid for by the Norwegian himself. The same is true of Mrs. Routledge's 1914 expedition, and it is interesting to compare those two private ventures and adventures, some four decades apart in time. Perhaps it's because the world no longer has room for the old-style gentleman or lady amateur who journeys for pleasure rather than for profession or profit, but for some reason there's a certain intensity and professionalism about the Heyerdahl expedition which Mrs. Rout-

ledge's, to her credit and our amusement, lacks. She
traveled to Easter Island not to prove a theory or make
great discoveries but only as a sort of lark. Mrs. Routledge
explains in the preface to her book, *The Mystery of Easter
Island: The Story of an Expedition*, that she and her
husband Scoresby "decided to see the Pacific before we
died" and that when they asked the British Museum to
recommend a place to go, Easter Island was suggested.

Mrs. Routledge is among the last of those inquisitive
amateurs—a great and now vanished species—possessing
the time and money to satisfy his or her curiosity. She is
what Mark Twain called the "unbiased traveler seeking
information," which he held to be "the pleasantest and
most irresponsible trade there is." Mrs. Routledge's book
is a delicious relic of that old tradition. She relates, for
example, how they organized the expedition: "It was
therefore decided, as Scoresby is a keen yachtsman, that it
was worth while to procure in England a little ship of our
own." As it turned out, the "little ship" they sought they
ended up building themselves—a 90-foot, 121-ton yacht.
Then they arranged for stores and for newspapers to be
delivered at ports along the way—*The Times*, of course,
and also journals of two societies for women's suffrage.

What is charming about Mrs. Routledge is that she is
both serious and not serious. She and her husband left
England in February 1913 and by Christmas found themselves moored in a cove in Patagonia. Mocking other
travel accounts, she writes: "It is, I believe, the correct
thing to give the menu on these occasions." She then
describes the holiday meal, listing such dishes as
"Pommes de terre de Punta Arenas," "Pouding Noël de
Army & Navy Stores," "Bonbons Peppermint à la School-
girl," and "Café de Rio de Janerio." The expedition
reached Easter Island in March 1914 and stayed seventeen
months. As usual, the natives were delighted to supply
legends and objects to meet the visitors' demands, and for
the most part Mrs. Routledge took their tales seriously
and took away their relics earnestly.

One of her greatest finds, so she thought, was the remains of Easter Island's last cannibal. The islanders practiced cannibalism until shortly after missionaries arrived in the mid-1860s, when two Peruvian traders received the honor of being the last people to be eaten. The tastiest parts were said to be fingers, toes, and buttocks. A doctor on the O'Higgins, a Chilean warship that visited Easter in 1871, noted a striking difference in the muscle tone and physical activity of the old male natives as contrasted with the young ones; the physician attributed the better condition of the older men to the presence of meat— human flesh—in their diet. There seems to be a sort of poetic justice—or perhaps it's just irony—in finding the fleshless bones of a man who ate human flesh. Mrs. Routledge became quite excited when one day at the top of Ranokao Volcano a native appeared from a crevice in the rocks carrying a thigh bone. She rushed into the opening and found a skeleton there. "Bones were in the department of the absent member of the Expedition," she writes, "but it was of course essential to collect them." After packing the bones in her lunch basket, Mrs. Routledge asked the natives to tell her the story about the cannibal, and the islanders willingly and quickly complied.

Ko Tori, as the last cannibal was called, lived at the opposite end of the island but he came to the cave on Ranokao to dine. There used to be a cooking place there, Mrs. Routledge was told, but stones now covered it. When the man died, the story went, he wanted to be buried at the site of his feasts—a sentimental cannibal, he was—so the corpse was carried from the other end of the island over to the cave. Mrs. Routledge was then informed that an old man present that very day had been one of the bearers of the body. This upset her: Mrs. Routledge regretted disturbing the dead man's remains before one of his mourners. But far from being perturbed by this sacrilege, the islanders were greatly amused and laughed until they were "suffocating with mirth," explaining "between sobs of laughter" that Ko Tori was now being taken to England in a basket. Mrs. Routledge accepted that explanation of their amusement, and the bones were indeed carried across the sea to England for study at the Royal College of Surgeons. But perhaps the hearty laughter erupted not because of Ko Tori's posthumous trip abroad but because the gullible visitor had swallowed the cannibal tale, bones and all.

In contrast to Mrs. Routledge's delightfully amateurish adventures are the more professional—and even clinical—approaches to Easter Island. Dr. Stephen-Chauvet, a French physician, diagnosed from afar—never having visited Easter—the reason for the grotesque appearance of small wooden carvings of human figures, claiming that the "moai-kava-kava" statuettes were modeled after natives who themselves were deformed by endocrine gland or thyroid conditions. Where does that sort of scientific approach to Easter lead? One man's bones are another's research data. In a paper written by a professor of anthropology about the cranial findings of Heyerdahl's expedition there appears this representative sentence: "The grouped males in Table 13 show mostly a pentagomid or ovoid shape in the norma verticalis, and a characteristic hausform shape in the norma occipitalis."

That somehow seems as remote from Mrs. Routledge, her cannibal bones in a picnic basket, and the old days of the "unbiased traveler seeking information" as Easter Island is from the rest of the world.

—3—

For over two and a half centuries now, visitors from the outside world have gaped at Easter Island and its inhabitants. At the same time, the islanders have observed the outsiders come and go, viewing them, as one visitor put it, "merely as a species of fauna that comes seldom and soon departs." Whether unbiased travelers seeking information or professional investigators, the strangers are all

fauna of the collecting species: they come to gather legends, souvenirs, and solutions to mysteries, all of which
the natives are only too glad to furnish. The locals view
the visiting fauna as a source of income and as bearers of
scarce goods from the distant outside world to be bought,
bartered for, or, preferably, lifted. It is the inquisitive
meeting the acquisitive.

Roggeveen, whose narrative of his discovery of the island anticipates virtually all the principal themes related
by subsequent visitors, told how the natives boarded his
ship and proceeded to pinch sailors' hats as well as a
tablecloth, a sufficient warning to him "that one must take
special heed to keep close watch over everything." Almost all the crews of subsequent ships experienced the
same light-fingered behavior. Captain Cook called the islanders "expert thieves." La Pérouse tells of being "robbed
of our hats and handkerchiefs," after which two officers
inform him that "the Indians had just committed a new
theft"—a daring underwater raid to cut a cable and remove the grapnel of the *Astrolab*, La Pérouse's ship.
Paymaster Thomson reported that when he and his associates quit work early on Christmas Day in 1886 and
returned to camp for their holiday meal, he "found that
our Christmas cheer had been reduced to 'hard tack' and
island mutton by the léger-de-main of our native as-
sistants." In more recent times it was said that, although
the island's largest industry was sheep raising, its most
profitable industry was sheep stealing. By the time
Metraux reached Easter in 1934 as a member of the
Franco-Belgian expedition, stealing on the island had
become so legendary he could say about a woman who
grabbed a pack of cigarettes and ran off with it that "this
theft delighted us," for it transported Metraux back to the
old days of the early explorers, such as Cook and La
Pérouse.

But it would be wrong to leave the impression that the
natives are but a band of thieves. For one thing, it should
be realized that because the people live on such a remote

and isolated island they've always been forced to sca-
venge goods and materials from any possible source. For
years, for example, the islanders had to rely on residues of
shipwrecks washed ashore for their wood supply. To the
locals, visitors simply represent a source of supply. And
from the perspective of the natives, thieving is perhaps
only doing unto the outsiders what the strangers have
done unto them. The ships arrived and carried away both
the island's people and much of its cultural inheritance.
Europeans have removed some of the great stone statues
and all of the rongo-rongo tablets, as well as many small
wood and stone carvings and various other artifacts. In
her book, Mrs. Routledge offers thanks to the European
resident manager of the sheep ranch on Easter "for his
practical aid on the Island; since we left he has obtained
for us a skin of the sacred bird which we had been unable
to procure, and forwarded. . .it." You wonder how Mrs.
Routledge would feel if some foreigner came to her place
and lifted from her one of her sacred skins, or its local
equivalent.

From the very beginning, outsiders have given the islanders ample cause to be wary. Roggeveen's visit made
the natives gun-shy—literally—of foreigners. He relates
how his landing party of one hundred and thirty-four
armed men were proceeding inland when suddenly, at the
rear of the ranks, shouting and shots sounded—" 't is tyd,
't is tyd, geeft vuur" ("It's time, it's time, fire"), called some
of the men. Thienhoven, an assistant ship's pilot, and six
other sailors proceeded to shoot and kill ten or twelve
islanders and wounded a number of others. Later, when
the American whaler *Pindos* called at Easter in 1811, the
crew brought some women aboard for the night and, after
casting them into the water the next day, ship's mate
Waden amused himself and his fellow sailors by firing
rifle shots at the swimming women.

Usually, however, visitors used the women of Easter for
purposes other than target practice. When La Pérouse
arrived in April 1786 the natives offered to the *Astrolab*

crew the services of thirteen- and fourteen-year-old girls, but no Frenchman used "the barbarous right," the commander reported, cautiously adding, in case any exceptions were found, that "if there were some moments dedicated to nature, the desire and consent were mutual, and the women made the first advances." George Peard, a member of Captain Beechey's scientific voyage on the *Blossom*, which reached Easter in November 1825, vividly described in his journal the sirenlike scene on a rock near the shore which "was covered as thick as possible with females, I supposed by way of welcome, and that on our landing one of the Natives brought a fine young woman & offered her to us."

Perhaps the local women were so freely offered to outsiders not only for commercial reasons but also in order that the local race could be refreshed by the genes of imported fauna. Visitors serve as suppliers of new flesh and blood—useful for purposes other than as cannibal goodies—as well as purveyors of other less organic goods and materials. My guide and host on Easter, Daniel Tepano, told me that even in modern times the islanders encourage their children to marry Chileans from the mainland—"el continente," as the locals call it. Many of the islanders bear features suggestive of European ancestry. Daniel is no doubt a descendant of Juan Tepano, the guide used by Mrs. Routledge and by Alfred Metraux, and he may also be the great-great-great-etc.-grandson of Captain Cook.

As did his forebears, who met passing ships to barter with the sailors, Daniel Tepano meets the arriving flights to offer his services as a guide and his house as a residence for visiting fauna. On any island, arrival is a special event, and on one as remote as Easter it's a particularly important occurrence. Easter epitomizes remoteness, when Henry Miller wanted an image to evoke the quality in his *The Colossus of Maroussi*, he compares that strangeness, to him, of seeing a pair of businessmen and a stenographer on the Greek island of Crete to the isolated

Pacific land speck: "Imagine what it would be like to find two businessmen and a stenographer on Easter Island! Imagine how a typewriter would sound in that Oceanic silence!"

Even now, when the LAN-Chile plane touches down on Easter twice a week, once coming from Santiago and once returning from Tahiti, the arrival of the outside world on the island is an important occurrence. That frequency—as well as the air link itself—is a relatively recent development. It was only in 1951, on January 19, that the first flight from the mainland of Chile to Easter took place. The navigator, R. Parragué Singer, wrote a Saint-Exupéry-like account of the trip which appeared in the first issue of *Geochile*, Chile's Geographical Society publication. The radio compass and transmitter failed during the flight, and "from this moment, navigation depended exclusively on the accuracy of our calculations." The moon and the Southern Cross were used to keep the plane on course, and finally "the sun appeared like a red disc over a sea of clouds," and at 1:33 in the afternoon Easter Island slid into view. "In Mataveri we could see the landing strip marked with white lines. All the islanders were waiting next to the strip. We made two passes to study the best way to land. I finally decided to land after circling the volcano Rano Kao and passing over Ovahe." On arrival, the islanders surrounded the plane and sang the national anthem. "With this flight," Singer wrote, "the island and the Continent became connected in 19 hours, instead of 9 days by boat."

But not until the late 1960s was regular air service introduced. Before that the islanders were required to rely on the yearly visit of the *Presidente Pinto*, sent out by the Chilean navy to deliver supplies and pick up wool. The natives were so isolated from the outside world then that they developed no immunity to common ailments, and when the ship arrived many of them caught what they called "the Pinto disease"—cough, sore throat, and diarrhea. The boat brought only the most essential items. No

cereals or bread were included, for example, for the is-
land-grown sweet potatoes could serve as a bread sub-
stitute, as they had for years. It was for that reason that the
early missionaries had to use the word "food" in place of
the phrase "our daily bread" when they translated the
Lord's Prayer into the local language.

The arrival in January 1864 of the first missionary, Eugène Eyraud, was an event of some drama, one which
typifies much of the suspicion and fascination of the
islanders toward outsiders. Eyraud appeared not long
after the Peruvian slave raids, which partly explains why
the natives were not friendly. A scout sent ahead to survey
the situation on the island returned to Eyraud's ship and
advised him not to land, explaining that "the people are
horrible to look at. They are menacing, armed with lan-
ces," present "a dreadful appearance," and are shouting
"savage cries." This failed to deter Eyraud. Perhaps it even
encouraged him: the description indicated the natives
seemed ripe for civilizing and salvation. After landing,
the missionary and his party proceeded to establish themselves on the island in the face of harassment by the
natives who had so often been harassed by outsiders. Like
the guards assigned to watch Alfred Dreyfus on Devil's
Island, the Easter Islanders followed Eyraud everywhere
and observed every move he made. Once, members of an
especially unfriendly clan stripped him naked and aimed
a stone at the spot where it would hurt him the most.
Another time the islanders stoned a corrugated iron hut
Eyraud had raised; finding the noise a novelty, they
adopted the habit of dancing around the structure while
pounding it with their fists and raining onto it a hail of
stones. Eyraud again lost his trousers when forced by a
native to hand them over while working at the bottom of a
well. But eventually Father Eyraud won the people's con-
fidence, and by the time he died in 1868 he'd converted
nearly all of them—or at least baptised them, even if the
natives hadn't all grown up to be true believers.

That must have been a strange ritual for the islanders—

baptism and conversion under the hand and teaching of one of those many odd outsiders who had come to Easter from distant foreign lands. Some had brought firepower or buying and bartering power, while others arrived carrying "the Pinto disease" or left carrying away statues, rongo-rongos, and sacred bird skins. In 1965 a Canadian medical expedition appeared with a refrigerated Christmas tree which the visitors set up and decorated with aluminum foil used to cook fish; as the tinsel rattled in the breeze it filled the air with a fishy odor. Even for the most devout of the converted natives, that homage to Christ's birthday must have seemed an odd way to celebrate. Many strangers from the outside world have no doubt appeared even more strange and exotic to the islanders than have the locals to the visitors. From the viewpoint of the natives, perhaps the real mystery of Easter Island is the odd behavior patterns of the foreigners who visit the place.

Imagine this scene: a group of Spaniards arrive suddenly out of the blue—the vast blue Pacific—and circle and survey the island; they then land and proceed to the interior, there planting three small crosses atop three low hills, after which chaplains chant litanies, muskets shoot volleys into the air, and the foreigners' ships fire 21-gun salutes as the men shout "Viva el Rey." Then the visitors sail away forever. What would the natives make of a performance like that? That was no imaginary happening: it was the way a Spanish expedition sent from Peru behaved when its members showed up in November 1770 to take possession of Easter—which they renamed San Carlos—for the king of Spain. The narrative of Don Felipe Gonzalez y Haedo, captain of one of the ships, relates that the islanders who had gathered to watch the ritual repeated it along with the visitors. It must have been like some sort of strange game for the natives—a game whose rules they didn't really understand.

The settled rituals of the Europeans no doubt often seem strange and wondrous to so-called primitive people. On hearing French sailors playing the "Marseillaise," Tasmanian aborigines reacted by contorting their bodies and making strange gestures, one young native becoming so enthusiastic that he tore his hair out while emitting a series of loud cries. A similar sort of ceremony took place in a remote part of Africa when Samuel Baker, a nineteenth-century English explorer, was sent south from Egypt by Khedive Ismail to annex the Upper Nile to Egypt and suppress the slave trade in the area. After organizing his expedition in Khartoum, Baker headed south and in April 1871 he reached Gondokoro, a tiny settlement on the Nile in what is now Sudan. On May 26 Baker carried out a ceremony annexing the surrounding territory to Egypt. Men in clean uniforms paraded, and the Ottoman flag was raised on an eighty-foot pole. The territory was named Equatoria, and Gondokoro, chosen as the capital, was renamed Ismailia. The only spectators to this annexation ceremony were a few naked Bari tribesmen, who faded into the jungle after the festivities. One wonders what the natives thought about the curious doings of the visitors. A deed perhaps even more baffling to the locals occurred in 1814 when Samuel Marsden, chaplain to the New South Wales colony in Australia, purchased for twelve axes two hundred acres of land at Rangihihoura in New Zealand. Because the seller couldn't write, Marsden decided that in place of a signature the deed of sale should carry the chief's *moko*, or face tattoo. What did the observers make of copying their chief's tattoo onto a piece of paper?

The clash of cultures is especially pronounced on Easter, for the island is remote and few of its residents have ever left home. Departure for them—in contrast to an outsider leaving—is a major event. For the visitor, leaving Easter Island is an anticlimax. By then the visitor has heard the legends and seen the great stone statues, and probably acquired small, crude copies of them, and will soon return to his own familiar world. But to a native, leaving is the start of a journey to far, strange lands, places where muskets and missionaries and professors studying cranial shapes and a lot of other similarly curious things and people have originated. Even today, in the jet age, departure of an islander is an important event that is celebrated with old-fashioned rituals. Friends and family clad in white-feathered costumes dance in that gracefully swaying Polynesian motion to the strains of a guitar as the departing native is bedecked with strand after strand of seashell necklaces. It is the sort of performance a cynical traveler would say was sponsored by Kodak, but in this case it was spontaneous and natural, a heartfelt and tearful expression of farewell to one venturing out into the great and mysterious world beyond the familiar precincts of Easter Island.

As for the rest of us visitors waiting there for the plane, we were simply the most recent in a long series of specimens of a type by now well known to the islands: a somewhat strange species of fauna who appears out of the blue, gawks, pays, and soon departs forever.

—4—

Pablo Neruda's short poem about Easter Island under rain begins:

At night I dream that you and I are two plants
that grow together, with entwined roots,
and that you know the earth and rain like my
     mouth,
because of earth and of rain we are made.

It is that sort of organic sensation—the feeling of being linked with nature and with the past—that the great stone statues of Easter Island create in the visitor. For me, that is the most memorable aspect of a visit to the island. By those statues, the past dwarfs the present; through those statues, art and nature are linked.

The past exists on Easter with an almost tangible presence. Mrs. Routledge noted that "in Easter Island the past is the present; it is impossible to escape from it; the inhabitants of today are less real than the men who have gone." And Arnold Toynbee, citing Easter as an example of a culture developed in response to the challenge of adverse circumstances, compares the two races which inhabit the island—one of flesh and blood, the other hewn from stone—and he contrasts what he calls the primitive, degenerated, contemporary real-life Polynesians with the monumental figures that remain as evidence of the great accomplishments of the past.

The most striking group of figures are those located at what the islanders call "the factory"—a volcano quarry where more than two hundred statues lie in various stages of completion, and at the bottom of which about seventy completed ones stand. Those unfinished figures—typically about thirty feet long, with the largest over twice that size and weighing some sixty tons—lie face up nestled in niches cut out of the side of the volcano. Because each is to a greater or lesser degree a part of the natural material used to form them, you can see the creative process in progress as it evolves through successive stages. But the final stage was not reached: for some reason the figures there were abandoned before completion. They are not fallen statues but ones which have never risen, and there is something poignant about the stillborn—and, in a way, seemingly still being born—shapes emerging from the lava, inchoate order beginning to be carved out of a natural chaos like Michelangelo's *Slaves* still enslaved in the confines of the only partly cut marble blocks.

Those unfinished figures are neither art nor nature but something in between. You can both admire them from a distance as creations and tread on them as natural stepping stones up the volcano's flank. In addition, they represent tangible and accessible contact with a past that, through them, takes on an organic texture. Perhaps the only other places which offer such a direct, touchable—

and touching—link between raw material and creation and the present remains of past abandoned efforts are in Greece and in Egypt. In Greece there is another island statue factory on Naxos, where a thirty-four-foot marble Apollo lies on its back in the quarry. Intended for Delos, twenty-five miles away, the figure was never sent because the poor quality stone developed cracks. The technique of moving the statues carved there was to pry them open underneath with wooden wedges which were then water-soaked so they would swell and split loose the effigy, which would be taken on rollers to the shore and rafted to its destination. At Luxor in Egypt you can walk on a half-finished cracked granite obelisque in the quarry there.

A nineteenth-century traveler in Egypt, Charles Dudley Warner, went a step or two farther at Abu Simbel, where the huge stone Ramses II figures rise in the cliffside; he "climbed up into the lap of one of the statues; it is there only that you can get an adequate idea of the size of the body. What a roomy lap! I sat comfortably in the navel of the statue, as in a niche, and mused on the passing of the nations."

My visit to Abu Simbel didn't include a reflective pause in Ramses' navel, but at the statue factory on Easter Island the visitor can't help but stroll over the anatomy of those prone, unfinished figures. Alfred Metraux described the experience this way: "To reach the neighboring niches it is necessary to walk on bodies, to catch hold of noses, to step across blocks and outcrops of tufa transformed into statues or the embryos of statues. The visitor distinguishes one or two at first, then suddenly realizes that he is sitting on a gigantic eyebrow arch."

It is hardly possible to get in closer contact with the nexus between nature and art, past and present, flesh and earth than by sitting on those figures at Rano-Raraku volcano. There you are in touch with what lies beyond the self and the now. You feel connected in an organic way with what existed long before you and with that which will survive long after you have gone. You feel the way

Neruda expressed himself in the rest of his Easter Island poem:

> At times
> I think that in death we will sleep below,
> in the depths at the feet of the effigy,
> looking at
> the Ocean which inspired us to build and to love.

It is that sort of feeling—the organic connection with the vastness that is not you—that to me is the real mystery and the marvel you find on Easter Island.

4

Pagan

—1—

BURMA HAS ALWAYS BEEN A LAND APART.

These days, the visa the Burmese issue to visitors reminds you of the country's isolation: large red letters set in a long red rectangle warn and inform you, "Land Route Not Permissible." But even in the days when overland routes were permitted they were hardly hospitable to heavy traffic. To reach Burma from China, travelers must cross a wide belt of rough mountains; and from India the Patkoi range presents a barrier which is reinforced by wild tribes that inhabit the area. Burma has never been an easy place to reach.

These days, you are also limited by time. The Burmese now let you into their country for a week, a generous allotment only when compared with the twenty-four hours allowed tourists in the 1960s. Once there, most of your brief time is depleted traveling between the scattered points of interest, since transportation in Burma is unpredictable—except that you can always predict with certainty that it will be slow and unpunctual. Your limited time in Burma flies but not always your plane.

There is this to be said, however, for the difficulty of access and shortness of time: those limitations of travel to and in Burma accentuate the exotic nature of the country, and they make you feel transported, almost literally, into a civilization distant in both time and place. The challenges of reaching and seeing the place reinforce the impression that Burma is a land apart.

Already a half century ago, Joseph Conrad, in a preface to a book about Burma, complained that it had become difficult to find places foreign in aspect and ambiance: "the time for such. . . travel is past on this earth girt about with cables, with an atmosphere made restless by the waves of ether, lighted by that sun of the twentieth century under which there is nothing new left now, and but very little of what may still be called obscure." Burma may no longer be obscure as in centuries past, but its present sort of oldness is still new to contemporary travelers accustomed to finding twentieth-century encroachments everywhere; the richest and greatest residue of Burma's past is located in the country's ancient and now nearly abandoned capital of Pagan.

Pagan (pronounced pa-GAHN) lies on the Irrawaddy River about four hundred miles northwest of Rangoon, the present-day capital, and one hundred miles southwest of Mandalay. The ancient capital is known as "the city of five thousand pagodas"—an understatement rather than hyperbole, for some thirteen thousand pagodas and other religious structures were built during Pagan's golden age between 1044 and 1287. By now, however, only about five thousand of the temples still stand, or lie, in various states of repair.

Conrad would no doubt be pleased to know that even today Pagan is behind the times, for it is still not easy of access, as are so many other once remote places. Shortly after the turn of the century a traveler in Burma noted that the former Burmese capital is "the most difficult" of all the old towns in the country to reach, and as late as 1967 a visitor to Pagan described the trip as a "far from simple journey."

At the time of my visit to Burma six years later, the

journey to Pagan was still complicated. One possibility was to take a river boat up the Irrawaddy to Pagan. The Irrawaddy Flotilla Co. runs three-hundred-foot-long shallow-draft paddle steamers, the biggest ones in the world. As a lifelong resident of a Mississippi River city, that form of travel attracts me, but the limited time available was insufficient for such a leisurely cruise. The national airline flies, on occasion, from Rangoon to Pagan, but, as soon became apparent, the procedure for obtaining a place on the plane is at best haphazard and at worst an example of the mysterious East at its most mysterious. The final possibility was to take the train from Rangoon to Mandalay and then work back down to Pagan by plane or train or by whatever other means presented themselves.

A Dutch friend of mine and I spent an evening in the bar of our hotel in Rangoon, the Strand, discussing the alternatives. The Strand is a period piece: one of those faded hotels that in the old days catered to colonials sent out to run the empire and which now exudes not only more atmosphere than you can absorb but more than you want to absorb. A large, ferocious-looking lizard clung to the ceiling as if designed to be a part of it, and the warm beer was served up complete with a well-nourished floating mosquito. Ceiling fans squeaked slow, uneven revolutions overhead and the teak floor creaked underfoot. The mosquito drowned, the lizard slithered away, and my friend and I finally opted for the train. The next morning we found ourselves on a vintage carriage that might have dated from the beginnings of the Burma railway in 1887. At 7 A.M.—more or less—we pulled out of Rangoon station and started off on the road to Mandalay.

—2—

The nearly four hundred mile train trip to Mandalay took almost twelve hours. We passed through countryside untouched by the twentieth century or, for that matter, by any century since man first became agricultural. I noted only one tractor along the way; all the ploughing was otherwise being done by oxen or by hand. Huts woven out of wood strips and roofed with thatch seemed vulnerable to the slightest breeze. Bicycles, or more often grounded foot power, transported people along dirt roads or trails. At infrequent stops, women clustered around the train to sell fruits, water from jars balanced on their heads, and rice which was served on a matched set of large leaf plates. The train, so it seemed, was taking us not only to Mandalay but also into the past.

On the wooden bench opposite us sat a Burmese doctor wearing a colorful "longyi," a long wraparound skirt commonly worn by men in Burma. He kept his bare feet tucked up under his skirt and for most of the trip chewed on a betel quid—nuts and spices wrapped in a leaf smeared with lime. He continually spit onto the floor red saliva that looked like blood coughed up from tubucular lungs. The Burmese claim that no one can speak their language until one chews betel, but since the doctor spoke excellent English we passed up his offer of betel and passed the time and the miles chatting with him.

He was a man of few words, but perceptive ones. Although a Christian, so he said, the doctor in response to our question offered a succinct definition of the essence of Buddhism: "Contentment." (Another idea of the meaning of Buddhism found expression on a sign I later noticed in Mandalay: "Be kind to animals by not eating them.") And as to what the Burmese thought about possible threats from China, he replied, "They're indifferent," punctuating his answer by letting loose an exceptionally large clot of red saliva. Could not "indifference" be coupled with "contentment" to round out a description of the Buddhist mentality?

It was dark by the time we reached Mandalay. On arrival my Dutch friend and I, along with the few other foreigners on the train, were immediately surrounded by armed guards and conducted into a small room where officials interrogated us and ordered us to show our passports and to register. At the time, it was a somewhat unnerving experience but looking back it's easy to see that the procedure typifies the deep suspicion of the Burmese people toward foreigners. Such suspicion is hardly unreasonable: in the same way that outsiders often brought trouble to Easter Island, foreigners have usually come to Burma—as missionaries, traders, invaders, administrators—to exploit the country rather than to develop or enrich it. The language of the Burmese expresses their attitude toward outsiders: the word for man, "lu," is applied only to the people of Burma; Chinese are called "tayok"; the rest of humanity is referred to as "kala," which not only means "foreigner" but also carries a connotation of inferiority. (By way of contrast, in the Balinese language there is no word at all for foreigner.)

From very early days, Burma remained remote from and unknown to the civilized world. In the first century A.D., Pliny the Elder wrote about Ceylon from information gathered by envoys sent there by the Roman Emperor Claudius, and a century later Ptolemy included some areas of the East in his *Geographia*, but neither man mentioned Burma. Only over a millennium later, at the end of the thirteenth century, did the country come to the attention of Europe when Marco Polo visited and wrote about Burma—mainly Pagan—and it took another hundred years before the country was shown on a European map, the Catalan map of 1375.

The rise of Islam raised a barrier between Europe and the East, which for a time kept Asia shrouded behind the Muslim curtain. Then the great explorations of the East began. In the sixteenth century Portuguese missionaries, mercenaries, and adventurers traveled to Burma, among them Ferdinand Mendes Pinto, whose extravagant tales of his exploits in Asia were so unbelievable that European languages adopted his middle name as a new word for falsehood. Less mendacious accounts of sixteenth-century Burma appeared in two narratives collected by

Hakluyt, one the chronicle of Caesar Fredericke, a "marchant of Venice," and the other, much of it lifted from Fredericke, by Ralph Fitch, a London merchant.

Fredericke left Venice for the East in 1563, and six years later he arrived in Pegu, then the capital of Burma. This was three centuries after the fall of Pagan, but Fredericke's description of Pegu could in many respects well have been a description of the former capital city of Burma. He tells of a walled city surrounded by moats filled with crocodiles; especially impressive to him was the king's albino "eliphants": "he hath foure that be white, a thing so rare that a man shall hardly finde another king that hath any such." That rarity of whiteness, I might note in passing, struck me as auspicious: as one prematurely, or so I like to think, grey—"flags planted by the King of Death," the Burmese call white hair—I imagined the Burmese might treat me with special reverence during my visit there. However, to receive such attention one must, it seems, not only offer whiteness but also be an elephant, and so my qualifications were found lacking. The white elephant in the East is apparently a sort of living talisman. Prior to becoming the Buddha, Gautama's last incarnation was as a white elephant. It is curious that what in the East is a venerated beast signifies to an English-speaking person an undesirable possession—a "white elephant."

Fredericke goes on to refer to Pegu's golden religious structures—they were similar to those at Pagan (Marco Polo mentions a pagoda there "covered with a plate of gold an inch in thickness")—which "they call Pagodes, whereof there are great aboundance, great and smal, and these houses are made in forme of little hilles, like to Sugar loaves or to Bells, and some of these houses are as high as a reasonable steeple. . . . Also they consume about these Varely or idol houses great store of leafe-gold, for that they overlay all the tops of the houses with gold. . . . And by this means they make gold dearer in Pegu than it would bee, if they consumed not so much in this vanities." Still today "vanitie" shapes the use of gold in Burma: in Rangoon's National Museum is displayed perhaps the world's only yak tail set in gold.

Ralph Fitch, the first Englishman known to have visited Burma, also commented on the golden capital of Pegu: "a citie very great, strong, and very faire." All the walls of the king's pagoda, Fitch notes, "are gilded with golde," and he says of statues in other pagodas that "their expences in gilding of their images are wonderfull." Pagan must have looked something like that before the city fell at the end of the thirteenth century. Fitch left England in 1583 on the *Tiger*—the ship referred to by one of the *Macbeth* witches: "Her husband's to Aleppo gone, master o' the Tiger." After making his way by land to Goa, a colony of Portugal on the west coast of India, Fitch was arrested as a spy by the Portuguese authorities there. He managed to escape and then traveled on, reaching Pagan in 1587. By the time he finally made it back to England four years later, Fitch's relatives, supposing him dead, had already divided up his estate. Three centuries later his descendant, Albert Fytche, served in Burma as British Chief Commissioner from 1867 to 1871; Fytche Square in Rangoon is named after him.

From the seventeenth century on, the British dominated Burma. In 1895 they annexed the country to Britain's main Asian possession, India. Then came the "Burmese Days" described by George Orwell in his novel of that name: the era of "Kipling-haunted little clubs" and such colonial characters as MacGregor, deputy commissioner of an up-country district, who in one passage is archetypically described as struggling on a bamboo mat to keep himself fit by performing exercises from Nordenflycht's *Physical Jerks for the Sedentary*. Such were the days of Empire. Those days lasted until 1948 when Burma became independent and declined to join the Commonwealth—the first former British colony to sever all political ties with the mother country since the thirteen American colonies left the Empire in 1776.

Independence encouraged the Burmese to view the

future with a hope based on nostalgia for the long-gone time of Pagan—a period which has always represented to the people of Burma the greatest era in their history. An inscription written in the dark ages after the fall of Pagan refers to the kingdom as the "fairest and dearest of lands." Shortly before independence in November 1947, Burma's first prime minister, U Nu, voiced his hope that within five years Burma "will see once again such a golden age as Pagan."

Independence day was originally set for January 6, 1948, but then changed to 4:20 A.M. two days earlier when astrologers decided that January 4 was a more auspicious time for the event. Burma is perhaps the only nation in the world ever to select its independence day— and minute—based on astrological advice. But then Burma has always been a land apart.

—3—

The pervasive influence of astrology in Burmese life is perhaps one reason why Burma seems to Westerners to be a land apart. Mandalay, where my Dutch friend and I spent a day, is the astrology capital of the country. I don't know whether Mandalay astrologers advised the government in 1948 about the timing of the most auspicious moment for independence, but they do perform other important divinations, such as setting the day for the Burmese New Year. The year begins sometime in April when Thagyamin, King of the Nats—natural spirits worshipped by the Burmese—leaves Mt. Popa, Burma's equivalent of Mt. Olympus, to descend to earth. The day that event occurs is determined by Mandalay astrologers.

Astrology is as important in the birth of every Burmese baby as it was in the birth of the nation. Father Sangermano, an Italian missionary priest who lived in Burma at the end of the eighteenth century, wrote: "There perhaps is not an nation in the world so given to superstition as the Burmese. . . . No sooner is an infant born, than they run to some Brahmin [astrologer] to learn what is the constellation that presided at its birth, and this is written upon a palm-leaf, together with the day and hour of the birth, to serve for the divinations." Of course, one man's superstition is another's conviction—what would a Burmese say about the beliefs of a Father Sangermano?—but still today when a Burmese child is born an astrologer prepares his horoscope, and the document becomes the individual's most valuable possession.

Written on a palm leaf strip, the horoscope is called a "sadā" and is consulted by its owner throughout his life in order to fix auspicious days and hours for marriage, travel, important business deals, and other such special events. On one side of the sadā appears the person's name, the exact time of his birth, the planet then in ascendance, and a brief horoscope—Buddha's, for example, forecast that he'd become a great king or a famous ascetic—while the other side is decorated with a number of intricate geometrical designs used by astrologers for divinations.

I have such a horoscope—but not my own. I don't know whose destiny I hold in my hands, since I can read nothing on the sadā except the year 1841. The palm strip is over four feet long and less than two inches wide and bears an especially detailed series of shapes—squares, flower petals, diamonds, ovals—all bordered by a rectangle formed by a long chain of quarter moons. Even the writing seems to carry out the astrological theme: the round characters on the leaf look like little moons hung across a big sky. This "bubble writing," as Burmese script is called, was derived from Indian Pali writing, which was square, but because the long, angular stylus strokes tore the fibre of the palm leaves the angles evolved into circles.

The best horoscopes in Burma are said to be cast by the "ponnas"—astrologers—of Mandalay. We saw them around the city, the signs advertising their services often written, for some reason, in English: perhaps use of that language lent status to a *ponna*. On one such poster appeared the word "Astrologer," below which spread a painted pair of palms: maybe the *ponnas* read palms as well as palm leaves.

The pervasive influence of astrology in Burma gives an additional twist to the time warp one feels when traveling in that country. To find a similar situation in the West it would be necessary to revert to the Italian Renaissance, when astrology was very much in fashion with rulers, princes, and the great families of the time. Cities retained astrological advisers, and from the fourteenth to the sixteenth centuries, professors of astrology lectured at leading universities. In upper class families it was the practice to draw horoscopes of young children—in the Dresden Art Gallery a painting by, or after, Giorgione shows a white-bearded sage casting the horoscope of an infant lying at his mother's feet—and even the popes were influenced by astrologers. One pontiff, Julius II,* went so far as to rely on astrological calculations to set the propitious day for his coronation, much as Burma did for its independence in 1948. But, of course, Julius II's event occurred rather less recently than did Burma's independence: his coronation was in 1503.

We spent only a day in Mandalay, the shortness of the stay enforced by the one-week limitation on visits to Burma. As soon as you finally make it "up country" you have to start planning how to get back down to Rangoon so you can leave the country before your seven-day visa expires. At the Union of Burma Airways office in town we bought a ticket for the afternoon flight to Pagan. Acquiring a ticket, however, is by no means the equivalent of getting a reservation, nor does it even evidence the existence of a flight. The general procedure for flying in Burma may be described as follows: you go to the airport and wait. And

---

*Pope Julius was the greatest art patron in the papal line. He recruited Michelangelo to paint the Sistine Chapel ceiling, and he commissioned Raphael to create the now famous Vatican frescoes.

then you wait some more. And maybe, in time, something will happen—not necessarily the flight you want, but at least something.

Any recent visitor to Burma will have fond memories of the Union of Burma Airways. The organization—if that's the word—deserves a few lines, for UBA is one of the unsung wonders of the Orient. It is no Orient express, but it is certainly a wonder. For one thing, the airline always keeps you wondering; and for another, it combines in a wondrous way the seemingly contradictory characteristics of chaos and achievement. By some mysterious process, complete confusion results in getting you, sooner or later or much later, to your destination. Perhaps UBA's schedules are based on logical principles, or maybe even occult or astrological ones, but I could never figure them out—and I doubt if anyone else could either, least of all UBA personnel. It was the airline which passeth all understanding.

Our first contact with UBA was in the airline's main office in Rangoon, next door to the Strand Hotel. When you arrive your first impression is that no one is working and that no one knows anything about flights or anything else. Before long your impression is confirmed. After a certain amount of confusion—the UBA staff seemed not to know what to do with such strange apparitions as potential passengers—a functionary directed my Dutch friend and I upstairs to a special department. We never learned what was special about that section; in fact, it seemed just as confused as the rest of the place. But perhaps its specialness was because the man there spoke English—a very special sort of English. After a while we came to understand his version of the language or at least a few words of it. We asked about flights to Pagan. He consulted some papers, then informed us that he wasn't sure about schedules because one of the company's planes was being used by "him," the "him" being General Ne Win, Burma's prime minister, whose photograph was hanging on the wall. The UBA fleet—a misnomer as a noun, an incorrect description as an adjective—consisted of a few Dutch Fokker 27s and some DC-3s, those venerable Dakotas left over from World War II and earlier, but no one ever knew exactly how many planes were in use or when or where they would fly. Whatever the number, when the general requisitioned one that was enough to upset the UBA schedule, assuming there was a schedule to begin with.

We next asked the UBA man about the possibility of reservations from Mandalay to Pagan and then back to Rangoon. I wasn't sure that possibility had ever been raised before; in fact, I'm uncertain if the concept of a reservation was known at all to UBA. After a certain delay to ponder the request, the man bestirred himself and went to the shortwave radio and called someone. The signals crackled across the ether. There was a long conversation in Burmese. The words somehow even sounded round, like their letters, and it all sounded very official. But maybe he was only chatting with his second cousin once removed in Mandalay, or perhaps with his wife or his mistress just a few blocks away, because in the end the attendant was unable to tell us anything at all about UBA flights from Rangoon to Mandalay, from up-country back down to Rangoon, or, for that matter, from anywhere to anywhere else.

It was with that experience with UBA in Rangoon behind us that we went out to the airport in Mandalay. Our expectations were limited—very limited. We waited. For a long time nothing happened. That didn't surprise us. We kept waiting. Someone said that a plane from Pagan was supposed to arrive sometime in the afternoon; but for all we knew, "he"—or, if not Ne Win, someone else—was using one of UBA's planes, perhaps the UBA plane, that day. So we resigned ourselves to a long and possibly fruitless wait. A few aircraft did land and take off, but none of them for Pagan. Our anticipation was whetted by the pre-arrival procedure. A man on the roof of a building next to the terminal would sound a gong three times about a half hour before a plane was due; then a single gong signaled arrival in five minutes.

One plane which landed was supposedly going to Pagan, so we all piled aboard. I sat next to a young soldier lying on a stretcher; the bandaged, bleeding man had been wounded in a skirmish with guerillas in the Shan states on the border with Red China. Presently, the pilot appeared from the cockpit and asked how many passengers wanted to go to Rangoon. A clear majority raised their hands. Then passengers for Pagan cast their vote, raising their hands and a commotion, but the democratic process had set the flight's course; the Pagan contingent deplaned to await the next election.

The afternoon faded and with it our hopes to reach Pagan that day. The sun dipped and turned an orange the color of robes worn by Buddhist monks. But as the time leaked away, Western frustration rather than Buddhistic contentment dominated us. Hardly indifferent to the delay—especially in light of our limited time in the country—we fretted and paced, but our pacing got us nowhere. We waited. Finally the gong again sounded and resounded, and another plane landed. Once again, passengers for Pagan boarded and this time we took our places only tentatively. Then, on being informed the plane was bound for Pagan, we settled in, and seat belt buckles rattled and snapped shut with definitive clicks.

By the time we took off it was dark. Torch-lit flares bordered the airfield and outlined its perimeter. The engines on the creaky DC-3—it creaked like the teak floor at the Strand Hotel in Rangoon—started up and the plane wheezed into motion. We taxied to one end of the field, then paused briefly for a final warm-up before charging across the dirt runway toward the flares that flickered at the far end. None too soon we lifted, and the antique plane shook under the strain of the takeoff. A fingernail moon shaped like those that decorate palm leaf horoscopes hung in the sky high above, and below us the flares' flames gradually shrunk to dots, then disappeared;

somewhere ahead of us in the darkness lay the ancient capital where—if the stars and planets favored our night flight with an auspicious horoscope—we would soon return to earth and to the past that was Pagan.

—4—

The oldest ruin at Pagan is the Sarabha Gateway, the only structure remaining from the old city built in the ninth century before Pagan's golden age began. The gateway is unique in that all the other surviving structures in the former capital—and there are thousands of them— were built for religious purposes. Pagan first became important in the middle of the ninth century when its ruler enclosed the city within a wall. The main entrance of the east wall was the Sarabha Gate, which was, and still is, flanked by two small shrines that house Nats, or spirits, to guard the city. That gate and wall fragment are what remain of the beginnings of Pagan, and they also mark the scene of the end of the beginning, for a century after the city's first stirrings the founder and greatest king of Pagan's golden age, Anawratha, passed through the Sarabha Gateway on his way to death—he was trampled by a Nat which had assumed the form of a white buffalo.

King Anawratha took the throne in 1044, but not without intrigues. A little over a hundred years before that, an earlier ruler was one day found picking cucumbers from a field without asking permission of the farmer, named Sawrahan, who proceeded to kill the king with a spade handle. The king's attendant then proclaimed, "Farmer, he who slayeth a king becometh a king," but the farmer insisted he was quite happy to stay as he was and tend to his cucumbers. The attendant continued to tempt him. When the landowner finally agreed to give up his garden and become king, he was taken to the palace and introduced to the queen, who, as the *Burmese Chronicle* relates, "instructed the farmer to bathe in warm water and cold, and rub himself with bath powders to remove all dirt and disease." Sawrahan must have learned his bathing and other royal lessons well from the queen, for he remained on the throne for thirty-three years.

The garden incident which brought Sawrahan to the throne gave him the name "the Cucumber King." Sawrahan's problem with a cucumber thief was not unique to Burma; its analogue in Western lore appears in Isaiah 1:8, a biblical allusion to Zion being as desolate "as a lodge in a garden of cucumbers," referring to the practice of farmers erecting leaf and branch watch houses to use in guarding crops against poachers and then allowing the huts to collapse after the harvest ended. Cucumbers have a long history in the consciousness and stomachs of the West. After the cucumber was brought to Europe from northern India, where the vegetable supposedly originated, it received mixed notices. John Gerard, in his 1597 *Herball,* claimed that an oatmeal and cucumber mix would cure "flegme and copper faces, red and fierie noses." In 1761 Dr. Johnson opined that "a cucumber should be well-sliced, and dressed with pepper and vinegar, and then thrown out, as good for nothing." More recently, Alexander Solzhenitsyn, in *Cancer Ward,* affirmed that "cucumbers are the only thing that gives a kind of respite."

The cucumber lore of East and West meets in the person of the legendary Baron Munchhausen, who recounts in his book of *Travels* (or, to give the full title of the first English edition, published in 1786, *Baron Munchhausen, Narrative of His Marvellous Travels and Campaigns in Russia. Humbly Dedicated and Recommended to Country Gentlemen; And, If They Please, to be repeated as their own, after a Hunt, at Horse Races, in Watering Places, and other such polite Assemblies, round the bottle and fireside*) a curious tale curiously similar to the story of how Pagan's "Cucumber King" acceded to the throne. This "polite assembly" of two, scribbler and reader, which is this book—or, for that matter, any book being read—occa-

sions me to repeat the Baron's tale. Accompanying his
father to the East, Baron Munchhausen stopped on the
way to Ceylon at an island where he was told of a large
tree with "a man and his wife, a very honest old couple,
upon its branches, gathering cucumbers (in this part of
the globe, that useful vegtable grows upon trees)." A storm
caused the tree to fall on a local tyrant king, after which
"the people chose the cucumber-gatherers for their gover-
nors"—much the same way Sawrahan became "the
Cucumber King" after he killed Pagan's reigning monarch
in the cucumber patch.

Sawrahan's reign ended in 964 when a pretender to the
throne deposed him. The new king was then, in turn,
deposed by the Cucumber King's two sons. The usurper
was confined to the monastery where he lived with his
wife and son, a boy named Anawratha. A stray arrow
launched during a stag hunt accidentally killed one of the
Cucumber King's sons, and the other son died in a duel
with Anawratha, who in 1044 assumed the throne. It was
then that Pagan's golden age began.

The next two hundred and fifty years are known as the
golden age because during that time Pagan became the
religious, political, and cultural center of Indo-China, and
in that time span literally thousands of temples, pagodas,
and other structures were built. Burmese tradition has it
that King Anawratha began raising religious buildings to
atone for his killing of the Cucumber King's son. In a
dream, Anawratha was visited by Thagyamin, head of the
Nats—he's the Nat whose descent to earth marks the beginning of the Burmese New Year—who told the king that
he could redeem himself by building "many pagodas,
caves, monastaries, rest houses." Accepting the suggestion, Anawratha began construction in 1059 of the Shwezigon, the first of Pagan's great pagodas and the pro-
totype of Mingalazedi, the empire's final important temple, built in 1274 by its last king.

The site for Shwezigon was selected by a random—yet
putatively providential—method. A white elephant, car-

rying in a jeweled shrine a duplicate of one of Buddha's teeth, was allowed to roam until it stopped to rest. At that spot, the pagoda was built. It consists of a solid, bell-shaped structure which stands on three square terraces, all covered with gold that collects and reflects the sun's rays so that you can see the glittering monument from almost anywhere in Pagan. That golden temple links Pagan's golden age with Burma of today, for Shwezigon is one of Pagan's few buildings still in use. Buddhist monks stroll or meditate; children frolic through the grove of sacred "trees"—gilded trunks that bloom with gold-leaf leaves; an astrologer, his sign bearing a hand (and perhaps his hand bearing a sign), holds consultations in one of the pavilions.

Shwezigon serves as more than a link between the past and the present: the pagoda also represents an attempt by Anawratha to merge Nat worship—a pagan, though not a Pagan, cult—into Pagan's new Buddhist religion, which the king had adopted. Since Anawratha wished to wean his people away from their belief in Nats and convert them to Buddhism, he shrewdly put images of the thirty-seven principal Nats at Shwezigon, explaining: "Men will not come for the sake of the new faith. Let them come for their old gods and gradually they will be won over." The king's hopes were to an extent fulfilled: the people both adopted the new religion and retained their old beliefs, and still today Nats play a large part in the lives of Burma's Buddhists. Nearly every Burmese house, for example, contains a hanging coconut called an "oundaw"—honorific coconut—in which resides Min Mahagiri, the house Nat and the most famous of the thirty-seven.

Min Mahagiri started life as a blacksmith named U Tin De. Fearing that U Tin De would lead a rebellion, the king of the region married the blacksmith's sister, who then summoned her brother to the palace, where the king threw him into a fire, whereupon his sister, the queen, joined him in the flames. After they died, U Tin De and his sister became Nats and lived in the tree which grew at the spot where they'd perished. Because the Nats killed anyone who came into the tree's shade, the king ordered his aides to uproot the tree and throw it into the Irrawaddy River. That accomplished, the tree floated downstream and finally drifted ashore near Pagan. The king at Pagan listened to the Nats' story and then ordered their heads—the only part of their bodies that survived the fire—placed in a shrine on Mt. Popa, the sacred peak near Pagan. U Tin De then became Min Mahagiri, Lord of the Great Mountain and, eventually, guardian of Burmese houses.

That a Nat can simultaneously inhabit both Mt. Popa and coconuts hanging in houses might at first seem incredible, but the concept is no less believable than, for example, the idea that patron saints live in heaven as well as at their various shrines. And that Nats really do exist is not simply a fantastical notion of the mystical, mysterious East. Serious, scientific Westerners have believed in such spirits. After all, even a scientist such as Sir Thomas Browne, the seventeenth-century English physician, wrote in his autobiography about "apparitions and ghosts of departed persons," noting "that those phantasms appear often."

The great King Anawratha himself benefited from Nat power at the beginning of his reign. Before Pagan's golden age began one of Burma's most important kingdoms was at Thaton, in the southern part of the country, where King Manuha ruled. In 1038, two brothers from India were shipwrecked at Thaton and taken to a monastery where they acquired supernatural powers by eating the corpse of a magician preserved by the monks for medicinal purposes. One brother, Byatwi, died and became guardian spirit of Thaton, while the other brother, Byatta, escaped and, so Burmese legend has it, chanced to meet four soldiers sent by King Anawratha to Thaton to obtain copies of the Tripitaka, the Buddhist scriptures, from King Manuha. Anawratha had been converted to Buddhism the year before, in 1056, by Shin Arahan, a priest from Thaton, who'd urged Pagan's monarch to obtain copies of the holy writ possessed by King Manuha in Thaton.

King Anawratha sent a request to King Manuha in Thaton asking him for some copies of the Tripitaka. Manuha issued a curt refusal and that was his downfall: "Manuha, this great king of so high and joyous and excellent a realm, this lord of thirty-two white elephants, merely because he answered King Anawratha's messengers in discourteous wise, came to utter destruction." Anawratha ordered his soldiers south to Thaton, which they besieged for three months until the city finally fell. The conquerors fettered King Manuha in golden chains and brought him to Pagan along with the thirty thousand inhabitants of Thaton and all the kingdom's books, which were carried on the backs of the thirty-two white elephants. Thus ended the kingdom of Thaton in a way similar to how the kingdom of Pagan would end a little over two centuries later when the last king insulted messengers sent by Kublai Khan.

The books and documents brought to Pagan from Thaton were housed in the Pitakat Taik, the monastic library built by King Anawratha in 1058. The building still stands and is one of Pagan's most striking structures, even though it's much smaller than the monumental pagodas and temples. Built of the famous local brown brick—to this day the best type of brick in Thailand is known as "Pagan brick"—the library's ground floor, its mass lightened by window openings crisscrossed by stone latticework, is topped with a roof of five slanted tiers decorated by curved flamelike projections which recall carvings on the roofs of Norway's stave churches.

Anawratha not only built two of Pagan's most important structures—the Shwezigon Pagoda and Pitakat Taik library—but also laid the foundations for further development by consolidating competing people of varying cultures into one nation with a common language and religion, thereby creating for the first time a unified country in the territory which, approximately, Burma occupies today. In 1077, when Anawratha was on an expedition away from Pagan, court astrologers warned him that he'd die before reaching home. The king's response to this news was to put his soothsayers into chains. Returning to Pagan, Anawratha was just passing through the Sarabha Gate into town when an official told him about a wild buffalo that was terrorizing people nearby.

Anawratha turned back from Pagan to seek out and destroy the beast, but it destroyed him. The white buffalo, said to be an angry Nat, gored the monarch to death, and the great king's body disappeared forever somewhere in the jungle not far from the golden spires and towering temples of his kingdom.

—5—

The tale of King Anawratha typifies the mixture of fact and legend which is Pagan's history. The stories are—as the Burmese expression puts it—as countless as the temples of Pagan, and their content recalls the elusive butterfly dreamt about by Chuang-tze, a Chinese philosopher: "I was conscious only of my happiness as a butterfly, unaware that I was Chuang. Soon I awakened, and there I was, veritably myself again. Now I do not know whether I was then a man dreaming I was a butterfly, or whether I am now a butterfly dreaming I am a man." So it is with Pagan's past: it could be that the Nats on Mt. Popa really existed and regarded the people of Pagan as strange spirits, and perhaps the so-called legends are true, while what we suppose to be facts might well be stories fabricated to lend reality to what are supposedly mere fantasies.

Much of Burma's history is recounted in *The Glass Palace Chronicle of Kings*, an eighteenth-century compilation of earlier annals. After mentioning the sixty-four worlds that existed before the one we inhabit came into being, the *Chronicle* relates the history of our world as viewed from Burma. The narrative tells of Anawratha and how, after his death, his son Sawlu served as king for seven years until he was succeeded in 1084 by Kyanzittha, a warrior born to a court official and an Indian princess the official was bringing to Burma to marry Anawratha. In other names, it is the Lancelot and Guinevere story; and what Churchill wrote about the Arthurian legends could also be said about Pagan's history: "It is all true, or it ought to be; and more and better besides."

Kyanzittha, who ruled until 1112, was one of Pagan's great builders. He completed the Shwezigon, and to it the king added a series of poetic inscriptions containing noble sentiments: "his people shall be unto him as a child to its mother's bosom. . .he shall soften the hearts of those who intend evil. . .he shall exhort to speak good those who speak evil." Kyanzittha also built the Ananda Temple, probably the kingdom's most famous building and the one which represents the evolution of Pagan architecture from monolithic structures like Shwezigon into true temples with passageways and places inside for the display of Buddha statues.

When the foundation of Ananda was laid, King Kyanzittha ordered a child to be buried alive so the temple would enjoy a guardian spirit. This was a rite no more barbarous than the one attributed in 1 Kings 16:34 to Hiel, who, when he built Jericho, "laid the foundation thereof in Abiram his firstborn, and set up the gates thereof in his youngest son Segub." Kyanzittha, however, was even more fastidious than Hiel, for according to tradition Ananda temple so pleased the king that he executed the building's architect to prevent him from reproducing the structure elsewhere.

Ananda is one of the few ancient buildings at Pagan which is still used. Entering through one of the four corridors, you pass large, padlocked chests on which perch signs which request donations for such projects as "gilding. . .electricity. . .pavement. . .general use." I wondered which cause was the most favored by the locals.

You continue past stands displaying colorful lacquerware
on sale and then pass by great teak wood doors to reach a
chamber where there rises a thirty-foot-high gilded Buddha that glows from a touch of light artfully allowed to
enter the sanctuary from openings above. Outside, the
temple climbs in a series of seven square receding terraces
bordered with crenellations to a gilded spire, the only
part of the building not whitewashed, which peaks one
hundred and sixty-eight feet above the ground. Taken as a
whole, both outside and in, Ananda can fairly be called
an Oriental version of a Gothic cathedral. In at least one
way that comparison is not too farfetched: the four great
statues inside Ananda represent not only Buddha but also
a saint called Josaphat—the name under which Buddha
was canonized by the Catholic church.

After visiting Ananda we asked a Burmese girl to pose
for a picture holding a piece of the colorful lacquerware,
and after she primped her hair and smoothed her long
wraparound skirt—cosí fan tutte—she stood barefoot by
one of the large white guardian lions that flank the entrance to the main corridor. Pagan is the center of Burma's
lacquerware industry, and we later visited a shop to watch
the production process. The best lacquer is so elastic that
you can make the lips of a cup touch without the sides
cracking, but these days such quality is rare. The basic
ingredient is "thi'si," a black gum applied to wood which
is polished and then cut with a design formed by layers of
different colors.

The shop owner served us tea and sweets that tasted
like brown sugar candy, and after that pleasant interlude I
purchased a small lacquer picture of a typical Burmese
sight—a woman smoking a large white cheroot. Women
cigar smokers are more common in Burma than they are
in Denmark, and you see those half-foot-long, cone-
shaped white wrappers smouldering grey veils in front of
tawny Burmese female faces everywhere. In one of his
books on Burma, Sir J. G. Scott quotes a charming little
poem called "The Cigar Maiden of Madeya" (a town near

Mandalay) about women cigar smokers in Burma: "Thy cheroots, so deftly fingered,/Famous are in Burma's land,/ Many a chief has fondly lingered,/Watched the maiden's nimble hand."

We left the lacquer shop and climbed back in our antique jeep to continue the tour around Pagan. Riding in that World War II vintage vehicle takes you back nearly half a century—you half expect to see General Stillwell suddenly emerge from the jungle in another old jeep— and the next temple we saw, Thatbyinnyu, quickly took us back another eight hundred years. This is a large, square, whitewashed pile near Ananda, constructed in 1144 in the same style as that temple by King Alaungsithu, grandson of Kyanzittha. A brick's throw from Thatbyinnyu stands the smaller and more graceful Shwegu temple, which Alaungsithu also built and embellished with poetic religious inscriptions—he "would hatred calm. The immoral states,/Greed, hate, delusion, rooted all in self,/O may they die, when born in me!"—and where he died in 1167, smothered to death by his son, Narathu, who feared the eighty-one-year-old invalid king would recover and chase Narathu from the palace.

His father dispatched, Narathu next faced a threat from his older brother, Minshinsaw, who gathered his forces to march on Pagan from a provincial town where he'd previously been exiled by his father. Narathu decided to send his head priest to Minshinsaw with an offer to deliver the throne to him. At first suspicious, Minshinsaw finally accepted the offer and returned to the palace where, as promised, Narathu ceded the throne to his brother, even organizing a great feast in honor of the occasion. One of the dishes was prepared from a special recipe, and Minshinsaw died of food poisoning the same night, allowing Narathu, after a gap of only a few hours in his reign, again to become king.

Narathu lasted only three years—just long enough to start constuction of Pagan's largest temple, Dhammayangyi, a "grim mass," so it has justifiably been called—before being executed by assassins hired by the father of his wife, whom he'd previously murdered. The assassins gained access to the king by disguising themselves as astrologers, and when Narathu appeared for an audience they stabbed him to death and then killed themselves rather than fighting with the royal guards, for their orders were to execute only the king.

Although the next king, Narapatisithu, also faced troubles—after cutting off the export of elephants to Ceylon, a military crisis between Pagan and Ceylon developed—under his reign, the longest of the Pagan dynasty, Burmese culture reached its highest level. He was a prolific temple builder as well as a benevolent ruler. He chose his successor out of gratitude to one of his lesser queens, whose job it was to salve a finger sore that irritated the king by putting her mouth on the infection. On one occasion, the king was dozing and so she swallowed pus rather than wake him; the monarch gratefully selected as his heir her son, Htilominlo, who in 1211 built a temple named after himself. It was the last of the great Pagan temples. The walls of Htilominlo temple are inscribed with horoscopes added to protect the building against damage or destruction. The charms must have worked because the walls are still standing.

Pagan, however, soon fell and its golden age ended. The last king, Narathihapate, "being desirous of attaining the bliss of Nirvana," decided to build a pagoda, but the project was so costly that it threatened to bankrupt the kingdom. Astrologers warned the sovereign that the dynasty would come to an end when the monument was completed, a prophecy which gave rise to a phrase which soon became common in the kingdom: "The pagoda is finished and the country is ruined." At first the king abandoned the project, but he later changed his mind after the chief priest pointed out that, life being what it is, the dynasty would eventually come to an end whether or not the pagoda was completed.

The pagoda, called Mingalazedi, was finished. Its style

reverted to that of the Shwezigon, the kingdom's first notable pagoda constructed some two hundred years earlier by the dynasty's first king. Pagan had come full circle. Mingalazedi's bell-shaped dome, now brown brick, was no doubt once gilded, for the pagoda was probably the "pyramid of gold" referred to by Marco Polo in his description of Pagan in the late thirteenth century. Polo visited Burma—which he called "Mien" in his chronicle—as a representative of the Kublai Khan. The great Khan's attention turned to Pagan in 1271 when he sent an envoy to ask for tribute. King Narathihapate refused. Two years later another delegation arrived, this time with a letter from the Khan himself, who again asked for a tribute, warning, "Ponder well, O king, upon Our words." Just as King Manuha of Thaton had insulted Pagan's King Anawratha and brought destruction to Thaton, so Narathihapate insulted the Kublai Khan by killing his envoys when they refused to remove their shoes in the royal presence. Times may change, but apparently not kings: six hundred years later when Theebaw curtly rejected a British ultimatum—"Theebaw the Burma King/ Did a very foolish thing," Kipling wrote—Britain proceeded to depose the monarch and annex Burma to India.

The Kublai Khan proceeded to send his forces into Pagan's territory. Describing one of the battles, Marco Polo tells how the Khan's men shot arrows at the enemy's elephants, which then retreated in panic and trampled Pagan's infantry. As the invaders drew closer to the capital, King Narathihapate pulled down some six thousand of the pagodas so devoutly built by his predecessors in order to raise defenses against the advancing army. But the king finally fled the city, and the Khan's men conquered Pagan in 1287. The golden age was at an end.

Contemporary Pagan is nothing but a primitive village where the people live as their ancestors did before the golden age. Tourists are still so sufficiently rare that they are viewed with as much curiosity as they view the locals. The little village will probably be there forever, but someday, no doubt, all traces of Pagan's golden age will turn into dust and vanish for all time. Even the best preserved and most stately temples may be doomed. On July 8, 1975, two years after my visit, an earthquake toppled the towers of some of the most important monuments. In all, about eighty percent of the structures at Pagan were damaged. Those quake-stricken relics are by now starting to crumble away like many of the other stumps of brick and stucco which were once pagodas.

As we flew over Pagan bound for Rangoon, it was the ruined pagodas that caught my eye rather than the great stone piles of Shwezigon or Ananda or Htilominlo. The crumbling stubs seemed more haunting than the temples still intact, for the decayed structures better epitomized the vanished glitter of Pagan's golden age. As the plane advanced, I glanced back at the receding city, rich with legends and history but now filled with disintegrating monuments.

Pagan fell behind and already it seemed remote—as distant in space from the world I knew, and belonged to, as the golden age is in time from the twentieth century. Or is it? Perhaps Burma is not really a land apart, nor as different from our world as it first seems to be. Nats, bloody kings, legendary figures, myths, cucumbered crowns, astrology, and even paddle-wheel river steamers that would be at home on the Mississippi as much as on the Irrawaddy: of such elements is the culture of the West also comprised, for the fabric of our world is woven with similar threads of folklore, fantasy, and fact.

The antique airplane bucked and climbed—it was UBA at its bumpiest and most exciting—and the King of Death planted a few more flags in my already greyed head. I gazed from on high at Pagan, the one-time golden city. Then the plane suddenly passed into a cloud and Pagan disappeared, for me, forever.

5
Petra

A N EXCURSION TO PETRA HAS ALWAYS BEEN AN ADVEN-
ture, often a dangerous one. Never was a journey to
the two-thousand-year-old city hewn from rock cliffs in
southern Jordan more exciting than when John Louis
Burckhardt, a young Swiss adventurer, rediscovered the
abandoned settlement early in the nineteenth century. For
at least seven hundred years before that, since the time of
the Crusaders, Petra had remained lost and forgotten—at
least to the Western world. Then, on August 22, 1812,
Burckhardt spent a few hours in Petra, becoming the first
European in seven centuries to lay eyes on the hidden and
remote ancient trading town whose dwellings, temples,
and tombs were carved from rugged sandstone cliffs stra-
tegically located at desert's edge south of the Dead Sea
and east of the Mediterranean. Burckhardt was the first
Westerner in modern times to see Petra, but he wasn't the
first to hear about the long-lost city. That honor belongs to
an earlier traveler, a German named Ulrich-Jasper
Seetzen. Except for an unfortunate occurrence in 1811,
Seetzen would have no doubt been the first European
visitor to reach Petra since the Crusaders. Seetzen, how-

ever, found death in the sands of the Middle East rather than Petra, for in December of that year he was poisoned in Yemen by order of suspicious officials who thought the foreigner was a sorcerer. An excursion to Petra has always been an adventure.

Almost forgotten today, Ulrich-Jasper Seetzen is virtually unknown compared to the famous Burckhardt, but Seetzen's Middle East adventures were no less exciting than those enjoyed a few years later by the young Swiss traveler. Seetzen, in fact, was one step ahead of Burckhardt in visiting many of the Arab world's remote and exotic sights. Seetzen's advantage in this regard derived from his age: seventeen years older than Burckhardt, he enjoyed a headstart. Born in 1767, Seetzen studied natural sciences at Gottingen University, which Burckhardt also attended some years later; and then in August 1802 he left Europe for Constantinople on an expedition to the Middle East sponsored by the Dukes Ernest and August of Saxe-Gotha. Seetzen continued on to Syria, settling for a time in Aleppo, which he used as a base for excursions to surrounding areas. Burckhardt, too, later made Aleppo his headquarters for two and a half years, during which time he also traveled to points of interest in the region.

In 1806, Seetzen traveled farther afield, now heading south through Jordan to the Greco-Roman city of Jerash, a route Burckhardt later followed. He then decided to risk an excursion east of the Jordan River into areas no European had dared venture for years. It was during this phase of his travels that Seetzen heard about the existence of Petra. In a letter dated June 11, 1806, he tells of hearing Arabs in the neighborhood of Kerak, site of a twelfth-century Crusader castle—and of a twelfth-century B.C. Iron-Age settlement—speak of the ruins of "bedra," a day's journey south of Kerak. The supposed distance was wrong—Petra is more than a day's trip, by foot or by camel—but no matter: for the first time in centuries, long-lost Petra had come to the attention of a European. In a later letter Seetzen wrote that one of the sheikhs who spoke of the Petra ruins said they were so impressive "he had to weep when he saw them."

Seetzen, however, was never to see those ruins. Instead of continuing south from Kerak to Petra across a countryside hostile with forbidding terrain and suspicious natives, he went around the lower end of the Dead Sea, fifty miles due north of Petra, and then traveled on to Jerusalem, which he reached April 6. Encouraged by his successful excursion, Seetzen next decided to continue his explorations of south Palestine and Arabia; after crossing the Sinai Peninsula, where he visited Mt. Sinai and the Santa Caterina monastery nestled at the base of the peak, he arrived at Cairo. In the Egyptian capital he prepared for a pilgrimage to Mecca by announcing himself to be a Muslim. Little was required for the conversion: the first of the so-called Five Pillars of Islam provides that anyone can become a Muslim simply by reciting the words, "I believe that there is no god but Allah, and that Mohammed is His Apostle."

That said and done, Seetzen reached Mecca in October 1809. This was five years before Burckhardt's visit there. It is often thought that Burckhardt was the first Westerner to see Mecca. In fact, even Seetzen was not the first. Over a century before the German reached Mecca, Joseph Pitts, an English sailor captured by pirates off the Spanish coast, was sold into slavery in Algiers and taken to Mecca in 1680. After Burckhardt's 1814 visit, no European reached Mecca until 1845, when George Augustus Wallin, a Finnish scholar born in 1811, managed to enter the holy city.

Seetzen's foray into Arabia was facilitated by a traveler who had preceded him there by ten years. In 1799 John Lewis Reinaud, assistant to the British Resident in Basra, became the first European to reach Diriya, as Riyadh was then called. Later, on April 2, 1805, Reinaud wrote Seetzen from Aleppo offering advice about travel in Arabia and describing the town of Diriya.

On reaching Mecca, Seetzen was moved by the holy

precincts of his self-proclaimed faith. He visited the Kaaba mosque, which houses the sacred black stone, a meteorite, that Mohammed once touched (and which Muslim pilgrims still kiss), an historic event that transpired in 629, the same year the first clash between Muslims and the Byzantine Empire occurred at Mota, a village five miles south of Kerak. After his visit to the Kaaba mosque, Seetzen wrote: "This entire complex created in me a deep emotion of a kind I never felt anywhere else."

Seetzen next headed for Medina with a caravan that traveled by night and rested during the day. Ever the meticulous observer, this schedule upset Seetzen but he hastened to assure his potential European public—and perhaps himself—by writing: "I expect, however, that my readers haven't missed anything, for the Hedjas does not in this area contain very many interesting sights." Seetzen himself, however, became an interesting sight in the area. When the emir in Medina became suspicious of the German traveler, Seetzen departed and returned to Mecca for two months where he systematically observed the holy city and its inhabitants. To avoid attracting undue and unwelcome attention, the European conducted his observations in a discreet manner. Among his ambitious projects while in Mecca was an attempt to determine scientifically the exact geographic position of the city.

From Mecca Seetzen penetrated more deeply into the remote and unexplored—and dangerous—reaches of the Arab world. Still traveling in the relative coolness of darkness, he moved south across the desert into Yemen, noting that "you travel only by night, but more safely and quietly than you can walk through the streets of London or any other large city." These words were to come back and haunt him. On June 2, 1810, Seetzen reached Saana, the capital of Yemen, which he called the most beautiful city in the Middle East. In November he traveled to the south coast of Yemen to Al Mukha, a Red Sea port from where the Arabica coffee called "mocha" was originally exported to the West. Al Mukha is also the city where Seetzen wrote the last letter received in Europe from him.

Seetzen now started to retrace his steps, but his tracings soon ceased. During his journey through Yemen, Seetzen had collected a number of wildlife specimens, and on his way back to Saana the collection was seized from him by Arabs who accused him of being a sorcerer. Seetzen requested permission to continue on to Saana to ask the iman there for the return of his specimens, but Yemen turned out to be much less safe than "the streets of London or any other large city." Supposedly by order of the iman of Yemen, Seetzen was poisoned to death in December 1811. He died alone and far from home in Ta'izz, a mountain town between Saana and Al Mukha.

At the time of Seetzen's death, John Louis Burckhardt had already established himself in Aleppo, where he was studying Arabic and making periodic excursions into the surrounding desert. Burckhardt was then still a young man of twenty-seven, and still ahead of him were most of the explorations and discoveries that would make him famous. But it was Seetzen's pioneering travels that helped pave the way for many of Burckhardt's subsequent findings, for Burckhardt was well aware of his predecessor's itineraries and observations. As John Louis's relative, Jakob Burckhardt, the famous Swiss historian of the Renaissance, observed: "The true discoverer . . . is not the man who first chances to stumble upon anything, but the man who finds what he has sought. Such a one alone stands in a link with the thoughts and interests of his predecessors." In the region of Petra, for example, Burckhardt employed the same guide who'd accompanied Seetzen, and the young Swiss—he was only twenty-eight when he discovered Petra in 1812—no doubt learned from his aide much about the German's ideas and findings, thereby enabling Burckhardt to bring to a successful conclusion what Seetzen had begun six years previously.

Seetzen's account of his travels was, unfortunately for

him, published long after Burckhardt's narratives, and it is no doubt due to that tardiness that Seetzen remains a figure much more obscure than he deserves to be. Apart from *A Brief Account* of his journey through Jordan and around the Dead Sea published in London in 1813 by the Palestine Association, Seetzen's works only appeared nearly a half century after his death in three volumes printed in Berlin in 1854 under the title *Travels in Syria, Phonecia, in the country east of the Jordan, in Arabia Petrae and in Lower Egypt.* By then, some of the novelty of his account had been pre-empted by Burckhardt, and by now the intrepid Seetzen has all but been forgotten.

—2—

It is a pleasant, if idle, exercise to speculate on what Seetzen might have discovered had he lived longer. He was only forty-four when he died. Perhaps the career of Burckhardt, who died even younger at thirty-three, encompassed some of the accomplishments that might have accrued to Seetzen, for in those few years Burckhardt packed enough adventures and discoveries for any two, or even more, lives.

One wonders what manner of man it was to have left the civilized comforts of Europe in the early nineteenth century to venture into the wilds of the then relatively unknown, and absolutely dangerous, Arab world. What drove them, those early explorers? Some, no doubt, would've given anything to have been the first to discover Petra; one, Seetzen, gave everything, his very life, and yet he failed.

The most striking aspects of John Louis Burckhardt's life are his strong sense of purpose and his meticulous preparation. From early days, Burckhardt knew what he wanted to do, and he proceeded to train himself and acquire the skills to accomplish his goals. So it was not simply by chance that he was the first European in hundreds of years to lay eyes not only on Petra but also on the great stone statues at Abu Simbel on the Nile in southern Egypt near the border with Sudan. If fortune favors the prepared mind, then Burckhardt well deserved his good luck, for he was exceptionally well prepared.

Burckhardt was born in 1784 into a prosperous and venerable Swiss family. After the Burckhardts left the Black Forest area in Germany, they settled in Basel, Switzerland, in the early sixteenth century. A member of the same family, historian Jakob Burckhardt—who was born in 1818, the year after John Louis died—wrote in his essay "On Fortune and Misfortune In History" a sentence which might well be taken to describe the guiding principal of John Louis's life: "Every individual—we too—exists not for his own sake, but for the sake of all the past and all the future." John Louis immersed himself, intellectually and physically, in the past and its remnants, while to the future, which for the time being includes us, he left detailed accounts of his travels.

As for Burckhardt's own past, its early context has come down to us in an especially vivid form, for the family residence is now a Basel museum, the Kirschgarten, which has been preserved and furnished as the elegant eighteenth-century town house it originally was. Upon completion of the Kirschgarten on Elisabethenstrasse in 1777, Rudolf Burckhardt, a wealthy silk merchant, and his first wife—daughter of Basel's mayor—and their five children moved into the mansion, shortly after which they divorced. Burckhardt then married Sara Rohner, daughter of the secretary of Basel's hospital; the second son born to that marriage was John Louis.

Burckhardt's parents sent him to Leipzig University when he was sixteen, and there he quickly fell into debt, thanks to an extravagant way of life that included frequent gambling sessions. He then spent a year at Gottingen University, where Seetzen had also studied, and at age twenty-one Burckhardt moved to London where he looked for a job. By then the young Swiss had decided what sort of life he wanted to live and he began to prepare himself. To harden his body for the rigors of the un-civilized areas he hoped to explore, Burckhardt slept out-doors on the ground, took long walks wearing no overclothes, and restricted his diet to a vegetarian menu. He also had himself circumcised. As for his mind, for three years the young man studied Arabic and the history and culture of the Middle East at Cambridge and in London. Finally, in 1809, an opportunity presented itself, one for which Burckhardt was by then eminently qualified. Through the offices of Sir Joseph Banks, the naturalist who had accompanied Captain Cook on his first voyage, Burckhardt was retained by the African Asso-ciation of London. Founded the year of John Louis's birth, the organization had as its purpose not only investigating the "dark continent's" cultural aspects but also studying economic possibilities there. One major business oppor-tunity of the time was forbidden, however, for the group opposed the then lively commerce of trading in slaves. Young Burckhardt was made to order—self-made—for the association, which needed a trained, enthusiastic adven-turer to explore parts unknown, and in March 1809 he left Europe—forever, as it turned out—and sailed for Malta.

Burckhardt spent seven weeks in Malta, improving his Arabic and converting himself into the guise of a Muslim trader from India, the identity he adopted for his explora-tions in the Middle East. That sort of disguise was often used by early European travelers in the area. Charles M. Doughty, perhaps the greatest nineteenth-century Middle Eastern explorer that Europe produced, traveled "clothed as a Syrian of simple fortune," he noted in his classic *Arabia Deserta*. In earlier times it was a more serious matter to abandon European ways for the habits and re-ligions of the East. Nicolò de' Conti, a fifteenth-century Venetian trader who ventured beyond the Levant and spent twenty-five years in the East, disguised himself as a Damascus merchant and, for purposes of his journey, held himself out as a Muslim, a move which so bothered him he later sought absolution from the Pope for even pretending to have renounced his faith.

As for Burckhardt, from Malta he continued on to Aleppo, which Seetzen had also chosen as the place to make his home base away from home. Burckhardt remained there two and a half years. During that time he improved his Arabic—by, among other things, translating into that language an adaptation of *Robinson Crusoe*, which he renamed *Pearl of the Seas*—and he continued to study the culture of the Arabs. He learned much of the Koran by rote and became so expert in Koranic law that on occasion he was asked to render judgments. He also traveled widely, visiting such places as Damascus, Baalbek, and Palmyra, where bandits robbed Burckhardt of everything but his underpants, an omission an Arab woman tried to remedy when she attempted to take that garment as Burckhardt made his way back to civilization. The young Swiss lost his possessions but, unlike Seetzen, at least escaped with his life.

In February 1812, John Louis left Aleppo for Egypt, and it was on that journey that he discovered Petra. He passed through Lebanon and Damascus, then visited Jerash, a large and well-preserved Greco-Roman city in northern Jordan that Seetzen had discovered. After returning to Damascus, Burckhardt headed south and moved into the Petra region. In Shaubak, site of a Crusader castle south of Kerak and some twenty miles from Petra, the traveler bartered his spare shirt, a red cap, and half his turban cloth for food and a goat. Along his route Burckhardt had heard the Arabs speak with admiration of the ruins hidden away in the Wadi Musa—the valley in which the ancient stone city was secluded—and on August 22 he reached Ain Musa, the spring of Moses, located not far from the Siq, a narrow gorge leading into Petra itself.

Burckhardt was now in dangerous territory. For more than six hundred years no Westerner had seen Petra, and it was no secret that the locals were hostile to foreigners. Burckhardt's guide, Hamid, urged John Louis to leave the area while they were still alive, but Hamid was "silenced" when he heard Burckhardt's plan. "I pretended to have made a vow to have slaughtered a goat in honor of Aaron, whose tomb I knew was situated at the extremity of the valley," Burckhardt noted in his journal, published in London in 1822 under the title *Travels in Syria and the Holy Land*, "and by this stratagem I thought that I should have the means of seeing the valley on my way to the tomb. To this my guide had nothing to oppose; the dread of drawing on himself, by resistance, the wrath of Aaron completely silenced him."

Poor Hamid tried to get his employer to sacrifice the goat at Ain Musa outside Petra, but Burckhardt pressed on. In Elji, a village near the Siq, he paid with a pair of house shoes to hire a local guide, and then they continued on a short distance to the cliffs by the Siq. "And it is here," Burckhardt wrote, now nearing the end of his quest to find the long-lost hidden city, "that the antiquities . . . begin." But discretion dominated Burckhardt's curiosity and ambition: "Of those," he went on, "I regret that I am not able to give a very complete account: but I know well the character of the people around me; I was without protection in the midst of a desert where no traveller had ever before been seen; and a close examination of the works of the infidels, as they are called, would have excited suspicions that I was a magician in search of treasures." Burckhardt might well have been thinking of the death of Seetzen.

Soon after the party had passed through the Siq and inspected a few of Petra's tombs and dwellings cut into the sandstone cliffs, Burckhardt's fears were confirmed. "I see now," his guide said, "that you are an infidel, who has some particular business among the ruins of the city of your forefathers; but depend on it we shall not suffer you to take out a single part of the treasures hidden therein." Perhaps John Louis's blood ran cold on learning that the guide had guessed his true purpose, but he kept his composure; and it was the goat's blood, not that of the visitor, which was shed—a scrawny sacrifice, but one which nonetheless inspired Burckhardt's guide to prayer. "While I was in the act of slaying the animal, my guide exclaimed aloud, 'O Harun [Aaron], protect us and forgive us! O Harun, be content with our good intentions, for it is but a lean goat! O Harun, smooth our paths; and praise be to the Lord of all creatures!' "

After napping on the rocks, they returned to Elji in the dark because the guide wanted to get back early August 23 in time to catch a caravan to Ma'an, a nearby city. Of his fleeting look at the hidden city, Burckhardt wrote that "it appears very probable that the ruins in Wadi Musa are those of the ancient Petra," and he concluded: "Of this at least I am persuaded, from all the information I procured, that there is no other ruin between the extremities of the Dead Sea and the Red Sea of sufficient importance to answer to that city. Whether or no I have discovered the remains of the capital of Arabia Petraea, I leave to the decision of Greek scholars."

Burckhardt, of course, had indeed discovered Petra, and what is remarkable is not only that feat but the accuracy with which he recorded what he saw. Few details escaped his attention. Another great nineteenth-century traveler and orientalist, Richard Burton, himself a meticulous observer and recorder (he was born in 1821, four years after Burckhardt's death), once referred to "Burckhardt, with his usual accuracy" in a passage relating to Burckhardt's account of how fresh curtains are put on tombs of Moslem prophets when a new sultan ascends the throne. A few hours after his visit to Petra, John Louis managed to draw the first map ever made of the city, and his sketch can hardly be faulted for its accuracy. Of course, it was not only at Petra that Burckhardt exercised his powers of observation and description—that was a way of life with him. Nor was Petra by any means his only great discovery. Burckhardt's career was, in fact, so re-

markable that it is virtually irresistible to avoid following
the redoubtable young adventurer through the few years
which remained to him after he discovered Petra.

Burckhardt's other major find was the huge Ramses
statues carved in the side cliffs of the Nile at Abu Simbel
in southern Egypt. He discovered them less than a year
after his visit to Petra. From the rock city in Jordan he
continued on by camel caravan to Cairo, which he
reached September 4, 1812. The following January, Burckhardt set out for Nubia. Following the Nile southward, by
March 22, 1813, Burckhardt reached Abu Simbel, where
he found Queen Nefertari's temple, which Ramses II had
cut into the rock facade about 1260 B.C. for his favorite
wife. After exploring the temple, which Burckhardt supposed was the main sight at Abu Simbel, he began to
climb up the sand to the top of the cliff that towered over
the Nile. Shifting his course slightly to the south, "I fell in
with what is yet visible of four immense colossal statues
cut out of the rock . . . [which] stand in a deep recess
excavated in the mountain." He noted that "they are almost entirely buried beneath the sands, which are blown
down here in torrents"—sand that had covered the figures
since about 400 B.C., when Greek mercenaries had recorded their presence there by carving graffiti on a thigh
of one of the Ramses statues, then nearly a thousand years
old. Burckhardt thus became the first European—and perhaps the first man—to see the Abu Simbel statues in more
than two thousand years.

Burckhardt spent the next year in southern Egypt and
Nubia, arriving in June 1814 at the Red Sea, which he
crossed to Jedda. On September 9 he reached Mecca.
Although Seetzen had visited Mecca five years previously,
it was not exactly an everyday occurrence for a Westerner
to manage to enter the holy city of Islam. One must
therefore read the following evocative description—the
passage, from Burckhardt's *Travels in Arabia*, published
in London in 1829, is representative of Burckhardt's style

of writing (he wrote in English) and method of travel, and his attention to detail and precision of expression—in light of the fact that had the foreigner's true identity, or the journal he was keeping, been discovered, he no doubt would have been put to death:

About the middle of October I returned [from Jidda, where he had gone on September 15 to make travel arrangements] to Mekka, accompanied by a slave whom I had purchased. This boy had been in the caravan with which I went from the Black Country to Sowakin [port city on the west coast of the Red Sea from which he crossed to Jidda], and was quite astonished at seeing me in a condition so superior to that in which he had before known me. I took with me a camel-load of provisions, mostly flour, biscuit and butter, procured in Djidda at one third of the price demanded at Mekka, where, immediately on my arrival, I hired decent apartments in a quarter of the town not much frequented, called Haret el Mesfale. I had here the advantage of several large trees growing before my windows, the verdure of which, among the barren and sun-burnt rocks of Mekka, was to me more exhilarating than the finest landscape could have been under different circumstances. At this place I enjoyed an enviable freedom and independence, known only to the Kadhy [the chief religious judge, to whom Burckhardt was introduced in Mecca; the Kadhy regarded the Swiss traveler as a devout and learned Muslim] and his followers, who soon after took their departure. The Pasha [Mohammed Ali, then fighting the Wahabis, a fanatical tribe of Muslim puritans in central Arabia] and his court remained at Tayf [a verdant hilltown, called by Doughty "the Eden of Mecca," located southeast of Mecca and known as the summer capital; a shiny modern Inter-Continental Hotel now embellishes

Taif's garden-rich landscape] till the days of the Hadj [the November religious pilgrimage]. I frequented only such society as pleased me, and, mixing with a crowd of foreign pilgrims from all parts of the world, I was not liable to impertinent remarks or disagreeable inquiries. If any question arose about my origin (a circumstance that rarely happened in a place which always abounds with strangers), I stated myself to be a reduced member of the Mamelouk corps of Egypt, and found it easy to avoid those persons whose intimate knowledge of that country might perhaps have enabled them to detect the falsehood. But there was little to be apprehended even from the consequences of such detection; for the assumption of a false character is frequent among all eastern travellers, and especially at Mekka, where every one affects poverty in order to escape imposition, or being led into great expenses. During all my journies in the East, I never enjoyed such perfect ease as at Mekka; and I shall always retain a pleasing recollection of my residence there, although the state of my health did not permit me to benefit by all the advantages that my situation offered. I shall now proceed to describe the town, its inhabitants, and the pilgrimage, and then resume the narrative of my travels.

In January 1815 Burckhardt left Mecca by caravan for Medina and by June 24 he once again reached Cairo, after a two-and-a-half-year absence from the city. Burckhardt met Giovanni Battista Belzoni there. Belzoni was born in Padua in 1778, six years before John Louis; the Italian outlived him by six years, dying in 1823 on an expedition to Timbuktu. A one-time strong man in a London music hall, Belzoni went to Cairo to sell a waterwheel he'd invented to Mohammed Ali, pasha of Egypt. Burckhardt told Belzoni about the colossal figures at Abu Simbel, which the Italian visited and helped to excavate in 1817.

The two men also agreed to collaborate with Henry Salt, British consul-general in Egypt, in a project whereby Belzoni would transport from Luxor to the Mediterranean port of Alexandria a huge head they supposed was Memnon—in fact, it portrayed Ramses II—from the Ramesseum at Thebes.

Burckhardt next departed for a trip to the Sinai Peninsula. There in the Santa Caterina Monastery he saw on the wall of his room a penciled note dated April 9, 1807, written by the ubiquitous Seetzen, by then five years dead, listing the principal places he'd visited and signed with his adopted name, Mousa (Moses). After two months in the Sinai, Burckhardt, now thirty-one, returned to Cairo where he prepared to carry out his assignment for the African Society to explore the Niger River. He intended to join a large caravan scheduled to pass through Cairo on the way south in October 1816; but the caravan failed to appear, and John Louis spent the winter in Cairo working on his journals and papers.

The following October Burckhardt contracted a case of dysentery. In those days there was no cure for the sickness, and by the middle of the month his condition had severely worsened. Burckhardt knew he was dying. He summoned Henry Salt and asked the consul to record his last wishes. One instruction was to "pay up my share of the Memnon head"—to his last days Burckhardt was thinking of his role in reviving and preserving the past. In time, Belzoni did carry out his commission to remove the head, which was taken to the British Museum where it may still be seen. The dying man left his European books to Salt and the rest of his library to Cambridge University. He gave fifty pounds for the poor in Zurich and willed his male and female slaves to one Osman, a local Scottish friend of Burckhardt who was a Middle East traveler and a professed Muslim.

Burckhardt died October 15, 1817, at the age of thirty-three. But was he really still simply John Louis Burckhardt, a young Swiss? By then assimilated into the alien world he had chosen, Burckhardt was no longer an European outsider in Islam lands. He was buried in an obscure grave in the Muslim cemetery in Cairo near the Bab el-Nasr—the Victory Gate—as Ibrahim ibn Abdallah, the name he used in his travels. Thus by the end of his life the man born a Christian in Switzerland under the name Johann Ludwig Burckhardt had, by all appearances, become a Muslim known as Ibrahim ibn Abdallah.

At least some Arabs seemed to have accepted Burckhardt as one of their own. As Richard Burton wrote in *Pilgrimage to Al Madinah and Mecca*—Burton followed in many of the footsteps of Burckhardt and Seetzen—about his visit to John Louis's grave in Cairo: "Here lies the Swiss Burckhardt, who enjoyed a wonderful immunity from censure until a certain pseudo-Orientalist of the present day seized the opportunity of using the 'unscrupulous traveller's' information and of abusing his memory. Some years ago, the sum of 20 pounds (I am informed) was collected in order to raise a fitting monument over the discoverer of Petra's humble grave. Some objection, however, was started, because Moslems are supposed to claim Burckhardt as one of their own."

There is a sketch by Henry Salt done shortly before Burckhardt's death which typifies the Swiss-Muslim traveler. The drawing shows a European face, adorned with a stringy, Levantine-ish beard and bearing a sober expression, with a turban round the head and a baggy, bulky robe over the upper body. The sketch suggests the artful blending of East and West, which Burckhardt's remarkable career illustrates.

"Men's lives," Burckhardt wrote in *Travels in Arabia*, "are predestined; we all obey our fate. For myself, I enjoy great pleasure in exploring new and unknown countries and becoming acquainted with different races of people."

For all who came after John Louis Burckhardt, there were fewer new and unknown countries.

—3—

What sort of place did John Louis Burckhardt—and, giving additional credit where it's due but seldom paid, Ulrich-Jasper Seetzen—discover? Or, to put the matter more precisely, rediscover?

According to many subsequent visitors, Petra is a smorgasbord of sights on which to feast the eyes. You could make a fairly complete meal of the treats travelers imagined they saw in the rugged, ruddy rocks that form the hidden valley where Petra nestles. One observer compared the color to "reddish-mauve raw flesh" and another, Sacheverell Sitwell, wrote of the "wine-stained stone." In her book about Jordan's King Hussein, Winifred Carr described the weathered carved facades cut in the cliffs as looking "like vast edifices of raspberry, vanilla and blackcurrent ice-cream, melting in the desert sun." Kammerer, a Frenchman who produced a compendium of Petra lore in 1929, agrees with the choice of raspberry; but Julian Huxley chose chocolate as his Petra flavor.

For some strange reason, the English have outdone the French in serving up food comparisons at Petra. Huxley's compatriot, H.V. Morton, when walking *In the Steps of the Master*, as his book on the Middle East is called, found that "the mountains of Petra crumble like old Stilton . . . . If you can imagine an ancient Stilton cheese stained red, with a great hollow scooped in the middle, you have, more or less, a little model of Petra." But it is the description of Petra given by Edward Lear's chef which takes the cake: " 'O master,' said Giorgio (who is prone to culinary similies), 'we have come into a world where everything is made of chocolate, ham, curry powder and salmon.' "

The taste of more than one writer has run to serving up culinary comparisons to describe unusual landscapes. Charles Dudley Warner, a nineteenth-century American traveler, likens carved stone turbans on Turkish tombs to "the form of a mould of Charlotte Russe." In a 1936 review of the film "The Garden of Allah" Graham Greene saw the "yellow cratered desert" in which Charles Boyer and Marlene Dietrich cavort as a "Gruyère cheese." Far more delicious to Sacheverell Sitwell than Petra, where he found only wine stains, was the Lotfollah mosque dome in Ishfahan, Iran: "it is café au lait . . . or is it the colour of a mousse of coffee . . . . More, still, like the colour of marron, like the marron in a 'Mont Blanc' but without the cream in it, and with a drop of strawberry or raspberry juice added." In Patagonia Louis Simpson found an amphitheater-like formation with "a little conical hill, about a hundred feet high, down the sides of which are spilled streams of brown pebbles. It looks like a Brobdingnagian serving of ice cream, with chocolate syrup."

In contrast to observers who find a menu in the world at large, Proust saw the world in a meal. To him, an oyster surrounded by yellow grape leaves was "poetic and remote as a landscape." Perhaps these culinary comparisons arise out of writers' attempts to link our narrow reality with that which is not us, for is not food the one true tangible connection we have with the world that exists beyond the self? Ortega's famous phrase, "I am I plus my circumstances," might be amended to read, "I am I plus my last few meals." Vladimir Nabokov suggested that "food is our chief link with the common chaos of matter rolling about us." Eating, by reducing chaos to order, is, then, a form of power: fat represents control over the world; obesity denotes dominion.

Petra, of course, must be described as more than just a menu of treats. The delectable, colorful descriptions of the city—and of course the carved monuments of Petra themselves—were confectioned from richly tinted sandstone of a type apparently unique in the world (apart from some similar formations in nearby Lebanon). Throughout Petra appear those many-hued wavy bands mimicked in miniature by strata of different colored sandstone particles which the locals put into discarded gin bottles offered as souvenirs for sale to tourists. Because the bands undulate in random directions that don't conform to the strata of the rocks, geologists have concluded that the colors were created subsequent to the formation of the sandstone, which in its original state consisted primarily of colorless quartz grains cemented together with various compounds of calcium, aluminum, and iron. Those minerals showed their true colors when water percolated through the rock, causing chemical changes. Petra's history, then, can be said to have begun something like thirty million years ago when the earth's crust sank to create a great rift, of which the Jordan valley and the Dead Sea form a part, and to wrinkle the featureless sandstone plateau into cliffs and gorges. From those cliffs, the intaglio city was shaped.

Considerably less remote—almost the day before yesterday in historical terms—is the very early Neolithic village of Beidha, a Petra suburb an hour's walk north of the city, discovered in 1956 by English archeologist Diana Kirkbride and later excavated by her. This find updates the history of Petra from thirty million years ago to the relatively recent days of about 7000 B.C. During that era, Stone-Age settlers were among the first people to move into the protected and well-watered sandstone cliffs where many subsequent societies were also to find favorable living conditions. Evidence of Mesolithic settlements has been found beneath the Neolithic excavations. (During the Neolithic period, the third and latest subdivision of the Stone Age, man left the Mesolithic culture, when he depended for food on wild animals and plants, and began to cultivate crops and domesticate food animals. After the Neolithic Age, history—or should it be written History?—begins.) Beidha ranks with Jericho, where Neolithic findings also dating from about 7000 B.C. have been excavated, as one of the earliest Neolithic sites yet discovered anywhere. Europe entered the Neolithic Age about 3000 B.C., about five thousand years later than when that age had begun in the Middle East.

Starting about 2300 B.C., a Bronze Age civilization

established itself in the Petra region, but that culture was devastated around 1900 B.C. when the four Eastern kings swept into the area and conquered it. The region now for the first time enters recorded time in the form of biblical history. The kings' campaign is described, and Seir, thought to be Petra, is mentioned in Genesis 14. Some seven hundred years later Petra again surfaces in the Old Testament when Esau, who sold his birthright to his brother Jacob for pottage, migrated from Canaan to Edom, where, as Deuteronomy 2:12 tells the story, his tribe conquered the Horims, troglodytes who at that time occupied the Petra area.

About the same time the Edomites were settling in Seir, Ramses II ruled Egypt. He was the pharaoh whose huge stone images John Louis Burckhardt discovered under the sand drifts in the cliffs at Abu Simbel and whose great stone head Belzoni floated down the Nile from Thebes for shipment to the British Museum. Ramses, who reigned between 1290 and 1244 B.C., was more than likely the pharaoh whom Moses (and Aaron) petitioned to "let my people go," for the Exodus is thought to have begun about that time. Traveling from the south toward the Promised Land, the first people the Israelites met were the Edomites at Seir—Petra. After smiting a rock to produce water which still today flows from a spring near Petra called Ain Musa—"the spring of Moses"—Moses, as related in Numbers 20:17, asked the Edomite king for permission to cross his territory: "Let us pass, I pray thee, through thy country . . . . we will go by the king's high way." The king refused Moses' request, thus touching off the very first of the innumerable quarrels which, over the next three thousand years, would transpire between Arabs and Jews.

"The king's high way" Moses wanted to take is a most venerable road. It was so named because the four Eastern kings used that route, which runs north and south through Transjordan, to invade the area. By Moses's time, the road was already seven hundred years old. Over a millennium later, the Emperor Trajan built a Roman road along the route, a thoroughfare still used and still known as "The King's Highway." Along the highway rise Roman "milestone" markers, the most interesting being a pair of well-preserved conical stones, bearing detailed information—in Latin, of course—which stand beside the road between Dhiban and Kerak. The Romans used the term "petra"—stone—to designate their mile, equal to about 1,480 meters.

About 1000 B.C. King David took power, after which he invaded Edom "and all they of Edom became David's servants" (2 Sam. 8:14). David conquered that land to the south not only because of the perennial friction between the Hebrews and the Edomites but also because possession of the area gave him control over the trade routes that crisscross Edom, routes which later were to contribute to the rise of Petra under the Nabateans. An additional reason for David's interest in the area was because Petra's colorful sandstone contained copper and iron ore. Nine hundred years earlier Moses had recognized the presence of valuable minerals in Edom. He told his people that after forty years of wandering the Lord had brought them to "a good land," one "whose stones are iron, and out of whose hills thou mayest dig brass" (Deut. 8:7,9).

After David's conquest, the Israelites controlled Edom for many years. The Edomites occasionally tried to break free, but without success. After one attempt, Amaziah, king of Judah, invaded Edom, killed ten thousand Edomites in battle, then captured Petra, which he renamed (2 Kings 14:7). There he cast another ten thousand people "down from the top of the rock" (2 Chronicles 25:12), thought to be the flat-topped mountain Umm el Biyara that dominates Petra and its history. That peak, nearly impregnable, was frequently used as a refuge and as a citadel by the inhabitants of Petra when attackers appeared.

Obadiah, who prophesied around 600 B.C., referred to Umm el Biyara in his diatribe against the "greatly despised" Edomites—those "that dwellest in the clefts of the rock, whose habitation is high; that saith in his heart, Who shall bring me down to the ground?" (Obadiah 1:2,3) Referring to the sack of Jerusalem by Nebuchadnezzar, king of Babylon, in 586 B.C., when Solomon's temple was destroyed, the Prophet Obadiah warns the Edomites, who joined in the attack on Jerusalem, that "as thou hast done, it shall be done unto thee: thy reward shall return upon thine own head" (Obadiah 1:15). The prophecy came to pass three centuries later when Edom was conquered by nomadic Arabs called Nabateans who had gradually infiltrated the area around Petra. That marked the end of the Edomites, who scattered to the north to form a new kingdom called Idumea, which some two hundred years later was defeated by the Judeans and integrated into that Jewish state; and it also marked the beginning of Petra's golden age.

Conditions in the Middle East were especially unsettled then. Alexander had conquered much of the area, but when he died in 323 B.C. the empire split into what might be called the African and Asian sections: Egypt, under the Ptolemys, and Syria, under the Seleucids. Jordan, including Petra, occupied a middle ground between the two competing kingdoms. By 312 B.C., Petra was enough of a prize for Antigonus, a Syrian king who was one of Alexander's successors, to covet the region, so he decided to raid the area.

The Seleucid empire, which tried to extend its dominion to the precincts of Petra, took its name from Seleucus, chief of the Macedonian cavalry under Alexander. After Antigonus forced Seleucus to leave Babylon in 316 B.C. he took refuge with Ptolemy in Egypt until 312. Seleucus then returned to Babylon, which he defended against attacks by Antigonus and his son Demetrius. Antigonus was defeated and killed in battle in 301, and twenty years later a son of Ptolemy stabbed Seleucus to death. What is noteworthy about the dynasty is that under it was founded the first widely used chronological era in history—the Seleucid Era, which began on April 3, 311 B.C., following Seleucus's return from Egypt to Babylon. The earliest surviving mention of an era is an Egyptian reference on a thirteenth-century B.C. monument of Ramses II, which is dated the year 400 of an era that began in Egypt about 1720 B.C. The Christian era was not used until the sixth century A.D. when Dionysius Exiguus ("Dennis the Little"), a Roman scholar, introduced it in 533. Because Dionysius forgot to count both the year zero between 1 B.C. and A.D. 1 and the four years when Emperor Augustus had reigned under his own name of Octavian, the reckoning was a few years off. It was only in 354 that December 25 was for the first time referred to as Christmas Day, that date being chosen perhaps because that day in ancient Rome was a secular festive holiday. Before Dionysius's new computation came into use in 533, Christ's birth year was 753, a calculation based on the number of years that had elapsed since the traditional founding of Rome in 753 B.C. Dean Burgon's celebrated line about Petra being "A rose-red city half as old as Time" might be revised to read, less poetically but more accurately, that Time—as now measured—is some three-quarters as old as Petra.

As for the attempt by King Antigonus to extend his empire to Petra, Diodorus Siculus, a Greek resident in Sicily who lived in the last half of the first century B.C., relates how Antigonus's general, Athenaeus, "seized the Rock"—perhaps the fortress peak Umm el Biyara itself—while the Nabateans were away from Petra. Later, when the invaders "were buried in sleep," the Nabateans returned to slaughter them, a result Diodorus comments on as follows: "Athenaeus' men then, while they succeeded at first, afterwards, on account of their own imprudence, met with disaster in their way. For slackness and contempt are commonly wont to follow success."

Having failed in his first attempt, Antigonus sent another expedition, led by his son Demetrius, to besiege Petra. The people removed themselves and their valuables to the rock fortress where they "easily prevailed on account of the strength of the position." Demetrius retreated and when he returned the next day to continue the siege, one of the Nabateans addressed the following moving appeal to him:

> O King Demetrius, what do you want, or what in-duces you to make war with us, who live in a soli-tude, and places which have neither water, nor corn, nor wine, nor absolutely any of those things that among you are considered necessities. We, refusing to admit of slavery on any terms, have fled for refuge into a country in want of all those things necessary to others, and chosen to live a life solitary and al-together wild, doing no harm to you. We beg, there-fore, both you and your father not to wrong us, but after taking gifts from us to lead off your army, and to consider the Nabateans your friends for the future. For even if you wish it you cannot stay here many days, being in want of water and all other necessities, nor can you compel us to love another life; but you will only have some captives as slaves with dejected minds and men who could not endure to live under other laws.

Upon hearing this supplication, Demetrius withdrew his army.

According to Diodorus, the Nabateans eschewed prop-erty in the belief that becoming slaves to material posses-sions would make it easier for the people to be enslaved by conquerors. "They have a law," he wrote, "neither to sow corn nor to plant any fruit-bearing plant, nor to use wine nor to build a house; and whoever is found acting in a contrary way is adjudged the punishment of death. This law they hold because they judge that those who possess these things will be easily compelled by powerful men to do what is ordered them because of their enjoyment of these things." Strabo, however, writing shortly after the beginning of the first century A.D., about the same time as

Diodorus, described the Nabateans as being extremely interested in wealth: "The Nabateans are prudent, and fond of accumulating property. The community fines a person who has diminished his substance, and they confer honors on him who has increased it." Strabo also relates a report "that the people were very wealthy, and exchanged their aromatics and precious stones for silver and gold, but never expended with foreigners any part of what they received in exchange."

Strabo's account is probably closer to the truth than that of Diodorus, for the Nabatean civilization rode on the backs of camels, as it were, which carried wares over the caravan routes which passed through Petra, the Nabatean capital. During the Nabatean era, which lasted for some two centuries just before and after the birth of Christ, Petra became an important way station and trading center, one of the largest in the Middle East; people and products converged on the city from all points of the compass. What the Nabateans offered the world of commerce was essentially a protected and efficient route tying together East and West, with Petra as the knot. One of the main routes, for example, permitted traders to reach the Mediterranean, without having to depend on either Egypt or Phoenicia, by passing from Aqaba at the top of the Red Sea across the Negev to Gaza. This was a sort of land version of the Suez Canal for the ancient world. Among the chattels traded along that route were human bodies. There was a famous slave market at Gaza, a commerce that caused God to punish the Gazans—"deliver them up to Edom" and "send a fire on the wall of Gaza" (Amos 1:6-7). Also sold there were such products as cloth in the form of gauze—a word thought to be derived from the place; damask—from, and named for, Damascus; and raw silk from distant China.

We are by now so used to certain common nouns that it comes as something of a revelation to recall the origins of those familiar words. Most often it is the case that proper names become generic, such as the way Al Mukha, the

Red Sea port visited by Seetzen shortly before his death, gave its name to the mocha coffee grown in the region. Occasionally, however, the process works in reverse. Pliny the Younger, for example, referred to China of the Han Dynasty—which, lasting from 206 B.C. to A.D. 220, existed concurrently with the shorter-lived Nabatean empire—as "seres," or silk, one of the materials from the Far East which passed through Petra on its way to points west. China lent its name to "china," but it is a linguistic oddity that only in English is that word used. For "china," German and French employ versions of the word "porcelain," a name given to the material by Marco Polo at the end of the thirteenth century because china's gloss resembled a marine shell of the genus porcellana, known in English as "cowrie," from the Hindu word "kauri"; in some Asiatic countries the cowrie shell was used as money. Petra's pottery has often been compared to porcelain: was it influenced by China? Of course, the best example of a generic name used as a proper one is the word "petra," which in Greek means "rock" and which, capitalized, became the name of the Nabatean capital.

The name Petra and the Nabateans became known far and wide—as far and wide, at least, as much of the known world then extended. Scattered about the Mediterranean basin were evidences of the Nabatean culture. At Puteoli, a port town near Naples where St. Paul landed after being shipwrecked and then stranded for two months on Malta, there was a Nabatean temple, perhaps built for a local colony of Nabateans but, in any case, used by commercial travelers from Nabatea. A similar temple also apparently existed on the island of Rhodes. Evidence of the worship of Allat, a leading Nabatean goddess, has been found as far west as Carthage and as far north as Palmyra, the Syrian desert city which, toward the end of the second century A.D., was to replace Petra as a caravan crossroads.

By then, Rome had absorbed Nabatea into its empire, thereby making Petra the first capital of the province called Arabia Petraea. Petra's prosperity had aroused

Rome's cupidity, and for some time the Romans attempted to conquer Nabatea. Pompey sent an army to attack Petra in 65 B.C. but the assault failed. Later, in 25 B.C., when Augustus moved troops into the area, Syllaeus, chief deputy of Nabatean King Obodas II, offered to guide the Roman soldiers through the desert to Petra. The Romans gladly accepted the offer, after which Syllaeus led them astray until most of the would-be conquerers died in the harsh desert. Finally, however, in March of A.D. 106 the Romans took control of Nabatea without bloodshed when Emperor Trajan instructed Cornelius Palma, the Roman governor of Syria, to annex the territory. Petra flourished under the Romans, at least for a time. To connect Bosra in Syria with Aqaba on the Red Sea, Trajan began a highway, completed under Hadrian, which passed through Ma'an, about thirty miles east of Petra. The road helped the rock city prosper under the Romans as much as it had under the Nabateans.

Urban renewal in the form of a full-fledged provincial town modernized Petra. The new regime built such typical Roman features as a columned "cardo maximus"—a "great hinge"-like main street—an amphitheater, temples, and baths. The Roman genius for taking over but not subduing foreign cultures is exemplified by the tomb of Sextus Florentinus, an important Roman official buried at Petra about A.D. 140: carved on the facade of the Nabatean-style sepulchre is a long Latin inscription—the language of the colonialists added to the architecture of the colony. Petra remained a center of commerce until the main caravan routes shifted to Palmyra. By the time of Emperor Severus (A.D. 222-235), Petra had lost its place as one of the Middle East's leading emporiums.

Petra now began to recede from history, but the rock city itself faded more slowly than did the Nabateans, who rapidly disappeared as a separate culture. That disappearance is one of history's curiosities, for although record-keeping in the Roman Empire under Emperor Hadrian (A.D. 117-138) was detailed and efficient, apparently no documents relating to the Nabateans survive. Eventually, the city, too, vanished from view and remained hidden for centuries in the remote, concealed valley that cuts through the craggy sandstone cliffs in the desert. In the fourth century, Christianity reached Petra, by then only a village, and it became the seat of a bishopric. The expanding sect converted some of the Nabatean monuments into churches. On the back wall of the Hellenistic-style Urn Tomb appears a barely legible inscription in red paint recording that Jason, Bishop of Petra, consecrated the chamber to Christian worship in 447. That seems to be the last known date directly connected with the city itself until Crusader times, although as late as 534 there is a reference to a bishop of Petra. By then, however, the seat of the archbishopric for Petra was at Kerak, the capital of the area.

When the Muslim conquests began in 636, a handful of people apparently still occupied Petra, but so unimportant was the place then that Arab historians of the expansion period fail to mention the rock city. In the late eighth century, after the Abbasid court moved from Damascus to Baghdad, the balance of gravity for the entire area shifted to the east and all of Jordan fell into obscurity.

At Christmas in the year 1100, Baldwin I became king of the newly formed Kingdom of Jerusalem. As part of his territory Baldwin claimed "Oultre Jourdain," as the Crusaders called Transjordan. Fulcher, the king's chaplain, described a trip they made to the area, reporting that they "came on the sixth day to a high mountain," the one from which Moses brought water by striking a rock. It's possible Baldwin I, or his representatives, entered Petra and realized its strategic importance, for the Crusaders built a small castle there which was captured by the Turks in 1144. Later that year, the thirteen-year-old king of Jerusalem, Baldwin III, led an army to expel the Turks from the fortress. Baldwin ordered olive and other trees to be cut down and burned near the castle, and the mere sight of the flames induced the Turks to surrender. But in 1189 the Crusaders were in their turn evicted when Muslim forces led by Saladin attacked and conquered Petra.

After that, except for one brief reference—and that not by name—Petra vanished until modern times. An Egyptian historian named Nowairi (died 1331) wrote an account of a visit to Petra about 1254 by Bibors, an Egyptian sultan or warlord who stopped off there on his way to Syria. "Through the mountain excavations have been made," goes the account—it was thought the Siq, the narrow gorge leading into Petra, was a man-made feature—"capable of being traversed by a man on horseback. At the left were seen stone steps and the grave of Aaron the brother of Moses; close by stood a castle called Aswit. The sultan visited the lofty castle, and found it extraordinarily strong, and built in a very singular manner." He then visited "the wonderful grotto-like architectural remains of the place. The houses, he says, were sustained by columns, the outsides of the doorways covered with sculptures; the whole was a mass of grottos. The houses were as large as those which the sultan was in the habit of seeing; within these were arched walls, vestibules, treasure vaults, harems—all, all hewn from the solid rock."

As did so many visitors who came after him, Bibors noticed the swirl of red, blue, and white across the sandstone of Petra. Now those bright stone ribbons and the delicately cut facades hewn from cliffs thrown up from the desert thirty million years before faded from view. After that, for nearly six hundred years—until John Louis Burckhardt laid eyes on Petra in 1812—the stone city in the remote sandstone valley lay lost and forgotten in the obscurity of the desert and the years

—4—

When John Louis Burckhardt spent a few perilous hours at Petra in 1812, he noted his hope that future visitors would be able to travel there under the protection of an armed force and, further, that "the inhabitants will become more accustomed to the researches of strangers." But it was a long time before trips to Petra became safe, and even today a journey through the southern Jordanian desert to the ancient rock city is tinged with adventure.

In 1816, only four years after Burckhardt discovered Petra, an Englishman named John Silk Buckingham arrived in Jordan. Buckingham published his opinion of the local people in one of those delightful nineteenth-century English travel books, *Travels Among the Arab Tribes.** Those were the days when leisure and curiosity combined to enable adventurous men to produce long, rambling, and, on occasion, slightly eccentric accounts of experiences in foreign lands. One can imagine Buckingham sitting by a roaring fire in his London club, brandy in his hand and reminiscences on his mind, regaling his all-ears companions with tales of far places. After quoting from Diodorus Siculus a passage written nearly two thousand years before to the effect that the Nabateans "live by robbing and stealing, and for that end roving up and down the countries far and near, they vex the inhabitants with their continual incursions and robberies, it being a very difficult matter to subdue them," Buckingham noted that "from their character at present, as compared with the earliest accounts of them, it appears indeed that they have undergone little alteration for many centuries past." Buckingham called the bedouins "a barbarous and unjust race" and warned "that no one, unless accompanied by an armed escort, or furnished with se-

*To the title of his book, published in London in 1825, Buckingham added the notation, "with an Appendix, containing a refutation of certain unfounded calumnies industriously circulated against the author of this work"—an attack on reviewers of a previous book who "have carried their insolence and injustice to a pitch beyond endurance," such critics being "slanderers" who "dip their weapons in poison, and care not who they wound." Buckingham viewed the reviewers with even more disdain than he did the bedouins.

curity, as well as pledges, from the sheikhs of the tribes, could with safety trust himself among them."

Ten years after Buckingham's travels among the Arab tribes, two Frenchmen, Léon de Laborde and Maurice Linant, later chief engineer for the Suez Canal, visited Petra accompanied by a small armed escort and a fleet of sixteen camels in the hope that a caravan that size would deter attacks by hostile desert tribes. Laborde was in a certain respect a Gallic Burckhardt, for he belonged to a prominent French family and had a thirst for foreign travel and adventure. Laborde's grandfather was the banker who lent money to the government of France during the Seven Years' War and who built a quarter in Paris which includes the Rue de Laborde, a short street parallel to Boulevard Haussmann in the 8th arrondisement near Gare St. Lazare. His sister Valentine was the mistress of Prosper Merimée, author of *Carmen*, for eighteen years; and Laborde himself enjoyed a distinguished career, becoming head of the Archives of France and a member of the French Academy. Petra enchanted Laborde—he called it a "magical" place—and he and his associate Linant escaped the area unscathed. In 1830 they published in Paris a three-volume work containing their findings and drawings of the main monuments.

A visitor in 1828, two years after Laborde and Linant were at Petra, found the bedouins "a cowardly race, both cruel and vicious . . . . They are exceedingly given to theft, and will steal the cover of a tin kettle, thinking it to be silver." It was necessary for him to hire "the wild Arabs of the desert to guard the luggage at night." This sort of protection racket is as much a part of Petra as the swirls of color embedded in the sandstone cliffs—and is very nearly as old. In the nineteenth century, when Petra was customarily visited by travelers from Cairo on the way to Jerusalem via Hebron (or vice versa)—rather than from Amman, the capital of Jordan, as is now the case—the British consul in Cairo, a man named Finn, went to the

rock city in 1851 to conclude an arrangement with Sheikh
Abdur-Rahman of Hebron for the safe conduct of travelers
from Petra to Jerusalem on payment of a fixed fee. Apparently little had changed in the area for centuries, for
Finn's agreement with the sheikh was an updated version
of the procedure mentioned by Herodotus some twenty-
three hundred years earlier in one of the few passages he
devotes (at the beginning of Book III) to the Nabateans.
Discussing the expedition of Cambyses, son of Cyrus,
against the Egyptians, Herodotus relates how Cambyses
"sent messengers to the Arabian king to beg a safe-con-
duct through the region." Herodotus figures in a passage
by Proust which, curiously, is an almost exact description
of Petra. A scholar "who has been studying in a distant
land the place-names, the customs of the inhabitants,"
Proust writes in *The Guermantes Way*, "may still extract
from them some legend long anterior to the Christian era,
already unintelligible, if not actually forgotten, at the time
of Herodotus, which in the name given to a rock, in a
religious rite, dwells surrounded by the present, like an
emanation of greater density, immemorial and stable."

By and large, it is money, not blood, which the den-
izens of Petra have sought, although they often threaten to
spill the latter in order to extract the former. At the turn of
the century an American visitor, University of Chicago
Professor George Livingston Robinson, was accosted by
Petra residents, who shouted "European dogs," threw
rocks and dirt, and aimed a flintlock gun at his party. "We
were considerably perturbed by their barbaric actions,"
Robinson wrote with genteel understatement in *The Sarcophagus of an Ancient Civilization, Petra, Edom and the
Edomites*. The episode ended—predictably, for the Middle East—when the Arabs announced that "they coveted
backshish!" Demands for "backsheesh"—Mark Twain
called it "bucksheesh"—plague the traveler in Middle
Eastern lands. One of the most descriptive, succinct, and
epigrammatic book titles I know is *Backsheesh! or Life and*

Adventures in the Orient, an account published in 1875 (complete "with fine steel-plate portrait of the author," Thomas W. Knox). A 472-page narrative of a trip to Egypt published in Paris in 1871 by Raoul Lacour, a French lawyer, begins, "Backsheesh,—that's the first Arab word which strikes the ear of the newly arrived traveler." The rest of the first chapter, entitled "Backsheesh," discusses the word and the practice it denotes, concluding that in Egypt "backsheesh is all-powerful, it rules! Backsheesh is king, Ismail-Pasha is only vice-king."

During his stay in Petra in 1900, Professor Robinson was told his throat would be cut if he climbed the sacred Mt. Hor to see Aaron's grave. Thirty-three years later H.V. Morton, the English travel writer, encountered the same sort of threats, the locals informing him he'd be shot or knifed—perhaps traveler's choice—if he made that climb. It was of course the desire for backsheesh, not the imperatives of piety, which so exercised the people of Petra. As Baedeker noted in his guide *Palestine and Syria* (fifth edition, 1912), "Travellers are warned against the exorbitant demands of the Sheikh of Elji, for opening the Tomb of Aaron and may cheerfully forego a visit to the uninteresting inner chamber." The inclusion of the word "cheerfully" assures the traveler that the advice is valid: if the meticulous Mr. Baedeker counsels that you can miss a place with good cheer, then you can be sure the site isn't worth seeing.

In 1921 authorities opened the first police station at Elji, the village just outside the Siq, which leads into Petra. The local bedouins promptly murdered the men sent to man the post. The people at Petra subsequently became less violent, but according to the description given by St. John Philby, they were still not quite civilized. The men, he said, "wear no more than a headkerchief and a dirty smock reaching to the knee," complemented "by a 'trinity' of tooth-pick, ear-pick, and tweezers to extract thorns from the feet." As for the women, Philby related that they'd scrape the nicotine-filled residue from earthen pipes smoked by the men and stuff the substance into the spaces between their teeth.

It is worth noting that Philby was among the last in a long line of European orientalists and Middle East adventurers and travelers, a line that extends from Seetzen and Burckhardt through Richard Burton and Charles Doughty and, in this century, to Lawrence of Arabia. Harry St. John Bridges Philby, who died in 1960, is certainly more colorful, even if less well known, than either T.E. Lawrence, whom he called a "genius," or his son Kim, the spy whom the press called "The Third Man." The "St. John" was included in his name not because his parents were devout but for a less pious reason—it was the designation of the bungalow in Badulla, Ceylon, where Philby, the son of a tea planter, was born in 1885. During his life Philby always disclaimed any desire to attempt to model himself after that early missionary. Following his student days at Cambridge, Philby entered the civil service and returned to the East, to India, where his son Kim was born New Year's Eve, 1912. Assigned to the Middle East during World War I, Philby was sent on a special mission to Ibn Saud in 1917, becoming at that time the first European to enter the holy area of the Nejd in central Arabia. After Saudi Arabia was created, Philby left the British Civil Service in 1925 to act as Ibn Saud's political advisor.

The following year, believing his usefulness to the king had come to an end, Philby left Jidda for England. He had no intention of returning to Arabia; but after a chance meeting in London with a friend who introduced him to City financiers, Philby went back to Jidda in the autumn of 1926 and founded Sharqieh Limited there, a trading company which dealt with European firms. It was rumored that Ibn Saud used Sharqieh Limited to purchase arms. Philby's wife, son, and three daughters remained in London. He became a Muslim and took additional wives in Arabia, including a girl he bought at a slave market. While running the trading company, Philby traveled throughout the Middle East, where he made a number of archeological discoveries; and he also became well acquainted with Petra.

On his last trip to England before the war, officials detained Philby for his pro-Nazi comments. After his release, Philby returned to Arabia, then later moved to Beirut, where he died in 1960 at age seventy-six—in exile from the West of his origins and the East of his choice. He was one of the last in the line of colorful European adventurers in the Levant. Perhaps the very last in that tradition is Wilfred Thesiger, an Englishman who published in 1980 at age seventy *The Last Nomad*, which tells of his "Forty Year Adventure in the World's Most Remote Deserts, Mountains and Marshes," as the book's subtitle puts it. In a passage on the deserts of Arabia, Thesiger says: "No man can live there and emerge unchanged . . . [for] that cruel land can cast a spell no temperate clime can match." It is that sort of experience—an experience which somehow forces you to change your view of the world— which, for the traveler of today, has become increasingly rare and hard to find. But he who has cast his eye upon the ruined pagodas of the one-time golden city of Pagan in Burma or upon the weathered, fading facades of Petra's ancient temples and tombs can no longer view the world as he has before.

These days, there is little danger in visiting Petra, apart from the ever-present possibility of war breaking out in the volatile region. The trip, however, still carries with it a strong sense of adventure. For one thing, the feeling of anticipation—especially if you've read about Petra and are familiar with its history and sights—creates increasing excitement as you advance across the desert toward the city. In *From an Antique Land*, which contains a long and richly descriptive section on Petra and its past, Julian Huxley lists the "ten places in the world which I have treasured in imagination as goals of pilgrimage." Among them are Bali, Machu Picchu in Peru, Peking, Angkor Wat, "and Petra, longer desired than any of the others."

Petra, it seems, holds a fascination for even the most urbane and widely traveled of men,* and seldom are they disappointed by a visit to the curious rock city. "Looking back over a life busy with journeys," wrote the English writer Hector Bolitho, who was there in May 1932, "I believe the adventure in Petra was the most romantic I have known." It was with alluring statements such as that one in mind that, with great anticipation, I set out from Amman for my visit to Petra.

—5—

There is, indeed, as Bolitho wrote, a certain romance in a visit to Petra. The desert of south Jordan you pass through on the way from Amman to the rock city is Lawrence of Arabia country. "Brilliant Petra," Lawrence called it; there, on October 21, 1917, in the first battle fought at Petra since Crusader times, Lawrence led a group of Arab troops in a successful ambush of Turkish

*Very few women figure in the story of Petra. One of them is archeologist Diana Kirkbride, who excavated the Neolithic village of Beidha. Another is Crystal M. Bennett, formerly assistant director of the British School of Archaeology in Jerusalem, who has specialized in the Nabateans and conducted excavations at Petra. Apparently the only female traveler-adventuress who has left an account of a trip to Petra is Harriet Martineau, who described her three-day visit there in March 1847 in *Eastern Life: Past and Present*, published the following year. In ancient times, another woman collaterally connected with Petra was the daughter of Aretas IV, the king who ruled the Nabateans from 9 B.C. to A.D. 40. At that time the empire included Damascus, and it was from Aretas that Paul escaped by climbing from a window in a Damascus house. The son of Herod the Great, Herod Antipas of Galilee—whom Jesus calls "that fox" in Luke 13:32—wanted to marry his niece Herodias, so he divorced his first wife, King Aretas IV's daughter, who fled to her father (in Petra, presumably), whereupon the king declared war on Herod Antipas. After John the Baptist criticized Herodias, her daughter Salome's veil dance before Herod led to John's loss of his head.

soldiers. Riding through the desert—which in places closely resembles the Wild West country of the United States—I visualized how Lawrence and his Arab bands might have appeared as they dashed across the sands on their way to conduct raids and other escapades in the area.

As we drove deeper into the desert, occasionally a unit of the desert police mounted on camels approached as if riding straight out of a movie. As the camels loped toward us I could hear the strains of "Desert Song" music playing in some too-romanticized realm of my imagination. The police these days ask not for backsheesh but for identification. At one control point a member of the camel corps studied my passport with great concentration for some time, but I was unsure what he saw in it because he held the document upside down. The men of the desert patrol are most colorful characters. Their ruddy faces are carved by the wind and sun, by time, by adversity, and perhaps by sorrow into creviced folds of skin that in color and contour recall the rugged rocks of Petra. Each man wears a high-necked khaki tunic with a skirt that falls to the ankles, and his crossed red leather bandoliers glitter with cartridges awaiting action in the rifle strapped on his back or the Colt dangling on the thigh. A small curved dagger in a shiny silver scabbard attached to a belt completes the arsenal. The standard headdress is made of a red cloth flecked with white dots and called a "kaffiah." My guide in Petra later told me the scarf is practical as well as decorative, for the desert people use it to protect themselves against sun, wind, dust, sand and insects and to filter spring water.

Near Ma'an, the main town of south Jordan, we passed a series of desert scenes—grazing, hobbled camels, each worth some $200 to their bedouin owners, whose long low tents stretched across the landscape, and derricks in the scrub land pumping not oil but water, a more valuable substance in that arid area. In Ma'an itself, welcome trees cast swatches of shade which we enjoyed along with refreshing bottles of American-brand cola that cooled us after the desert passage.

From Ma'an it's a short trip on to Alji, the village near Petra where once the local chieftain extorted money from tourists and where now the government maintains a resthouse built around a Nabatean cave tomb, its facade artfully incorporated inside the hostel. It was opened back in 1963 when the Jordanian government hoped Petra would become a major revenue producer for the country, and so it was—for a time. In 1966, the last year before the Six Day War, gross tourist income in Jordan was nearly $50 million, a figure the government expected to triple by 1971. But the collective violence now accomplished what individual threats against person and purse had previously failed to do: the war deterred visitors and reduced tourist traffic to a trickle. My Petra guide said that the number of visitors dropped from about five hundred people a day before the fighting to about ten afterward; and by the time of my visit, in 1973, the number of guides had dwindled to eleven, each working on a rotation basis only once every ten days or so.

The lack of tourists at Petra during the time I was there made the deserted ancient city seem especially empty and eerie and even a bit out of this world. Sir Alexander Kennedy, who visited Petra in the early 1920s, described the rock formations and landscape there as a "lunar chaos," a description which conforms to that given by one of the very few people who have seen both Petra and the moon. My guide, who'd previously conducted Neil Armstrong around Petra, told me that the astronaut commented that some of the rocks there resembled those he'd seen on the moon. My guide spoke impeccable English but not quite perfect American: he asked me if Neil Armstrong and Louis Armstrong were related.

Other visitors, earthbound but worldly and widely traveled, have also found Petra a forsaken place. H.V.

Morton, the English travel writer, wrote: "If I had to select one place among all the places I know in the world where the spirit of desolation might have its home, I would choose the dead city of Petra." A half century earlier, in the 1870s, Charles M. Doughty referred in *Travels in Arabia Deserta* to "that wild abysmal place which is desolate Petra."

The redoubtable Doughty was the first European to visit Madain Salih, Petra's almost unknown twin city deep in the Arabian desert, a place which even up to the present-day has scarcely been explored. Located some three hundred and fifty miles south of Petra and five hundred miles north of Jiddah, Madain Salih is tucked into cliffs carved with ornate facades in the same Hellenistic style as those at Petra. Doughty writes: "I visited Petra; and at Ma'an Settlement, which is a few miles beyond, heard of other Petra-like sculptured cliff monuments bearing many inscriptions at Madain Salih . . . [and] I resolved to accept the hazard of visiting them." It took Doughty a year to find a way to get there; finally, "I had taken the adventure of journeying thither in the great Damascus Caravan. Arrived at the place after three weeks' tedious riding amongst that often clamorous, mixed, and, in their religion devout pilgrim multitude, I find Madain Salih to be an old ruinous sand plain with sand rock cliffs."

On reaching the remote site, Doughty proceeded to survey the Petra-like carved facades. "Now I had sight at little distance, of a first monument, and another hewn above . . . . This ambitious sculpture, seventy feet wide, is called *Kasr el-Bint*, 'the maiden's bower.' " It reminded him of "the strange half-pinnacles of the Petra monuments; also this rock is the same yellow-grey soft sandstone with gritty veins and small quartz pebbles." Another facade, "sculptured architecture with corniced columns," is "as all those before seen at Petra." In addition to the rock carvings, another resemblance between Petra and Madain Salih appeared: "What wilt thou give

me," asked Doughty's guide at Madain Salih, "to see the
monuments? and remember, I only am thy protection in
this wilderness."

Apart from the virtually inaccessible Madain Salih,
there are a few other places around the world which are
more or less comparable to Petra. Victor W. Von Hagen
suggests in *The Aztec: Man and Tribe* a resemblance between the ancient Jordan city and Malinalco, a fifteenth-
century Aztec temple town—located between Cuernevaca
and Mexico City—whose structures are hewn from rock.
In the Goreme Valley of Cappadocia in central Turkey the
abandoned troglodyte city of Zelve, carved into the reddish rock walls of a small cul-de-sac canyon, struck me as
being quite similar to Petra. In central Afghanistan on the
way to Bamian, Arnold Toynbee traveled through an area
that reminded him of Petra: driving up the Surkhab valley,
"I felt as if I were revisiting the eastern approaches to
Petra . . . [for] in these eastern approaches to Bamian the
landscape of Petra has been reproduced on a gigantic
scale," Toynbee writes in *Between Oxus and Jumma*. On
my trip to Bamian I saw but a vague resemblance to the
approach to Petra and that only by stretching my imagination nearly as wide as the spacious valley. The reddish
rock on the way to Bamian, however, does recall the hues
of Petra's sandstone, and the Shahr-i-Zohak—The Red
City—fortress atop a magenta-red cliff ten miles east of
Bamian is reminiscent of a Petra-type structure. The most
curious example of a place that resembles Petra is a certain corner of Europe described by Evelyn Waugh in his
essay "Labels": "The walls of the building, which stands
at a corner, are faced with rough sandstone, pierced by six
courses of windows. These are made to look like caves,
having no sharply defined outlines or any straight line
anywhere about them, sides, top and bottom being all
wildly and irrelevantly curved, as if drawn by a faltering
hand." Waugh was discussing an apartment building in
Barcelona designed by the famous Spanish architect An-

toni Gaudí, but the passage is an almost exact description of a Petra-style sandstone monument.

A half century before Charles Doughty's visit to Petra, John Lloyd Stephens, one of the very few Americans to adventure in the Middle East—perhaps nineteenth-century Yankees were too busy building their own society at home to bother with visiting remnants of ancient cultures abroad—saw during his stay at Petra only one lone Arab, "a mere wanderer among the ruins . . . the only living being we saw in the desolate city of Petra." Like others before him, Stephens traveled to Petra disguised as a Muslim merchant; and, also like his predecessors, and followers, his guide demanded ever greater amounts of money as they drew closer to their destination. Stephens tells of his adventures in *Incidents of Travel in Egypt, Arabia Petraea, and the Holy Land*, a two-volume travel narrative which, on publication in 1837, became a great success. Edgar Allan Poe praised the work when it appeared, and John William Burgon was inspired by Stephens' account of his trip to the rock city to compose the famous poem about "rose-red Petra," a place Burgon himself never visited. In *Redburn*, Herman Melville tells of seeing John Lloyd Stephens in church one day, a "wonderful Arabian Traveller . . . who had been in Stony Arabia and passed through strange adventures there, all of which with my own eyes I had read in the book which he wrote, an arid-looking book in a pale yellow cover."

It was most unusual for an American in the early nineteenth century to visit a place as exotic as Petra. But even back in those days Stephens seems to have traveled in much the same way as his compatriots would a century later. At Petra, he didn't "dwell upon details" but "hurried from place to place, utterly insensible to physical fatigue . . . and made the whole circuit of the desolate city." Perhaps John Lloyd Stephens was the first "typical" American tourist—in fact, he became known as "the American traveler." As an archetypal American tourist it's fitting that Stephens was the first of his countrymen to visit Petra, an accomplishment which pleased him: "I was the first American who had ever been there . . . [and] I felt what, I trust, was not an inexcusable pride, in writing upon the innermost walls of that temple [the Khazne, or Treasury] the name of an American citizen."

In his book on Petra, Sir Alexander Kennedy complains about this sort of defacement, a practice all too common for centuries: over two thousand years before Burck-hardt's rediscovery of the Abu Simbel statues in Egypt, Greek mercenaries had cut graffiti onto a thigh of the Ramses II image. "I am afraid it must be confessed with shame," Kennedy writes, "that a considerable number of the English-speaking visitors speak with pride of finding the names of former Englishmen or Americans scratched or chalked on the walls of the monuments. One gentlemen even goes so far as to point out that it is only English-speaking people who are civilized and educated enough to do this!" Among the numerous grafitti on the wall of a cliff-side grotto at Bamian in Afghanistan is the rhyme, "If any fool this high samooch explore/Know Charles Masson has been here before." Masson, one of those adventurous nineteenth-century English travelers, visited Bamian in 1835 and was the first to present an account of the valley to the West.

Apart from Stephens, perhaps the only other early nineteenth-century American adventurer in the Middle East was George Bethune English. Born in 1787, he graduated from Harvard and was sponsored by John Quincy Adams for a commission in the U.S. Marines. After leaving his ship in 1820 when it docked at Alexandria, English changed his religion to Islam and his name to Muhammad Effendi, then signed on as an aide to Egypt's Pasha Muhammed Ali. He eventually left Egypt for Constantinople, where he represented the U.S. government. But English was no match as a traveler compared to John Lloyd Stephens, who, after his Middle Eastern journeys, visited the jungles of the New World and in 1841 published a best seller entitled *Incidents of Travel in Central America, Chiapas, and Yucatan*.

Stephens was justifiably proud of his "first"—to be the first American to visit Petra. By now, most everything has been done, and every place seen, for the first time. The only sort of first times left for travelers these days are the personal initial experiences of each individual, experiences which are, admittedly, second best, but what else remains? The moon, Everest, the Poles, Petra have all been reached for the first time. Poor Seetzen—although he prepared the way for Petra's discovery, he enjoys little or no credit for his pioneering efforts, for it was Burckhardt who first reached the rock city.

People will go to almost any lengths to claim a first—"that vanity which urges one to try to discover new or unknown places for oneself," English art critic James Pope-Hennessy called it. A colleague of Constantine Rafinesque, the nineteenth-century American naturalist, complained that "he is too fond of novelty. He finds too many new things. All is new!"* Years after Stephens had become the first American to reach Petra—too many years, as it turned out—it was another American, Professor George Livingston Robinson, of the University of Chicago, who thought himself to be the first outsider to see Petra's Great High Place, a well-preserved religious shrine atop a ridge thirty-four hundred feet above sea level and six hundred feet above the rock city in the valley below.

I spent the better part of an hour up there, lounging on a sacrificial altar and taking the sun. The High Place is a splendid vantage point, and even if, on a clear day, you can't see forever, you can see quite far enough—sufficiently so that the view remains fixed in your memory nearly forever. In her mystery *Appointment with Death*, Agatha Christie highlights the High Place: "You have not

---

*Quoted in Joseph Kastner, *A Species of Eternity* (New York: Alfred A. Knopf, 1977), p. 242.

been to Petra, M. Poirot? If you go, you must certainly climb to the Place of Sacrifice. It has an—how shall I say?—an atmosphere!" After Robinson reached those heights during his 1900 Petra expedition, he felt "the thrill was something glorious!" Robinson eagerly made notes, measured, photographed, drew plans and diagrams, all the while, "One supreme thought completely obsessed me, namely, 'I have found a high place! I have found a high place!'" Excitement, however, eclipsed reality, as Robinson related in *The Sarcophagus of an Ancient Civilization:* "It never dawned on me at the time that any other civilized man had already *seen* it and described it." But, alas, eighteen years before, in 1882, Edward C. Wilson, an American photographer, had discovered the Great High Place.

Wilson described the find as follows: "The afternoon was waning, and I was obliged to make haste. The summit must be gained." He kept climbing, descended some rocky steps, then "crossed a short depression, ascended another stairway, and came out upon a summit." Another climber, better known than Wilson, described his conquest of the heights in quite similar terms: "Time was passing and the ridge seemed never-ending . . . . I went on step cutting . . . . I looked upward to see a narrow snow ridge running up to a snowy summit. A few more whacks of the ice ax in the firm snow and we stood on top." That was Edmund Hillary atop Mt. Everest—the Great High Place of the world. To Wilson, discovery of the High Place at Petra was no doubt as exciting as the ascent of Everest was to Hillary, even if the former feat was less enthralling to the world at large.* As for poor Professor Robinson, only number two to reach Petra's Great High Place, he managed to salvage some glory for himself by

---

*In the early 1960s, a team of British archeologists at Petra engaged a Himalayan mountaineer named Joe Brown to pass across the sheer facade of Tomb Number 67 to reach a previously inaccessible attic room. It turned out to be a burial chamber.

affirming that at least he was "the first to have recognized its religious value, and to have interpreted it to the world."

When John Lloyd Stephens wanted to record his presence as the first American at Petra, he entered his name on a wall of the Khazne, or Treasury, so called because it was thought that the urn atop its facade once contained a treasure trove. This tomb-temple is the ancient city's most famous monument and its best preserved. It is also the first monument you see after leaving the Siq, the narrow gorge you pass through to reach Petra. The Khazne's sudden appearance there, just beyond the Siq at the entrance to Petra, is surely one of the great sights in the world of travel. Beginning with the very first look at the Khazne in modern times and continuing up to the present time, the elaborately carved classical facade has, justifiably, fascinated visitors to Petra. Burckhardt called it "one of the most elegant remains of antiquity existing in Syria [now Jordan]," adding that its "situation and beauty . . . make an extraordinary impression upon the traveler." Irby and Mangles, commanders in the British Navy, who spent two years in the Middle East and visited Petra in May 1818, wrote that there was "scarcely a building of forty years standing in England, so well preserved in the greater part of its architectural decorations." In our day, Sacheverell Sitwell found the structure "one of the most mysterious and intriguing buildings in the world."

But apart from the Khazne's perfect placement, its excellent state of preservation, and its elegance and mystery—no one is certain exactly when or by whom it was built or what its function was—the monument bears another feature which impresses itself upon the visitor and which remains in the mind long after his brief moments at Petra are over. On the facade is cut a group of now faded stone images which give a haunting reminder of the once-thriving trading center's decline and of its disappearance for a millennium until it reappeared as a long deserted relic. Those effaced faces and figures—the central one has been identified as Isis bearing a cornucopia—are exceptions to the Khazne's otherwise well-nigh perfectly preserved facade, timeworn exceptions which echo Francis Bacon's observation that "there is no excellent beauty that hath not some strangeness in the proportion."

It is the excellent beauty of the Khazne, combined with those vanishing and by now rather ethereal medallions of carved sandstone, that best summarizes what is Petra—and, more, what is past. Those half-here and half-disappeared figures seem to mock the passing visitor and to make him appear more transient than he would like to acknowledge. The vanishing carvings recall the shadowy skeletal forms found on the floor of a Bronze-Age tumulus at Elp in the Netherlands, where acid in the sand ate away the bones, leaving behind only their dark outline, a design that looks like a primitive cave drawing. Or they recall the simultaneous sense of presence and absence pictured by Vermeer in his painting, *A Lady Reading at the Window*, in the Dresden Museum: in the lower right-hand corner of the glass of an open window appears the vague, insubstantial reflection of the downward-tilted head of a beautiful young woman reading a letter, her fading, ghostly reflected image a kind of strange foreshadowing of her inevitable disintegration and disappearance.

Someday in the not-too-distant future—in half a million years or so, say, a mere instant as cosmic time goes—all the intricately carved sandstone facades at Petra will have crumbled into grainy nothings. Already many of the carvings, like those fading images on the Khazne, are showing signs of time: perhaps they, like the crumbling pagodas and temples of Burma's Pagan, will disappear long before the lapse of that cosmic instant. Then what we know as Petra will be no more. The rugged sandstone cliffs will revert to their original state, raw and unembellished, as they were thirty million years ago when convulsions threw them up from the desert terrain. Then, once again, they will be as they were before man's hand cut into them the strange beauty that was the Khazne; before Burckhardt rediscovered the long-lost city; before the Romans and the Nabateans inhabited the rock valley; before Moses passed by leading his people to the Promised Land; before, even, the formation of man's consciousness through which was to flow the concept, and the corrosion of time.

6

Benjamin Constant

—1—

FROM THE TIME I FIRST STARTED PLANNING MY TRIP TO South America, Benjamin Constant intrigued me. Browsing on a large-scale map of Brazil, I came across that name printed in the tiniest of type and lost in the vastness of the Amazon jungle. The little dot of a place seemed as remote as the Southern Cross and considerably more mysterious: we name the constellations for what we see in them, but why was an obscure Amazon jungle settlement named after a cultured and civilized early nineteenth-century French novelist?

What is there about a name which can so stir our imagination? In *Tropic of Capricorn* Henry Miller tells of his fascination with another Brazilian name, that of Santos Dumont, the aviation pioneer: "About his exploits we were not much concerned—just the name .... Santos Dumont was a magical word which suggested a beautiful flowing moustache, a sombrero, spurs, something airy, delicate, humorous, quixotic." Such is the incantatory effect of certain names. What person, with even the slightest instinct in his blood toward the romance and adventure of travel to remote places, could fail to feel the

175

stirrings of wanderlust on reading or hearing names such as Devil's Island or Easter Island or Petra, to give but a few examples. The very writing of those names instills in me a feeling like that described by D.H. Lawrence in the first sentence of *Sea and Sardinia*: "Comes over one an absolute necessity to move."

After I finally did move from the soft life of my easy chair and travel books to the long, hard road through South America, a vast, incontinent continent, the name Benjamin Constant, that most incongruously labeled outpost in the remote Brazilian jungle, continued to activate my imagination. Not that Benjamin Constant is the only place name in Brazil foreign to that country. Others include a river in the Madeira Basin called Theodore Roosevelt, a Cleveland and a Filadelfia, and even a settlement named Americana, founded in 1866 by post-Civil War exiles from the American Confederacy, where the residents still speak English with a Southern drawl and bury their dead in a cemetery marked with a painted Confederate flag. Those American names, however, somehow seemed less strange and out of place in Brazil than the name Benjamin Constant. I wondered if Benjamin Constant was the Gallic analogue to Americana: perhaps the place had been settled by exiles from France who still spoke French. And as my trip through South America unfolded I began to wonder if anyone from the outside world ever visited that speck of civilization—or whatever it was—lost in the Brazilian jungle.

From time to time I attempted to imagine the jungle village into existence. I saw it in my mind as a typical French provincialish town, one of those sleepy little places with tree-lined streets, a few fountains, a couple of "haute cuisine" restaurants, maybe even a museum and a theater to lend at least the appearance of culture; and in that remote spot perhaps there was also an Alliance Française to spread French culture and language into the Amazon jungle. After visiting Manaus, a Brazilian jungle city on the Amazon fifteen hundred miles downriver from

Benjamin Constant, I was able to furnish my imaginary village with real settings.

Manaus is truly a European outpost deep in the Amazon jungle. The city flourished during the rubber boom in the last half of the nineteenth century. Its squares, wide streets, fountains, and smattering of European-style buildings combine to give Manaus the air of a French provincial town. Profits from products cultivated in the jungle were used to buy the goods and services of a cultivated, cultured Europe. During the boom times, the rich of Manaus would send their shirts to London to be ironed. The stone blocks used to build the customs house and lighthouse in Manaus were imported, piece by piece, from England. The famous Manaus Opera House, where Sarah Bernhardt, Anna Pavlova, and most of the other renowned European artists of the time performed, is an Old World amalgam: Swedish steel beams structure the building, blue and gold tiles from Alsace-Lorraine decorate the dome, and the interior is embellished with Italian Carrara marble, English furniture, Venetian glass chandeliers, and paintings and murals by French and Italian artists. On the gracefully curved balcony appears a constellation of names from a distant culture foreign to the Amazon: Shakespeare, Molière, Goethe, Lessing, Corneille, Gil Vincente, Beethoven, Mozart, Verdi, Racine.

As my South American trip rolled on, I continued to imagine Benjamin Constant as a sort of mini-Manaus. Never supposing I'd ever see the place, I contented myself with that imaginary version of the village. The elegantly named jungle settlement was as inaccessible as the Southern Cross and, in one way, even more so, for at least I could see the stars in their religiously regular pattern. But, in time, chance happened to lead me to an out-of-the-way area of the Brazilian jungle; and a few months after visiting Manaus, having traveled down the east coast of South America and back up the west, I found myself in a dugout canoe floating down the Amazon headed for—of all places—Benjamin Constant.

—2—

The original Benjamin Constant was born in 1767 in Switzerland—where, in Lausanne, there is an Avenue Benjamin Constant—but he lived a French life and wrote a very French book called *Adolphe*, published in 1816. The novel is a psychological study of how the love of Ellénore, an older woman, increases as the infatuation of Adolphe, the detached and introspective young intellectual, wanes. It is what the French call a "roman d'analyse." Much of the story is based on Benjamin Constant's seventeen-year affair, from 1794 to 1811, with Madame de Staël, who ran the era's most refined and cultivated literary and political salon at Coppet, the Lake Geneva chateau owned by her father, the banker Necker.

A second, and later, Constant was a turn-of-the-nineteenth-century Paris artist named Jean Joseph Benjamin Constant, a portraitist who painted a wide variety of late Victorian figures, ranging from Jay Gould to Queen Victoria herself.

Then there was a third Benjamin Constant. His full name was Benjamin Constant de Botelho Magalhães. (In Portuguese, the spelling is "Benjamim.") Born in Brazil in 1833, he, like his friend, journalist Ramiz Galvão, who at age twelve adopted the strange—for Brazil—name of Benjamin Franklin, called himself after another Benjamin— Constant—because of his admiration for the republican French writer. The Amazon jungle village was named after the Brazilian, a national hero and a very versatile one. He entered the Brazilian army in 1852, became a captain in the engineers, then fought in the war against Paraguay. He served on the staff of the *Jornal do Commercio*, and later in the late 1880s he wrote articles for the *Gazeta de Tarde* supporting the military against the House of Braganza, the royal family of Brazil. He was also an astronomer at Rio's Observatory and he founded that city's Institute for the Blind, now known as the Benjamin Constant Institute. As Minister of Public Education, Constant instituted important education reforms, and in 1889 he played a leading role in the overthrow of Emperor Dom Pedro II and in the subsequent establishment of the republic which Constant served as Minister of War until his death in 1891.

Benjamin Constant was more than a military and political figure. As a follower of August Comte, the French thinker who developed the philosophy of positivism, Constant was one of the founders of the Brazilian branch of positivism; he also served as the idealogue of his country's republican movement. It was Constant who added to the star-cluttered Brazilian flag the positivist motto originated by Comte—"Ordem e Progresso."

But in spite of all his service and accomplishments— or, thanks to his rivals, perhaps because of them—the founder of the Brazilian republic was honored by a pitiful sort of memorial. The village bearing his name is more an insult to him than a tribute; as I soon discovered, the poor little settlement lost in the Amazon jungle shows little order and even less progress.

—3—

The dugout canoe floated easily with the current as we drifted down the broad, gently flowing Amazon heading for Benjamin Constant, Brazil. They say you can also get there by airplane, but in the Amazon country they tell you lots of tales. Looking at the jungle that bordered both sides of the river, it was hard to believe the dense tangle of vegetation could be cleared for a landing strip, let alone a village or, for that matter, for any other sort of human presence. But somewhere ahead of us lay Benjamin Constant, that remote settlement that had for so long stirred my curiosity and teased my imagination.

The jungle looks the same everywhere—monotonously so, in fact—but man, his sense of territory acute even in that out-of-the-way overgrown wasteland, has managed to partition it into political units. We started off from Leticia, the southernmost outpost of Colombia, drifted past Ramón Castila in Peru on the opposite bank, and then passed Marco, Brazil, a mile or so downstream. The three countries border each other there, or so the map has it, but no markings or barriers show you that you've crossed an international boundary. The jungle, invariable, yields no clues to how men have cut it up politically. In that part of the world the only states are states of nature.

Life—both plant and human—is primeval out there. Primitive huts raised on poles above flood level and topped by large-leaved roofs rise at scattered points along the shores. From time to time a small dugout canoe of a type used on the Amazon since time immemorial approached, passed, or followed us. After an hour's ride we left the Amazon and turned into a tributary called Rio Solimões, then continued on for another twenty minutes before finally reaching Benjamin Constant.

We docked. I left the canoe and walked along the unpainted wooden pier, gingerly stepping on the weathered, splintery grey planks while taking care to step across the open spaces left by missing boards. Shabby shacks lining the boardwalk offered for sale only the barest necessities—batteries, flashlights, flour, tinned goods, work clothes, candles. The pier led to the village's main shopping street, a dirty dirt road bordered by more shacks. I ambled on into the center of Benjamin Constant, then advanced a few blocks to the outskirts where a wall of jungle rose to block my way.

I wandered through some of the outlying dirt streets, carefully avoiding the dead rats that lay decomposing in the brutal sun. Low over the village glided vultures, natural counterparts to the makeshift tattered paper kites jerked through the air on short strings by unwashed, barefoot little boys. The ragged bits of airborne paper reminded me of the brighter and more elegant cloth kites I'd seen soaring high over Rio's Copacabana beach. Rio now seemed a long way away. But once upon a time, even that great city, I suppose, was as primitive as Benjamin Constant.

I continued my stroll. Humidity blanketed the jungle settlement with an almost tangible pressure. There wasn't very much to see. Even Baedeker would've been hard pressed to contrive a paragraph on the sights of Benjamin Constant. I managed to find the following points of interest: a small electric power station; a brick factory, vintage 1900 or earlier; a sawmill with some fairly new machines, including a band saw and a lathe; the concrete shell of an unfinished church which, so I imagined, was permanently under construction. There was also said to be a rubber factory a short distance from town, but at the time I visited Benjamin Constant the plant was flooded and under water.

Benjamin Constant is the sort of place where you'd expect to come across a character like Dr. Livingston or a Mr. Kurtz. But I discovered no Livingston, and the local Kurtz—if there had ever been one—was indeed dead. From what I could see, nothing much happened in Benjamin Constant; nothing, except that they produced children there—lots of them—and life, of a sorts, went on. Otherwise, nothing.

But it wasn't for nothing that I'd traveled to Benjamin Constant, nor did I journey there simply out of idle curiosity. I was perhaps the only person in many months—maybe ever—to visit the isolated settlement on official business. When I landed a few days earlier in Leticia, in Colombia, the immigration officer there advised me that I needed a visa to enter that country. The man let me into Colombia with the understanding I'd get the visa abroad—from the Colombian consul in Benjamin Constant. It was for that reason I left Colombia and took an international excursion to Brazil.

The consul's place was the most attractive house in Benjamin Constant—but only by default. The official seemed quite pleased with my visit, no doubt because I gave him something to do, much as was the case with

Fitzroy Maclean who, on arrival at Alma Ata in Kazakhstan, reported to an official bureau where, he recounts in *Escape to Adventure*, he found "a zealous young Kazakh who assured me that he was delighted to see me as he felt that my arrival justified his existence." Similarly, the Colombian consul in Benjamin Constant saw my presence as a reason for his existence: the functionary could now function. But he didn't function very efficiently, and it soon became apparent to me that he was out of practice—if, in fact, he'd ever been in practice. I observed him—first patiently, then impatiently—as he fumbled for forms, reviewed regulations, and studied instructions. Finally, he was ready to begin processing the papers.

The diplomat first copied information from my passport onto a sheet of paper. He worked slowly, deliberately. After completing that procedure the consul transferred the information from the paper to official forms, this time typing on an antique machine at a pace somewhat slower than hunt and peck. The inevitable ceiling fan wafted vague wrinkles of slow hot air through the room. The heavy breeze circulated more quickly than my visa application. Eventually, the papers were seemingly completed and delivered to me for signature; but then the consul realized he'd forgotten to enter my passport number in some of the appropriate places and so he retrieved the forms and remedied the omission. That took another few minutes. In time, all the papers were completed and, over an hour after my arrival, I left with my visa. The consul seemed sorry to see me go.

Lunch at a cafe on the wharf boardwalk provided in taste what it lacked—so I imagined—in hygiene. The menu would have pleased natural food addicts: large-grained rice, stew, potatoes, green beans, peas mixed with strange-looking and strange-tasting green herbs. During the meal a sort of floor show played out by my chair. A furry, mangy dog toyed with a large insect—a cross between a roach and a grasshopper—by pawing and biting the bug. The dog finally crushed and broke most of its toy's parts, leaving the insect supine and able to move only its pincer mouth in futile spasms. Then it stopped moving.

Such is life—and death—in Benjamin Constant, Brazil. In one scene of Benjamin Constant's *Adolphe*, the hero and his mistress, Ellénore, stroll through a landscape where the trees are bare, the sky birdless, the grass frozen, and where "the sun seems to cast a dismal light over the greyish countryside, as though looking down in pity upon a world it has ceased to warm." The French writer's imaginary world is most unlike the reality that exists in his namesake village in the Brazilian jungle. There, trees, birds, and grass proliferate everywhere, and the sun burns down on the green chaos with an unforgiving, pitiless glare. Unlike Constant's imagined sun, the real sun, of course, is too high in the sky to pity the world it nourishes from such a far distance.

—4—

Now the dugout canoe fought its way upstream, struggling against the Amazon's current, as we returned to Leticia. Benjamin Constant had disappeared from view, but it remained vivid in my mind. The isolated village intrigued me even more now, after my visit, than it had previously in my anticipation and imagination. The jungle hybrid, with its evocative European name and ramshackle tropical appearance, epitomized to me the essential duality of the culture of South America, where the Old World's refined civilization both complements and contrasts with the natural, primitive life of the New World.

The European country most influential in South American life is France. It is curious that the Spanish and Portuguese intellectual communities in the New World looked to Paris, rather than to Madrid or Lisbon, as their cultural home. It is as if educated North Americans had learned German as a second language and gravitated to Berlin and Gottingen, rather than to London and Oxford, for their Wanderjahr. In *The Honorary Consul,* a novel set in South America, Graham Greene notes that "Rousseau and Chateaubriand were a greater influence in South America than Freud—there was even a city in Brazil named after Benjamin Constant." Benjamin Constant is hardly a city (although, it might be added parenthetically, Constant's *Adolphe,* an analysis of the psychology of love, can in some ways be considered a Freud-ish sort of work), but there is no doubt that France is the school of Latin America.

Perhaps one reason for French dominance in matters of the mind in South America stems from the desire of once colonized countries to distance themselves from their former motherlands. In that way, cultural independence supplements and reinforces political independence. In addition, the literature of France is richer than that of Spain or Portugal; and, during much of the twentieth century at least, it has also been freer. Furthermore, the French attempt to export their culture and language around the world with a zeal that rivals the export by Yankees of Coca-Cola. Although such problems as gender, irregular verbs, and the subjunctive have in many countries been no match for the pause that refreshes, in Latin America the French language, brother to Spanish and Portuguese, is less arcane than in other lands. Finally, France has always extended a congenial reception to students, artists, exiles, and, for that matter, anyone who wishes to adopt Paris as his second home, which no doubt includes nearly everyone who's lived there long enough to get to know the city.

The proverbial "American in Paris" in fact encompasses not only North Americans but also transplants from the Latin countries of America. In *Cousin Bette,* Balzac depicts an archetypal South American in Paris—the rather uncouth and unsophisticated Brazilian Baron Henri Montès de Montejanos. The Baron's very name—the French "Henri" combined with the repeated reference to mountains, not to mention the two-faced figure hinted at by the "janos," which might also refer to "Janeiro"—suggests his situation in the story: a man of nature from the wilds of South America enmeshed in the jungle of drawing-room love intrigues of Parisian society. No match for the scheming Valérie Marneffe, with whom the Baron is infatuated, he is Constant's Adolphe turned inside out. Valérie thinks of her pursuer as a "half primitive Moor of Rio de Janeiro." The Baron's own words match his brutish image: "I am a Czar," he proclaims. "I've purchased all my subjects, and nobody can leave my kingdom, which lies a hundred leagues from any human habitation, and which is bordered by the land of the savages of the interior and separated from the coast by a waste land as big as your France."

From the wild country such as Baron Henri Montès described were collected such fauna as "monkeys in cages, domestic animals in pens, parrots and cockatoos, a Noah's Ark from South America," a Brazilian cargo carried by the steamship *Navarro*, which, in 1866, Hans Christian Andersen saw on boarding the boat, just arrived from Rio, to sail from Lisbon to Bordeaux after having visited Portugal. In Portugal he'd seen such refinements of European civilization as cathedrals, monasteries, art galleries, the venerable university at Coimbra, and seasoned "old Belém" in the western suburbs of Lisbon on the Tagus River, some thirty-eight hundred miles distant in space, and light years distant in ambiance, from Brazil's raw new Belém at the mouth of the Amazon. Cathedrals and cockatoos: an ocean, and worlds, apart.

The contrast between the primitive and the civilized— and America and Europe—found in the fictional character of Balzac's Baron Henri Montès is evident in the persons and works of two of South America's best known contemporary writers, Argentina's Jorge Luis Borges and Pablo Neruda of Chile. Neruda's poetry is deeply rooted in the natural, organic aspects of his continent. "I began to write," he wrote in *Viajes* ("Trips"), "by a vegetal impulse and my first contact with the grandeur of existence was my dreams on moss, my long wakings upon the humus." Elsewhere, Neruda says that poetry "shouldn't be pure form, or refined, or cultured. It should be rocky, dusty, rainy and daily." He speaks to the uneducated, to the people of the soil: "I write for the people/Although they can't read my poetry with their rural eyes," Neruda affirms in his *Canto General*.

Borges, on the other hand, is anything but rural. He is, rather, urban and urbane. In contrast to Neruda's native naturalness, Borges is cosmopolitan and literary. In his essay on "The Argentine Writer and Tradition," Borges discusses Ricardo Güiraldes' 1926 novel, *Don Segundo Sombra*, a book which romanticizes the figure of the gaucho and his struggle with natural forces by showing how a green, undisciplined boy develops into a responsible cowboy through coping with nature on the pampas under the tutelage of Don Segundo Sombra, a cowherder. Written in the Neruda tradition of nature and the land, the book is thought of in Argentina as a "nationalist" novel, but Borges argues that its metaphors "have nothing to do with country speech but a great deal to do with the metaphors of the then current literary circles of Montmartre." Borges goes on to suggest that the story was influenced by Kipling's *Kim*, and he concludes that the English writer "and the metaphors of French poets were necessary for this Argentine book, for this book which, I repeat, is no less Argentine for having accepted such influences." (Noting elsewhere that the Royal Spanish Academy has ruled that the word "viking" should be written "vikingo" in Spanish, Borges muses: "I suspect that quite soon we'll be hearing about the works of Kiplingo." But Borges, true to his cosmopolitan outlook, in the Spanish original of his essay on *Don Segundo Sombra* sticks to the English form of "Kipling." Gabriel García Márquez in his novel *The Autumn of the Patriarch* refers to an Ambassador Kippling, an alternate spelling which would perhaps both satisfy the Royal Spanish Academy and be respectful to the name's original version.)

So while Neruda's writings stem from his native and natural environment, Borges' refined works are produced within the European intellectual tradition. Borges eschews both his country and the land of his native language: "When I write, I do not think of myself as an Argentine or as a Spaniard." Such, in any event, are the ways Borges and Neruda think and write—in cosmopolitan and in indigenous terms, respectively.

But, curiously enough, those two South American writers have both lived their lives exactly opposite to how they wrote. Neruda was the most cosmopolitan of men. From age sixteen, when Ricardo Basoalto adopted as his pen name that of Czech poet Jan Neruda, to the end of his days, much of the Chilean writer's life was influenced by and spent in countries other than his native land. After joining the diplomatic service, he represented Chile as consul in such distant posts as Burma, Ceylon, and Java. He traveled extensively and often in Europe, as well as in the Americas, including the United States, and for a time he lived in Italy. And Neruda ended his life as the Allende government's ambassador to France, serving in Paris until February 1973, the year he died in September at age sixty-nine.

In contrast to Neruda, Borges for the most part stayed close to home. His family took him twice to Europe when he was a young man, but after the age of twenty-five Borges established himself definitively in Buenos Aires, where he lived for the next half century with only very occasional short trips abroad, not to live but only to lecture or receive honors. In his first book, *Fervor de Buenos Aires,* Borges wrote how he felt about his native city:

"This city that I thought my past/is my future, my present;/the years that I have lived in Europe are illusory,/I was always (and will be) in Buenos Aires." As the fourth generation of native-born Argentinians, Borges often refers in his writings to his ancestors. By a curious, Borgian sort of coincidence his first job was at a library on Avenida La Plata named after Juan Crisostomo—who died in 1824, "in exile," notes Borges—an ancestor of Borges to whom his essay "A New Refutation of Time" is dedicated.

In 1955 Borges was appointed director of Argentina's National Library. It was there—in his "lair," as he put it—that I met and spoke with him in December 1971 during my South American trip. He wanted to discuss the political situation in Argentina more than world literature; and when I asked him why politics interested him so much, Borges replied, "This is my country. I feel very Argentinian." To my response that he was very international, Borges countered by disagreeing, referring to his Argentine ancestors and especially his grandfather, a cavalry colonel who died in 1874, about whom Borges wrote a short poem called "Allusion to the Death of Colonel Francisco Borges." Later in the conversation, when we spoke about foreign travel, Borges said he had no plans and no desire for a trip abroad. "I'm an old man, and it's too hard for me to travel," he said, adding that he felt little nostalgia for Europe.

There is something archetypically South American about these two paradoxical figures—Neruda, a world traveler whose poetry sang of his homeland, and Borges, a literary internationalist who stayed in his hometown to live. Each had his mind in one place and his heart in another. This, I think, tends to make you rather skeptical about the connection between a poet's life and his art; and it makes you wonder if the poetry is in fact a sort of anti-mirror that reflects the opposite of the man's inner reality, just as the designation "Benjamin Constant" suggests a false picture of the squalid reality of the little Brazilian jungle village which bears that European name.

—5—

The contrast—tension, even—between the civilized and artful and the primitive and natural appears in many different forms all over South America and is probably the continent's defining theme.

A few days before meeting Borges I attended a performance at the San Martin Municipal Theater in Buenos Aires of tango music and dancing presented to mark the twentieth anniversary of the death of Enrique Santos Discépolo, a famous Argentine lyricist who wrote songs of a rather melancholy and cynical sort. Ricardo Güiraldes, author of *Don Segundo Sombra*, wrote a poem in Paris in 1911 entitled "Tango" in which he calls it a sad dance of love and death; and Santos Discépolo himself once wrote—typically, for him—"I remember that among the things used at school was a small globe of the earth. I covered it with a black cloth and I didn't return to uncover it. It seemed to me that the world should always remain that way—dressed in mourning."

In contrast to the tango's modulated music and melancholy words are the primitive rhythms and lively lyrics of the samba. The derivation of the music's name—it comes from "semba," an ancient African drum dance brought to Brazil by slaves—suggests its content. For the samba the world is not a crepe-draped globe but a roulette wheel to be spun. The refrain of Ernesto dos Santos' "Pelo Telefone" ("On the Telephone"), the first samba published and recorded, and the hit of the 1917 Carnival, says: "The Chief of Police/On the telephone/Informed me/That in Rio/There's a roulette/That can be played."

Friends in Rio took me one night to an "escola de samba," one of those informal groups which vie with each other in the dance and costume competitions at Carnival. Unlike the well-rehearsed tango performance in Buenos Aires' modern San Martin Theater, the escola de samba event was a happening—spontaneous and primitive—held in a cavernous rough concrete building in the

Catumbi section of Rio, an unfashionable but vibrant quarter of town; it was a remarkable spectacle.

After reaching the overgrown shed about midnight, we climbed to a balcony that overlooked the jammed dance floor below. At one side stood a group of sweat-drenched drummers beating out a samba rhythm that never stopped. The hundreds of people who crowded the floor twisted and undulated to the music. The wild movement and lively contortions represented the antithesis of those stony figures, petrified in place and frozen in time, that decorate Petra's Khazne. Many of the dancers, animated to a frenzy by the hypnotic beat, seemed lost in a trance as if possessed by some primitive tribal instinct. Almost without exception, the women were stunning in appearance and copious in body and energy; long, slender legs beneath short shorts or miniskirts moved to the rhythm as breasts swung and bobbed under tight jersey shirts. The samba's contagious drumbeat quickly infects everyone, and soon my friend and I joined in the dance, contorting our bodies to the sensuous music. The chaos of dancers, along with the din and the haze of cigarette smoke, combined to lend the scene a strange and even surrealistic appearance, like a passage from Dante come alive. But that is too bookish, too Borgian; in fact, it was all quite real and completely natural.

All this frenzied activity is by way of preparation for the Carnival competition. In *An Age of Mediocrity*, C.L. Sulzberger describes a performance on Rio's Copacabana beach by the samba school that had won at the Carnival in 1971, the year of my visit: "There were hundreds of men and women dancers in extraordinarily lavish costumes, red, white, silver, long feathers: a kind of pageant of the arrival of an African king. The samba dancers, who pay for their own costumes and the buses that bring them here, were at least 95 percent black (or mulatto). They all come from very poor districts." A similar sort of scene used to transpire at the nineteenth-century voodoo ceremonies in New Orleans: "While the wild chanting, the

rhythmic movement of hands and feet, the barbarous dance, and the fiery incantations were at their height, it was difficult to believe that we were in a civilized city of an enlightened republic . . . it was so wild and bizarre that one might easily imagine he was in Africa or hell."*
Such was the scene at Catumbi that night: it was in civilized Paris where the "last tango" was danced, but at the escola de samba in Rio I saw the dark underworld of Black Orpheus, a primitive New World celebration which Neruda, in his poem "Dancing with Negroes," described as a "dance of blood and joy . . . body and soul."

What the tango is to dance in South America, the San Martin Municipal Theater—where the Discépolo tango performance took place—is to architecture. Built in the 1950s, the theater is artfully structured into a proportioned whole consisting of three cubic sections of different heights arranged one atop the other. The theater is considered one of Argentina's finest public buildings; and, as such, its equivalent in Brazil is Rio's Ministry of Education and Public Health, a large, boxy office building constructed in the late 1930s by the renowned Brazilian architects Oscar Niemeyer and Lucio Costa. Their design was greatly influenced by Le Corbusier, the European whom they consulted on the ministry building and who had visited Brazil in 1929. The two Brazilian architects later collaborated on Brasilia, Costa working out the city plan and Niemeyer acting as director of architecture for "Novacap," as the project was called.

That Orwellian designation epitomizes Brasilia. The fabricated city represents order and logic gone haywire. In a way, the expression "planned city" is a contradiction in terms. The new capital is planned—no question about that—but it's hardly a true city, a settlement accreted piece by piece by and for people. Novacap, in fact, lacks all connection with life; completely unorganic, Brasilia

*C. D. Wagner, quoted in *Voodoo in New Orleans* by Robert Tallant (New York: Collier Books, 1969).

has been grafted onto the red earth like an oversized toy town transferred whole from the drawing board to the earth's surface without inclusion of the human element.

You have to look very carefully to find even the slightest human touch at Brasilia. One spark of spontaneity among the rigid buildings and severely straight streets is a footpath which winds its irregular way past the large box that contains the Congress Hall. Writing about the organic connection between man and land in South America, a Colombian priest, German Guzman, referred to what he called "the sense of the path"—a sense "that integrates peasant life." Maybe that worn, somehow forlorn little footpath in Brasilia evidences such a sense, one overwhelmed and overshadowed by Novacap's towers.

Another part of Brasilia that fails to conform to the architecture and arrangement decreed by the city planners are the jumbled "favelas" (slums) and "burracos" (shanties) located a short distance from town. Of these exceptions to the terrifying symmetry of Brasilia, Lucio Costa has said: "This is Brazil, not a civilized European country . . . . Of course half the people in Brasilia live in favelas. Brasilia was not designed to solve the problems of Brazil. It was bound to reflect them." What Costa observed about Brasilia is true also of all of South America: the order and progress of the planned city surrounded by a jungle of slums find their equivalent in the mixture of civilization and the natural that forms the continent's fabric—a synthesis typified by a remote and primitive village bearing the elegant name of Benjamin Constant.

But as my primitive little dugout canoe struggled against the current to climb the Amazon from Benjamin Constant, Brazil, up to Leticia, Colombia, all of that—culture, books, ideas, art, architecture, poetry—seemed out of place. There in the jungle twilight, natural history prevailed over world history, that artifact of past time created by men; Benjamin Constant was nearer to me, and to my thoughts just then, than the Europeanized town of Manaus, fifteen hundred miles downstream. If Freud was right, "the evolution of civilization may . . . be simply described as the struggle for life of the human species." But, as Graham Greene noted, "Rousseau and Chateaubriand were a greater influence in South America than Freud"; and somehow all the hopes and fears, the laughter and tears of that long Freudian struggle of man to emerge from a state of nature to civilization seemed irrelevant in the face of the pervasive and indifferent Amazon jungle and the quickly gathering darkness.

Dusk rushed across the great jungle. The first stars began to dot the darkening sky. Somewhere up there, those distant glimmers of light which man, in his passion to name nature—to civilize it—calls the Southern Cross would soon appear. "The Southern Cross," said Machado de Assis, the great Brazilian writer, "is too high in the heavens to distinguish between man's laughter and tears."

7

Mount Athos

—1—

A TRIP TO THE REMOTE, MILLENNIUM-OLD GREEK MONAS-
tic community of Mount Athos is as much a journey
into the inner reaches of your being as it is a voyage across
space and back in time. Lawrence Durrell's observation
about Greece—"Other countries may offer you discoveries
in manners or lore or landscape; Greece offers you something harder—the discovery of yourself"—is especially
true about Athos. A visit to that venerable holy enclave
perched on the tip of a peninsula in northern Greece
fairly forces you to examine your way of life in the greater
secular world left behind while you tour the isolated
ancient religious settlement. If, as Henry Miller believed,
"there is only one great adventure and this is inward
toward the self," then a trip to Athos is a step on the way
to that adventure, a beginning on the "longest journey . . .
the journey inwards," as Dag Hammerskjold put it: as you
visit Athos, Athos visits upon you the imperative to discover yourself.

Like one's inner being, Athos is remote and difficult of
access. Even today the peninsula—although only one
hundred miles from Salonika—is inconvenient to reach,
notwithstanding the complaint made early in this century

by F.W. Hasluck, librarian of the British School at Athens from 1906-1915, that "much of the difficulty and not a little of the romance of a pilgrimage to Athos has vanished with the coming of steam." One indication of how isolated Athos remains, in this day and age of ubiquitous instant and incessant communication, is that on the holy peninsula you are beyond the reach of both of those two pervasive word networks, the telephone and the postal service. Telephone communication with the outside world ends at the tiny port of Daphne, where authorities check arriving visitors for documentation—special permits are required to enter Athos—and for gender, for no females are allowed in the holy community. As for letters, the Greek postal service will carry them to Karyes, Athos's odd little capital—a comic opera village, as it was once described—some three hilly miles inland from Daphne, but no farther. Karyes boasts a post office—the post office, in fact, on Athos—and it is there where all mail reaches the end of the line.

A few places still exist today that lack access to the telephone network, but the absence of postal service is truly unusual and suggestive of how remote Athos really is. How many areas in the world are there outside the postal system? Virtually everywhere a traveler can take for granted the means to receive mail. Written communications are always possible—except at Athos—and they are an important element in pleasurable travel, for mail tethers us to a familiar world. A letter validates your temporarily tenuous existence in the distant context abandoned for travel: though out of sight you are still in mind.

Letters also act to palliate curiosity, a demon trait which is perhaps the fundamental force that moves us to travel, to read, to face tomorrows. Winston Churchill complained in a letter* written September 1898 from a remote

*This was actually a dispatch to London's The Morning Post in the form of a letter to Oliver Borthwick. Unable to receive a commission to

camp in the Sudan north of Khartoum: "The postal arrangements here are very bad and I will charitably conclude that the fact that I have received no letters from you is due to this cause .... It is a symptom of the contrariness of life that we always want to be informed of some place other than that in which we are." If the desire for mail is a sympton of life's contrariness, the letter itself is a symbol of its plenitude—the people, places, and events that exist beyond and without us. A letter represents the epitomy of the world which transcends the individual; and the writing of a letter, which demands thoughtfulness—even in those cases where little thought is required—is a selfless act. A character in Henry de Montherlant's *The Girls* pleads in a letter to a famous author she's trying to reach: "Write to me anything you like, but write to me. Be it only an empty envelope . . . .": even simply mailing an addressed envelope is an act of human communication.

There is virtually no escape from the written communication. When H.V. Morton, the English travel writer, visited El Deir, high in the cliffs of Petra and one of the most remote corners of that remote rock city deep in the Jordanian desert, he found himself within the purview of word from the outside world. He tells of receiving there a telegram, delivered by an Arab Legion soldier, addressed to "Morton, Petra," inviting him to attend a feast given in Amman by the pasha. El Deir is no doubt one of the most improbable sites in the world for a person to receive a written dinner invitation. At Athos, however, you are finally out of touch, beyond the reach of the familiar, for the writings end once you leave Karyes. You then leave behind communication with the world, your world; and, lacking outside resources—mail, phone, wheels, others— you are thrown back on your own. Mail-less Athos be-

---

act as an official correspondent for Kitchner's Sudan campaign; Churchill resorted to the subterfuge of writing privately to Borthwick; by a certain coincidence, he happened to be the proprietor of *The Morning Post*.

comes, in a way of speaking, like a certain cluster of mountains in nearby Macedonia called Agrapha, "the unwritten," so called because no one was able to enroll the population there for tax purposes. Beyond Karyes you are traveling in uncharted territory: the trip through Athos, and your journey inward, begins.

Athos's remoteness is more than simply geographical. There is also the distance of time. *The Go-Between*, a novel by L.P. Hartley, begins, "The past is a foreign country: they do things differently there," a notion that might serve as an apt introduction to Athos. The sense of "foreignness" begins long before you reach the Holy Mountain itself, for permits to enter Athos are issued under the jurisdiction of the Greek Ministry of Foreign Affairs. Shortly after the founding in 963 of Grand Lavra, the first monastery, Emperor John Tsimiskis issued a decree providing that Athos was to enjoy the sovereignty of an independent state; and so the monastic community has remained, in theory at least, if not always in practice. The decree, known as the Tragos—Greek for "he-goat"—because it was written on goatskin, was signed and sealed by Tsimiskis in 972 and is now in the archives of the Holy Synod in Karyes. It is the oldest existing Byzantine imperial document bearing an emperor's signature.

After passing through customs and passport and gender control at Daphne, you proceed to Karyes by an antique bus, one of the community's two motorized vehicles—the other is an old truck—and there you register with the police, who give you an impressive looking document called a "Diamonitirion." The certificate is embellished with the Byzantine two-headed crowned eagle, a tax stamp the size of half a playing card picturing the Holy Mountain, and an even larger purple-ink, rubber-stamped impression of the Virgin Mary. The number of my document was 5683, dated May 2, 1973. Written in Greek, this "License of Stay" is addressed to "The Twenty Sacred and Reverend Monasteries of the Holy Mountain," and it recites that the bearer was "recommended to us by the Ministry of Foreign Affairs." It requests that the visitor be afforded "in addition to a courteous welcome, every possible hospitality and attention toward fulfillment of the purpose for which he has come here." The document is signed in neat Greek letters by four Elders.

It doesn't take long to realize that you are in a country foreign in atmosphere as well as in law. The extent to which Athos is separated from the outside world is a function of time no less than of space. A hint of this added dimension of remoteness appears in a list of "Instructions to all visitors to the Holy Mountain," which the authorities give the newly arrived outsider. After setting forth a number of procedural matters, the instructions conclude:

> Finally, all visitors must be decently dressed.
> Entrance is forbidden to men with long hair; foreign priests without their uniform; visitors in shorts. Visitors disobeying will be expelled.
> All musical instruments are forbidden, on pain of confiscation.
> Motor boats with women in them may not enter the harbours of the various monasteries or Daphni.
> Movie cameras and record players are not allowed.
> Eating meat in the restaurants of Karyai on Wednesdays and Fridays during Lent is forbidden.
> Entering the monasteries with dogs or other animals; singing and whistling are not allowed.

Reading these rules suggests that you are entering a new world—or, more accurately, an old one that predates the one with which you are familiar. In addition to the absence of telephones and letters, movies and music and women are banned: Mount Athos is indeed a foreign land.

As a foreign country located in the past, Mount Athos presents a certain paradox in that many of its buildings are, in fact, of a relatively recent date. Most of the monasteries were constructed between the seventeenth and nineteenth centuries. Simon Petra, for example, the most striking of the monasteries—perched atop a thousand-foot seaside cliff, with tiers of wooden beam-supported balconies clinging to its side that seem to tempt gravity—was built in 1893 after a fire had destroyed the previous building two years before. (Fire is a recurrent hazard at Athos. In December 1976 a blaze at Zographou monastery killed one of the fifteen resident monks and destroyed a number of art treasures.) The Holy Mountain's oldest, and most attractive, phiale—holy water basin—is that at Grand Lavra monastery, but it dates only from 1635. Apart from the tenth-century churches at the monasteries of Grand Lavra and Vatopedi and the Protaton Church in Karyes, few buildings on Athos are older than the sixteenth century.

The past is present in Mount Athos, then, less in what meets the eye than in what the mind gradually absorbs there. Athos is an attitude—a beatitude, as it were—rather than a spectacle. The banning of movie cameras is hardly fatal to a fulfilling visit: life at Athos cannot be caught on film, Robert Byron's comment about the spectacular Simon Petra—in *The Station*, his account of a mid-1920s visit to Athos—notwithstanding: "To portray a building whose dissimilarity from its fellows on this globe robs metaphor of its natural function is best left to other means than words . . . . A film might suffice. Unfortunately, this is a book." Athos, in any event, is more a still life than a moving film. It's a place where the visitor is solemnly informed that an icon of the Virgin, on being sent into the outside world for display at an Orthodox cathedral, wept out of being homesick for the Holy Mountain. Or where he's told that, once upon a time, when a shark swallowed a swimming monk up to the armpits, the victim put his arms out—in the shape of a cross, it's emphasized in the telling—to avoid being completely consumed. Eventually the predator devoured him, but his fellow monks then caught the shark and buried it with religious services out of respect for the monk within. In other words, on Athos the world is described and explained in ways foreign to the ears and sense of the visitor.

The best description I've found of the other-world atmosphere at Athos is a passage that pertains not to Athos itself but to another seemingly similar place. A scene and mood described in *The Diary of a Russian Priest*, written in the 1920s and 1930s by Alexander Elchaninov, a Russian intellectual who in 1921 left his homeland with his wife and child to settle in Nice, France, and who in 1926 decided to enter the priesthood, evokes a sense of the odd forlorness Elchaninov felt when visiting a monastery in the Georgia Causasus during his school days. Just as he enters the monastery, "a small bell rings in the tower. It is such an unexpected sound in this isolated mountain dwelling. It rings again and again: today it is Saturday. But how strange to hear this bell on the top of a bare mountain—nobody will hear it, nobody will come. The very aimlessness of this tolling makes it more moving, more significant." That isolated mountain might be Mount Athos, where men of a bygone era enact hermitlike, hermetic rituals set within a context of remoteness and isolation. The very incongruity of those ancient and, to the visitor's mind, foreign rites are, when contrasted with the modern world beyond the Holy Mountain, more moving, more significant.

But it would be a mistake to take as the defining characteristic of Mount Athos the existence there of a civilization which has elsewhere long since vanished. While it's true you can see on that isolated sliver of land jutting into the Aegean the virtually unchanged remnant of a Byzantine way of life dating from a millenium ago, that is not the Holy Mountain's most distinctive trait, as many visitors have so facilely concluded. A goodly number of places exist in today's world where the atmosphere of the past survives no less than it does at Athos. Strolling the streets of Verona, especially at night, you are back in olden days in a Renaissance city where you can reasonably expect to see Juliet and Romeo—though, admittedly, perhaps not together—out for an evening walk. Along the banks of the Nile in Egypt you see scenes that predate biblical times, while Muezz ly Dine Allah, the street that runs between Bab Zuwaila and Bab El-Futuh in Cairo's old quarter, can't have changed much in the last five hundred years. Villages near Katmandu in Nepal appear untouched by time, but even those seem the last word compared to the hamlets of rural India. To say, then, that the unique and essential quality of Athos is the past you find there is to miss the point—or to avoid it.

How, then, does Athos differ from those other residues of outdated time and—for that matter—from anywhere else on earth? It is that Athos is a living community which represents a way of life diametrically opposite to that existing in the outside world. The visitor finds there a functioning aberration, a society which operates in a manner not previously encountered, based on a state of mind incarnating an attitude thought long obsolete. To the foreigner such discovery raises the possibility that his world and ways, previously accepted without reflection, are inadequate. You begin to consider the possibility that we of the contemporary world are, in fact, more out of step with the basics of existence than the Mount Athos monks, who at first impression appear to be so far removed from twentieth-century life.

Athos, then, presents that most disturbing of problems, an alternative. For that reason, the visitor soon begins to resent the Holy Mountain in the same way that harassed middle-aged businessmen resent Gauguin for his escape to paradise, or in the way would-be soldiers of fortune, and chroniclers thereof, lament their misfortune in not being Lawrence of Arabia or Hemingway, or in the way frustrated adventurers begrudge Richard Halliburton or Richard Burton, either the nineteenth-century English traveler and orientalist or the other contemporary and, these days, more famous Burton. Those men—role-models for prisoners of the conventional—represent alternative ways of life; but the mentor is also tormentor.

Unwilling at first to recognize the possible validity of the Athos ethos, the stranger tends to mock the monks and their seemingly strange way of life. Such is how Nikos Kazantzakis and Zorba, his alter ego, reacted on visiting the Holy Mountain. Near the end of his life Zorba sent a postcard from Mount Athos bearing a picture of the Virgin Mary with the message, "No chance of doing business here, boss! The monks even fleece their fleas! I'm leaving." Before departing, Zorba writes, he gave his pet parrot—a paradigm, perhaps, of the monkish muttering of the liturgy—to a monk who'd taught a blackbird to whistle "Kyrie Eleison"—"Lord, have mercy." In *Report to Greco*, Kazantzakis, in a similarly jocular vein, refers to a blackbird—apparently a different bird than the one Zorba mentioned—which sings, "Lord, I Cried unto Thee." The Greek writer further observes how the Athos hermits, supposedly solitaries, are always so eager to chat; and he tells of a monk who describes the devil as being the abbot of the monastery. Kazantzakis goes on to note that on the Holy Mountain the air has never been soiled by female exhalations: it has been soiled only by male exhalations. Finally, nearing the end of his visit, Kazantzakis becomes more serious and curious, and he begins to wonder if perhaps the Athos way may not have something to offer him; so the writer climbs to a remote cave to ask an ascetic how he can be saved. Salvation is attained only by renouncing the world and giving up the comfortable life, the hermit replies, not unexpectedly. Kazantzakis, not unexpectedly, declines to give up the good life. When the wasted old man says "mockingly"—must not the monks mock our way of life as visitors often do theirs?—"Regards to the world," the young visitor retorts, "Regards to heaven. And tell God it's not our fault but His—because He made the world so beautiful."

Kazantzakis's version of that almost tangible tension which exists between two opposed ways of life—Athos's and the world's—is not without its poignancy; but it was a real-life encounter at Athos, not a bookish one, which for

me illuminated even more vividly the problem of alternatives that a visit to the Holy Mountain starkly raises.
Some three miles beyond Karyes on the peninsula's east
coast stands the Stavronikita Monastery, the first one
we—a Swiss doctor I'd met in Salonika and I—visited.
You could say that the monastery resembles a medieval
fortified French chateau, with its square, crenellated
tower rising above solid stone walls and the small vine-
yard growing just by the entranceway; but the appearance
is deceiving because it was in fact only relatively recently
rebuilt after a fire in 1879. We found there the usual
collection of frescoes, reliquaries, and icons, at least one
of which, a portrayal of St. Nicholas with an oyster shell
stuck in the saint's forehead, is considered miraculous.
But we also found at Stavronikita a rather sad-looking
man with a resigned, if not defeated, air. A Greek who'd
resided for a time in Canada—and thus spoke good English—the man now lived with his wife in Athens, where
he painted and worked as an architect. Once a year, he
told us, he traveled to Athos to visit his "spiritual father,"
the abbot at Stavronikita.

We chatted for a few minutes about various church
subjects—the theory and purpose of the icon, Orthodox
rules and rituals, the life led by hermits and ascetics on
Athos—and finally, after detecting in him a strong strain
of piety, mixed with more than a little mysticism, I asked
the man if he'd ever wanted to become a monk.

"Yes, and I still do," he replied. Now he paused. Then,
his voice low and slow, he went on, "But you see, by now
it's too late for me. I've lived too long in the outside
world—and that has spoiled me for any other life."

And now he seemed to retreat into himself, and soon I
could see written on his face all the pain of the dilemma
of his existence and his regret at having spent his life in
the world rather than on the Holy Mountain. He was, in
other words, a man whose trip from his home to the
monastic community had taken him on a journey far

longer and more difficult than that from Athens to Athos:
he was a man who had traveled on the journey inward.

—2—

Mount Athos had a past before it became a monastic
community. But after it became a religious colony in the
tenth century the Holy Mountain had virtually no future,
for life there was for the most part frozen in place, in time.
Robert Byron's comments about the artwork at Mount
Athos might well be taken as an accurate description not
only of the paintings there but also of the life. "Its
frescoes," he wrote in *The Byzantine Achievement*, "ex-
hale an atmosphere of piety and quietude, and a sobriety
of light, which, if tending sometimes to weakness, be-
speak the dignity of spiritual repose, of unshaken faith in
the hidden world amid the mounting catastrophes of this
. . . . There are strange qualities about the Antarctic of the
Greek world." Apart from the polar extremes, only a place
such as Athos, as extreme in time as are the Poles in
space, can fairly be called "Antarctic": there on the Holy
Mountain, life jelled early and has changed, if at all, only
at a glacial pace. The tenth-century ambiance has continued to this day with a continuity seldom disturbed by
the ebb and flow of events that swirled around the outside
world.

If it is the case that change rules the world, then Athos
is without a sovereign. The Holy Mountain is impervious
to change. It is said that the two stately cypress trees that
grow in the courtyard of Grand Lavra were planted in the
tenth century by Athanasius, who founded that monastery in 963. Perhaps this is true; and even if not, it's hardly
the most incredible tale a traveler hears during his trip
around Athos. Still today at Dionysiou—among the most
mystical of the monasteries, not to mention the most
hospitable, and the one with the best food on the penin-

sula—the monks pray for the Trebizond emperors, the monastery's patrons at the time of its founding. That dynasty fell over five hundred years ago. Similarly, in 1873 a memorial was erected in the courtyard of the Bulgarian monastery Zographou to honor twenty-six martyrs who had been burned there by emissaries of the Pope because the monks refused to submit to the reunion of the Greek and Roman churches. The martyrdom so commemorated occurred six hundred years before.

In his *Manuel d'Icongraphie Chrétienne*, the Frenchman Didron tells of visiting Esphigmenou monastery in the 1830s, where he watched a monk painting a wall scene while consulting and following in every detail the *Guide to Painting*. This manual was written in the eighteenth century by Denys of Fourna based on rules set forth by Athos's most famous artist, Penselinos—"full moon," so called because he shined brighter than all the others—who painted in the early sixteenth century. Simonides, a melancholy Greek poet—a contemporary of Pindar, he died in 467 B.C.—said that poetry is "painting that speaks"; Athos painting, little changed for six hundred years, is by now poetry that is mute.

Long before the hermits and ascetics settled at Athos and made the Holy Mountain holy, the peninsula figured in Greek history—or mythology. In the *Iliad*, Homer tells how Hera, after leaving Olympus to visit the earth below, departed "from Athos" to cross "the foaming sea" to Lemnos to ask Sleep, Death's brother, to lull Zeus to sleep so she could seduce him. She did. In Aeschylus's *Agamemnon*, Clytemnestra, explaining how the news that the Greeks have taken Troy could so quickly reach the palace of Agamemnon in Argos, relates that fire signals—a "golden courier"—were passed from peak to peak and "flashed to Athos, lofty mount of Zeus." Athos was then the seat of the Greek gods, who occupied the Holy Mountain before moving to Olympus.

The land was named after Poseidon's son Athos, who picked up the peninsula from its original site in central

Thrace and hurled it at his father, the sea god, in a fit of anger. (A more compatible father-son relationship appears in Joyce's *Ulysses*, in which the dying wish of Leopold Bloom's father was, "Be good to Athos, Leopold." Joyce might have named the dog Athos to suggest Argus, Odysseus's dog.) Furious that the peninsula was dedicated to Zeus instead of to him, Poseidon took to stirring up storms in the waters around the tip of Athos. It was one of those storms which, as Herodotus relates, destroyed the fleet of King Darius in 492 B.C., thus saving the Greeks from the Persians for twelve more years.

In 480, Xerxes, Darius's son and successor, decided to try to bypass the wrath of Poseidon that had sunk his father's fleet by cutting a canal across the top of the peninsula. The canal was about a mile and a half long and wide enough for two triremes abreast of one another to pass through. Herodotus tells how the sides of the trench kept falling in, requiring the workmen to excavate the canal twice, a frustration which led Plutarch in his essay on "Contentment" to point out—arguing that one should be satisfied with his station in life—that "whenever you call Xerxes blessed . . . look at the poor devils digging at Athos under the lash." The reason for the channel's construction puzzled the Greeks—Herodotus suggests it was built for show rather than for use—because the Greeks conveyed their ships across the Isthmus of Corinth on a wooden track with rollers, the famous Corinth "diolkos."

Heinrich Schliemann—with a long perspective of time and a fairly long one of distance—recalled those ancient events as he viewed Athos and the surrounding area on October 26, 1871, while standing on Hissarlik, a small hill about a hundred feet high four miles south of the Dardanelles—the Hellespont, to the ancients—where the archeologist was excavating for Troy:

The view from the hill of Hissarlik is extremely magnificent. Before me lies the glorious Plain of Troy, which, since the recent rain, is again covered with grass and yellow buttercups; on the north-north-west, at about an hour's distance, it is bounded by the Hellespont. The peninsula of Gallipoli here runs out to a point, upon which stands a lighthouse. To the left of it is the island of Imbros, above which rises Mount Ida of the island of Samothrace, at present covered with snow; a little more to the west, on the Macedonian peninsula, lies the celebrated Mount Athos, or Monte Santo, with its monasteries, at the north-western side of which there are still to be seen traces of that great canal which, according to Herodotus (vii. 22–23), was made by Xerxes, in order to avoid sailing round the stormy Cape Athos.

In comparison to the archeologist's evocative description of the storied terrain, only a laconic comment about Athos was offered by a fictionalist. Herman Melville saw Mount Athos from the deck of his ship bound for Salonika—"rather conical," he noted in his *Journal* for December 6, 1850, his sole observation about the peak. Mount Athos is the name both of the monastic settlement, which occupies an area some forty miles long and an average of four miles wide at the lower part of the eastern Khalkidiki peninsula, and of the 6,450-foot-high mountain which dominates the landscape and, as Schliemann saw, is visible from afar. Perhaps the most original perspective on the area was that enjoyed by C.L. Sulzberger, *New York Times* foreign affairs columnist, who, in his memoir *A Long Row of Candles*, describes a flight made June 16, 1948, over the Holy Mountain: "Spent a wonderful hour skimming around Mt. Athos Peninsula like a huge swallow, inspecting one after another famous old monastery at roof-top level."

As for the ancient sea struggles that swirled around the peninsula, the Persian fleet managed to avoid the treacherous Athos currents only to be sunk by the Greeks in the naval battle of Salamis in 480 B.C. Later, a century and a half after Xerxes had built the canal and led the Persian attack, Alexander began his campaign to conquer the Persian empire. The great king's court sculptor, Dinocrates,* proposed carving on the grey-white limestone peak of Mount Athos a Greek version of Mount Rushmore showing Alexander, as Strabo wrote, "pouring a libation from a kind of ewer into a broad bowl, and to make two cities, one on the right of the mountain and the other on the left, and a river flowing from one to the other." Alexander refused, supposedly on the ground that it was enough that another king showed his arrogance by cutting a canal through the peninsula; and the project was dropped. But in 1721 Austrian architect Fischer von Erlach sketched a rather romantic version of the idea. The engraving—which appears in *Athos and Its Monastic Institutions Through Old Engravings and Other Works of Art*, by Paul M. Mylonas—shows a huge, seated figure of the king tucked into the side of the mountain; both his arms are outstretched, and over the right one runs a river that flows down and across his lap past a town and into the sea, while the left hand holds a blocklike building, the largest in a village which extends along a flat ridge halfway down the mountain. The helmet atop the king's head rises to near the top of the peak, while his feet lie on the lowland near the sea.

At about this time, another plan was prepared for

---

*In Ephesus, on the Turkish coast, the Artemis Temple, devoted to the pre-Hellenic cult of Artemis, was the only shrine of Ionia spared by Xerxes; but, by a curious coincidence, the temple was then burned down by a madman called Herostratus on the night Alexander the Great was born. Herostratus apparently wanted to perpetuate his name by performing that deed, but the general assembly of Ionian states passed a decree consigning him to oblivion; as proved by this footnote, however, the decree failed to accomplish its purpose. Subsequently, Alexander offered to rebuild the temple, but the Ephesians declined and decided to do the job themselves, employing Dinocrates as the architect. Later, St. Paul converted the people from idoltry to worship of the Virgin Mary, so the Artemis Temple was disused and no traces of it now remain. Nero looted the temple and the Goths destroyed it, but some of its columns survive and are used in St. Sophia in Istanbul.

Mount Athos, one which was carried out. In 316 B.C. Prince Alexarchus of Macedonia founded Uranopolis—"the city of heaven"—on the peninsula. The settlement had its own coinage; and Alexarchus invented a special language which, like the esperanto of today, he hoped to make universal.* Nothing came of this utopian experiment, and the city soon vanished. Athos then became an uninhabited peninsula occasionally frequented only by warlocks—male witches—who would venture there to gather medicinal herbs.

Now religion—not of the Greeks but of a new sect—reached Athos in the person of Mary. According to one tradition, when the Apostles cast lots to determine which part of the world would be allocated to each of them, Mary, asked to join in the lottery, received Athos, Georgia, and Iberia. Another tradition holds that in A.D. 49 Lazarus, then a bishop on Cyprus, asked the Virgin to visit him; when a storm forced her ship off course, she reached Athos, landing just below where Iviron monastery now stands. When she stepped ashore all the pagan idols fell and were broken, so the story goes; Mary then proceeded to baptise the inhabitants and claimed Athos as holy territory. It is sometimes called "the Garden of Mary."

But the real beginnings of the monastic community took place nearly one thousand years later with the founding of Grand Lavra. This event not only represents the beginning of the religious settlement that has come

---

*Perhaps even more fanciful than the Mount Rushmore-like project or the City of Heaven plan was the suggestion made in the 1920s that the Athos monasteries be closed and the peninsula turned into a holiday resort with a casino. As for the carved mountain monument concept, William Rothenstein, the early twentieth-century English art figure, refers in his memoirs *Men and Memories* to a similarly grandiose project proposed by sculptor Eric Gill, who in 1910 wrote Rothenstein "that [Jacob] Epstein & I have got a giant scheme of doing some colossal figures together (as a contribution to the world), a sort of twentieth-century Stonehenge."

down to us, little changed, over the past millennium but also exemplifies a theme which a visit to the Holy Mountain makes apparent: the tension created by the pull between two opposing ways of life, the world's and that of Athos.

The story begins in the middle of the tenth century when a Greek general named Nicephorus Phocas and a young man named Athanasius met. Athanasius was handsome and charming and so bright a student that his classmates petitioned the Byzantine emperor to appoint him a professor. This resulted in Athanasius's own professor lecturing to an empty classroom. But for some reason a melancholy disposition possessed the young man, and he sought to escape "the world" in favor of a life of the spirit. Athanasius introduced himself in Constantinople to Michael Maleinos, abbot of a monastery in Bithynia, on the Sea of Marmara, and he spent the next four years there. During that time the abbot's nephew, Nicephorus Phocas, visited the monastery and expressed his hope of one day becoming a monk. However, for the time being, Phocas wished to remain a man of the world, a world in which he was rapidly accumulating wealth and power. Athanasius, on the other hand, decided to distance himself even farther from the world; and in 958 he left the monastery, retreating from it to avoid being named abbot, and fled to the remote and then almost unknown peninsula of Mount Athos.

Athanasius lived on Athos under an assumed name; but Phocas sent an agent to seek out the young man, whom the emissary discovered in Karyes one Christmas during the "synaxis" there—the annual gathering of hermits who lived the rest of the year scattered about the peninsula. They were greatly impressed that such an important man had sent a representative to contact Athanasius, but he withdrew and removed himself for a year to the tip of the peninsula—near where he was soon to found Grand Lavra—to pray and meditate. But Phocas finally managed to persuade Athanasius to join him as a spiritual advisor for the general's campaign in 961 to liberate Crete from the Saracens. In March of that year Phocas launched his attack and crushed the Arab occupiers, a conquest which made him known as "the white death of the Saracens." Phocas attributed his success to the presence and prayers of Athanasius, and so after his victory the general gave part of the booty to the monk with instructions to build a monastery at Athos, to which Phocas promised to retire.

Athanasius returned to Athos where he began construction of Grand Lavra in the spring of 963. Meanwhile, Phocas enjoyed further military success, and in the summer of that year he acquired both the throne and the wife of the late Emperor Romanus II. The wife was considerably more hazardous than the throne. Theophano was a beautiful but sinister woman who, rumor had it, had poisoned her husband Romanus to death. When news of Phocas's marriage reached Athanasius on Athos, he abandoned construction of the monastery and rushed to Constantinople to berate the emperor for his continuing and increasing interest in the pleasures and power of the world. The man who had often expressed a desire to retire and become a celibate monk had instead become an emperor and a husband. Claiming his tenure as ruler was only temporary and reaffirming his wish to become a monk, Phocas pacified Athanasius by presenting him with a "chrysobul," a document formally recognizing the new monastery, as well as with a number of gifts that included a jeweled Bible bearing a dedication to the monk handwritten by the emperor and a fragment of the True Cross, both of which may still be seen at Grand Lavra.

Phocas remained emperor for only a short time, but for reasons other than his expressed desire to retreat to a monastery. On the night of December 10, 969, the emperor was sleeping in the palace on a tiger skin when an intruder suddenly kicked him awake and slashed his face with a sword. After this rude awakening, his assailant roped Phocas's legs and dragged him to John Tsimiskis, Empress Theophano's lover. After ripping out Phocas's beard, Tsimiskis killed the emperor with his sword and then succeeded him both on the throne and as the husband of the redoubtable Theophano.

The death of Athanasius's powerful patron encouraged some of the monks on Athos to air their previously muted complaints that the new, big monastery would ruin the holy community. In 970 the monks who preferred a life more solitary and less organized than the one dominated by a monastery sent a delegation to Tsimiskis to protest against the opulent new institution and the "modernization" of Athos. The protesters bitterly accused Athanasius of bringing "the world" to the Holy Mountain. Tsimiskis, however, favored the monastery in preference to the scattering of hermits throughout the peninsula, so he doubled the annual stipend allotted to Lavra; in 972 he issued the Tragos—the charter written on goatskin which formalized the status of Athos and its monasteries.

As for Athanasius, he was killed about the year 1000 when the half-finished dome of the Grand Lavra church collapsed and fell on him. Thus, both of Athos's founding fathers—the monk and the emperor, Nicephorus Phocas—died before they could fully enjoy the withdrawal from the outside world to the more removed world that the holy community affords. For them, time ran out and death cut short that great adventure—the search inward toward the self.

—3—

The monks of Athos still refer to all that lies outside the precincts of the Holy Mountain as "the world." Surrounded on three sides by the sea—it is called the Holy Sea, in no case to be confused with the Holy See—and on the fourth by rugged country which divides the sacred section of the peninsula from the secular part, the religious enclave is well protected from "the world." Although outsiders have occasionally managed to invade the self-contained little community that is Athos, the intrusions seem to have left no lasting effects.

Even high church officials outside Athos found it difficult to influence the Holy Mountain. In 1753 Patriarch Cyril V tried to make Athos a center of religious culture by founding an academy for monks there. Appointed to head the school was Eugene Boulgaris, a famous German-educated philosopher of the time; but his ideas were too wordly for the Athos monks. Accusing him of heresy, they forced his transfer to Constantinople, after which, in 1806, the academy was closed. Near Vatopedi monastery on a hill by the sea lie the ruins of the school: it, like other incursions from the world, had in the end come to nothing.

Most of the other intrusions from the outside were more violent than the academic invasion of Boulgaris. From the very beginning the monks saw the outside world as hostile to their existence; and the leaders tried to fortify the community against foreign influences, not only spiritual ones—kept at bay by locking the inmates into a narrow routine of religious rituals—but also those of a more material nature. Around 870 a monk named John Kolobos founded a fortified settlement in order to improve the security of monks—then living in small and dispersed groups—against Arab pirates based in Crete who would periodically raid Athos, among other Mediterranean communities, and carry away hermits to sell as slaves.*

*Eight centuries later, John Covel, the first known English visitor to Athos—he was there in 1677—noted in his *Journal* the "many castles or towers" by the seaside, adding somewhat wistfully: "They are useless for defense since Guns have been invented." While serving as Anglican chaplain to members of the Levant Company stationed at Constantinople, Covel found time to amass a fortune for himself in the silk trade. It was perhaps his business dealings with Greeks that led Covel to give as his opinion of them what Iphigeneia said of the Greeks in Euripides's play: "Trust them and hang them."

Saracen corsairs continued to plague Athos until finally in the thirteenth century the monks appealed for protection to—of all people—the Pope. Innocent responded immediately, hoping by his assistance to reunite the Orthodox and the Roman churches; and the Holy Mountain fell under the sway of the Vatican, at least nominally and, in any event, only temporarily.

It was in the following century that Athos sustained one of the most damaging invasions in its history. At the beginning of the fourteenth century the Byzantine Emperor Andronicus II was confronted with the rising power of a group of Turks led by Othman, whose name came to designate the dynasty that ruled Turkey until 1923. To combat the Ottomans, the emperor hired a band of mercenaries known as the Catalan Company. The Catalans (the company in fact also included men from other provinces of Spain) were led by Roger de Flor, a soldier of German origin whose family name "Blum"—"flower"— was transmuted in Spain to the more redolent Latin syllable "Flor." At the end of 1303 Flor arrived in Constantinople with his company of about sixty-five hundred men and half again as many women and children—wives, mistresses, and offspring of the mercenaries. Before agreeing to lead his men into battle against the Turks, Flor exacted from the emperor four months' advance pay and the hand of his niece, Maria Asen. The Catalan Company then marched to the east, where it defeated the Turks, after which, in 1305, it returned to the European side of the Hellespont. Flor found there not more glory but a gory end, for emperor Andronicus's eldest son murdered the mercenary leader.

Seeking revenge, the Catalan Company now swept through Macedonia wreaking havoc, and in the autumn of 1307 it invaded Mount Athos and launched an attack against Chilandari monastery. A nineteenth-century frescoe at Chilandari is said to represent the Catalan invaders being repulsed by a miracle, but in fact that monastery was sacked; an eyewitness wrote of the "horror" of the siege. The monks of Grand Lavra hastened to send two emissaries to King James II of Aragon requesting his help against the invaders. In a letter dated July 1, 1308, the king gave his assurance that he'd ordered the Catalans to spare the monks on Mount Athos. The royal order failed to impress the Catalans, however, and the raids at Athos continued for another two or three years until the marauders, having devastated most of the monasteries and slaughtered many of the monks, turned their attention elsewhere.

The Catalan Company now marched on Athens; and after defeating the Franks there, in March 1311, the invaders established themselves in the city for some eighty years. One of the changes the Catalans made during their occupation was to convert the Parthenon into the Church of the Holy Virgin. Finally, an invasion of forces from Navarre ended their domination and their appearance in history—except for one curious remnant: still today in the vernacular of Athens the word "Catalan" is used as an insult, a female of bad character sometimes being referred to as "a Catalan woman."

Oddly enough, it was the Christian mercenaries from Spain who damaged Athos far more than the infidels who soon came to dominate the region. After the Turkish leader Murad II captured Salonika, some one hundred miles west of Athos, in 1430 the monks decided to submit to the Turks in exchange for a confirmation by the invaders of the privileges and immunities enjoyed by the Holy Mountain. With minor exceptions over the next five centuries, the Turks kept their promise to leave Athos in peace. As a result, the monastic community was one of the few enclaves to escape the turmoils of the times from the fifteenth century to the present. Only once during their 482 years of rule did the Ottomans actually enter Athos. That occurred during the Greek revolution in 1821 when three thousand Turkish troops occupied the Holy Mountain to dampen the monkish enthusiasm for the revolutionaries. The invasion was not without provocation: in March 1821 Emmanuil Papas, a leader of the insurrection, established a revolutionary headquarters at Esphigmenou monastery and enrolled a number of monks into his army. The Turkish soldiers were quartered in the monasteries for nine years, during which time about five thousand of the six thousand monks deserted Athos for the world; but after 1830, when the troubles ended, most of them returned to resume life as it had been lived on the peninsula during the previous nine hundred years.

The Turkish occupation in the 1820s was virtually the last contact between "the world" and Athos, apart, of course, from individuals who came to the Holy Mountain as visitors or as refugees. Most of those refugees became monks, hoping to escape the rigors of life in the outside world or at least to exchange those difficulties for the otherworldly obligations they assumed in the Orthodox community. During World War II, however, Athos also served as a refuge for Allied soldiers fleeing from the Germans. One of the main escape routes was across the Khalkidiki Peninsula and into the haven of the Holy Mountain. Other than occasional sightseeing visits to the monasteries or the pursuit of enemy soldiers, the Germans left Athos to itself during the war. As Allied sympathizers, the monks willingly sheltered the escaping men, some of whom wore beads and cassocks to disguise themselves as monks when German search parties appeared. Dionysiou monastery was said to have housed both German hunters and Allied hunted, often at the same time.

If "the world" has only rarely come to Athos, even more seldom has Athos entered the world. One such contact occurred in the late sixteenth and early seventeenth centuries, during the long period of peace under the Ottoman Empire, when some Athos monks ventured outside the Holy Mountain to travel to Abyssinia in an attempt to convert the Ethiopians to the Orthodox church. Some of the pictures painted by Athos missionaries in Abyssinia are in the Trocadero Museum in Paris.

The most bizarre episode of an Athonite mingling with
the wide world beyond the little religious enclave, however, involved a young Macedonian named Metrophanes
Critopoulos, who was born in about 1589. When the boy
was twelve his eloquent readings of services attracted the
attention of his region's metropolitan. Metrophanes was
inducted into the church and eventually sent to Mount
Athos, where, in 1613, he happened to meet Cyril Lu-
caris, then Patriarch of Alexandria. The boy's intelligence
greatly impressed Cyril, so when the patriarch received a
letter from George Abbot, Archbishop of Canterbury,
inviting the Orthodox prelate to send young Greeks to
study theology in England, Metrophanes was one of the
students Cyril chose. On May 1, 1616, the patriarch wrote
George Abbot, telling the archbishop of Metrophanes's
selection and highly recommending the young man. Toward the middle of the following year Metrophanes arrived in London, where he somehow managed to obtain
an audience with the king. In time, the Athos traveler
went up to Oxford, where he attached himself to Balliol
College.

Most likely the archbishop had steered young Metrophanes to Balliol, for that had been Abbot's college during
his Oxford days. Abbot, an extreme Puritan, spent the
early part of his career at Oxford. While there, he wrote a
narrative modestly entitled *A Briefe Description of the
Whole World*; in 1605, he sent one hundred and forty
undergraduates to prison for wearing hats in his presence
at St. Mary's church. Appointed Archbishop of Canterbury in 1611, Abbot was apparently destined for greatness
from an unusually age—prebirth. As Aubrey relates in his
Brief Lives:

> When Arch-Bishop Abbot's Mother (a poor Cloath-
> worker's Wife in Gilford) was with Child of him, she
> did long for a Jack or Pike, and she dreamt that if she
> should Eat a Jack, her Son in her Belly should be a
> great Man. Upon this she was indefatigable to satisfy

her Longing, as well as her Dream. She first enquir'd out for this Fish: but the next Morning, goeing with her Payle to the River-side (which runneth by the Howse, now an Ale-house, the Signe of the 3 Mariners) to take up some Water, a good Jack accidentally came into her Payle. She took up the much desir'd Banquet, dress'd it, and devour'd it almost all her selfe, or very neare. This odd Affair made no small Noise in the Neighbourhood, and the Curiosity of it made severall People of Quality offer themselves to be Sponsors at the Baptismal Fount when she was deliver'd. This their Poverty accepted joyfully, and three were chosen, who maintained him at School, and University afterwards, his father not being able.

At the time Metrophanes reached the university, Balliol College had become something of a center for Greek students, so the young Athos scholar fitted in well there. Among the Balliol men of the time were a number of linguists who'd traveled in the Levant and, so it was said, "to whom the great Avicenna might speak and be understood without an interpreter." The first Greek at Balliol was Christopher Angelus, from the Peloponnesus, who arrived at the college in 1610 after leaving Greece because of Turkish persecutions. Angelus would display his Turk-inflicted scars to generate sympathy from his fellow students at the college. The best-known Greek was a Cretan named Nathaniel Conopios—like Metrophanes, he was one of Patriarch Cyril's disciples—who became famous for drinking a strange substance known as coffee. In his *Diary* entry for May 10, 1639, John Evelyn, a fellow Balliol student, remarks: "There came in my tyme to the Coll: one Nathaniel Conopios out of Greece, from Cyrill the Patriarch of Constantinople. . . . He was the first I ever saw drink Coffè, which custome came not into England til 30 years after."

The introduction of coffee to England must have been a memorable event, for it was also noted by Oxford historian Anthony Wood, who in 1676 in his *Life and Times* mentioned that he was told "that Canopius, a Graecian, of Ball. Coll., drank coffey every morning at Ball. Coll. of his owne making 40 yeares before this time." Only after another ten years or so, however, did the new beverage catch on; the first Oxford coffeehouse opened around 1650 in a house between Queen's and St. Edmund Hall colleges. Conopios brought religious intrigue as well as coffee to England. After receiving his degree at Oxford, he was appointed by Archbishop Laud as a cannon of Christ Church College; but in 1647 Puritans expelled the Greek from Oxford because of his connection with Laud, and he became Archbishop of Smyrna. Conopios's patron, Patriarch Cyril, also suffered from religious intrigues but with more serious effects. Working under the influence of Calvinistic theology, Cyril attempted to reform the Orthodox church, but his opponents choked off the patriarch's efforts by arranging for him to be strangled to death on June 27, 1638.

As for Metrophanes, another of Cyril's proteges, the wayward Athonite learned very quickly at Balliol, so it seems, to become a man of the world. He ran up large debts, which Archbishop Abbot felt morally obligated to pay; and he used the archbishop's enemies in an attempt to intrigue himself into royal circles. When the time came for Metrophanes to depart, Abbot agreed—gladly, no doubt, in order to be rid of the audacious young man—to pay his fare. But the Greek refused to take a cheap passage on a boat of the Levant Company, as Abbot requested, preferring instead to travel through Europe on a lecture tour. Metrophanes's escapades are discussed in a series of fascinating letters* exchanged between Archbishop Abbot and Thomas Roe, English ambassador to the Ottoman Empire in Constantinople. On August 12, 1622, Abbot wrote:

---

*They are collected in *Bibliographie Hellénique Au Dix-Septième Siècle* by Émile Legrand (Paris, 1903), vol. 5, pp. 192–218.

The Grecian Critopolus Metrophanes hath taken his journey very lately into France or Holland, pretending from thence to go by land to Constantinople. I bred him full five years in Oxford with good allowance for diet, clothes, books, chamber and other necessaries. . . . I sent for him to Lambeth, taking care that, in a very good ship, he might be conveyed with accommodation of all things by the way. But by the ill counsel of somebody, he desired to go to the Court at Newmarket, that he might see the king before his departure. His Majesty used him well; but then he was put into a conceit that he might get something to buy him books to carry home to the patriarch. The means that he gaped after were such as you can hardly believe; at first that he should have a knight to be made for his sake; and then, after that, a baronet. . . . I caused my chaplains to dissuade him from these things. . . . I lodged him in my own house, I sat him at my own table, I clothed him and provided all conveniences for him, and would once again have sent him away in a good ship, that he might safely have returned; but he fell into the company of certain Greeks, with whom we have been much troubled with collections and otherwise; and although I know them to be counterfeits and vagabonds (as sundry times you have written unto me), yet I could not keep my man within doors. . . . I found that he meant to turn rogue and beggar, and more I cannot tell what; and thereupon I gave him ten pounds in his purse, and . . . I dismissed him. I had heard before of the baseness and slavishness of that nation; but I could never have believed that any creature in human shape, having learning and such education as he hath had here, could, after so many years, have been so far from . . . any grateful respect.

To this tirade by Abbot against the young Greek, Thomas Roe replied from Constantinople on June 24,

1623: "I have let the good patriarch know the devious course taken by Metrophanes, of your bounty and care for him, and all the circumstances of his departure. At the first, he seemed somewhat astonished; but his affection towards him prevailed to make his excuse. He hath given orders to write to Holland, France, and divers other parts to recall this stray sheep." A year later, on June 20, 1624, George Abbot wrote Roe to advise that Metrophanes had asked the archbishop for some favors the previous February or March, to which Abbot responded that "now I would not know him; he might go where he list, and might do what he pleased. I thought then he had gone away; but now, two days past, being in my coach in London, I saw him go by me." Metrophanes was proving hard to get rid of.

In December of the same year, Roe informed George Abbot: "I have acquainted the patriarch with your Grace's first and last letters concerning Metrophanes: who can hear nothing against him, that affection doth not interpret the better. He expects him daily, and your worthy present of books, I fear they will be pawned in the way. Of wandering Greeks there is so great store, that I am forced daily to deny my passports." On March 30, 1625, George Abbot, now at a loss for words in regard to the errant Greek, wrote to Roe, "I know not what to say to the patriarch touching Metrophanes. His roguist countrymen did unto him. . . . I do much fear that he hath fared so well in these parts, that he will hardly reduce himself to the strict life . . . in the Greek church."

Roe concluded the exchange of letters by advising George Abbot that Patriarch Cyril finally received from Metrophanes in Nuremburg "a strange discourse, that Gondomar did seek to debauch him and send him to Rome; but failing, attempted his life, which made him foresake England, with many other frivolous adventures. I wished the patriarch to believe little; but he willingly hears nothing against him, upon whom he hath set his affection."

During the years covered by this correspondence, Metrophanes was making his way across Europe lecturing and holding himself out as a personal representative of Patriarch Cyril—and reaping the benefits of such position. After traveling through Germany for about three years he reached Switzerland in 1627. Well armed with letters of recommendation from important figures in Berne, Metrophanes continued on to Geneva, where the Consistory of Clergy and professors received him on October 6, 1627. Minutes of the session relate that the Greek visitor gave the meeting to understand that, acting under the authority of Cyril, the purpose of his travels through Europe was to help unite the Western and Orthodox churches. This sort of appeal was always good for attracting sympathy and support, both spiritual and financial. For centuries, enlightened men had dreamed of merging the two branches of Christianity. Erasmus, for example, refused to join the rising Lutheran movement because he was unwilling to give up his ideal of Christian unity. Metrophanes, however, failed to find the canny, cautious, and conservative Swiss an easy touch. Noting that the visiting Greek had failed to present any tangible evidence of his commission from the patriarch, they simply expressed a willingness to "extend our arms to such a holy and great work"; and then they sent Metrophanes on his way after giving him fifteen talers and—perhaps more valuable but less costly—letters of recommendation written in Greek and Latin.

Metrophanes continued on to Zurich and then proceeded to Venice, where he arrived November 1, 1627. During his stay in Venice he tried to pressure a publisher into printing some controversial material, and while waiting to receive shipments of books from western Europe he is thought to have lectured at the Greek colony school in Venice. In the fall of 1630 Metrophanes left for Constantinople, where he prevailed on Cyril to appoint him to a church position at Memphis in Egypt. In September 1636 the wandering Greek became patriarch of Alexandria, and three years later he died. He had come a long way since his early years in the sheltered precincts of Mount Athos.

The worldly Metrophanes Critopoulos, however, is by far a great exception to the Athos tradition. More typical are the hermits and ascetics—so curious to outsiders but perfectly normal to other Athonites—who shirk all contact with their fellowmen and with the ordinary comforts of life. One of the most fanatic was Maximos, a four-teenth-century ascetic who periodically burned down his hut so that he wouldn't become accustomed to its comforts. An Athos "skete," or small colony, called "kapsokalyvia"—"the burnt huts"—is named after him. Then there was Saint Makarios, whose remorse after swatting a mosquito which bit him was so great that he inhabited a mosquito-filled bog for six months, becoming so covered with sores that when he emerged his friends were unable to recognize him.* Makarios later left his monastery, which he found too wordly, and removed himself to a mountaintop until deciding that it, too, had become too busy for him; he then buried himself up to his neck in a hole near the Hellespont and relied on passersby for bits of bread and sips of water.

Retreat from life, of course, is a possible approach to living, and it is that approach which the monks of Athos have chosen. Still today you can catch occasional glimpses—from afar, from the deck of the little ships that plow the rough furrows of the Holy Sea around the peninsula—of hermits who dwell in caves high on the cliffs in the same way that Peter the Athonite, the very first of the Athos hermits, lived for some fifty years at the end of the ninth century. For a thousand years life—of a sorts—has gone on unchanged at Athos: but what is a brief millennium compared to the eternity for which the monks are

---

*Pierre Belon, a sixteenth-century French naturalist whose visit to Athos is referred to in the next section, wrote that while traveling in Egypt his face became so covered with mosquito bites he at first supposed he'd caught the measles.

preparing? After Peter died, one of his followers collected his bones, but they were quickly taken from the acolyte by force by monks from Klementos monastery, located on the site where Iviron is today, for display as holy relics.

But bones of the more obscure hermits are not so coveted. One day the basket which the recluse lowers to obtain a few morsels of food remains unemptied—a signal that the cliffside cave dweller no longer needs bodily nourishment. A monk then descends to the cave to remove the corpse and free the space for the next inhabitant. The wasted body is buried somewhere, in an unmarked grave no doubt; and the bones and flesh then begin their gradual, ineluctable disintegration into the earth of the Holy Mountain—the soul, presumably, is elsewhere—and the monk, at long last, is finally lifeless and truly frozen in time forever.

—4—

Athos and "the world" have seldom crossed paths or swords. Apart from the occasional exceptions mentioned in the previous section, the Holy Mountain has for the most part been left to not develop on its own.

What sort of men have chosen the retarded way of life found at Athos, and how do they live? Even the monks themselves would no doubt admit that they could fairly be described as fanatics. But those of us who live in the febrile world of the twentieth century are also in many ways fanatics. Because the Athos sort of fanaticism is outmoded, it strikes us as strange; as modern fanatics, comfortably in tune with the times, we of the outside world are normal—or so we view ourselves. But it is the complete lack of balance at Athos, rather than the religious fanaticism, which best defines the religious community's ambiance. When Aristotle said that a gentleman ought to be able to play the flute, but not too well—in effect, a definition of the well-rounded person—he

couldn't have been referring to Athonites, for at Athos
there is no such person as the whole man—only the holy
man.

A sociologist who studied the Athonite society in the
1930s described life there as "truncated, oppressive, and
gloomy," concluding that Athos was an "abnormal" community—"abnormal in the sense that both its basic philosophy and a portion of the practices of its inhabitants
negate, or tend to negate, the fundamental aspects of both
the social and natural life of man."* More colorful was the
description of Edward Lear, the English humorist, who
visited Athos in 1856 and vowed never to return—

> . . . so shockingly unnatural, so lonely, so lying, so
> unatonably odious seems to me all the atmosphere of
> such monkery. That half of our species which it is
> natural to every man to cherish and love best, ig-
> nored, prohibited and abhorred . . . [by] these mut-
> tering, miserable, mutton-hating, man-avoiding,
> misogynic, morose and merriment-marring, monoto-
> ning, many-mule-making, mocking, mournful
> minced fish and marmalade masticating Monx!

Lear proposed that Parliament pass a law to send "dis-
tressed needle women" to the Holy Mountain where, after
landing, they would "make a rush for the nearest monastery; that subdued, all the rest will speedily follow."

The absence of women represents the most obvious
"abnormality" of the Holy Mountain, and it is that characteristic most often seized on by visitors to indicate the
strangeness of the Athos way of life. The ban on females
was originally imposed not to keep the monks chaste so
much as to honor the Virgin Mary, patroness of Mount
Athos. One legend relates that when the devout, early
fifth-century Empress Galla Placidia—whose mosaic

---

*Black Angels of Athos, Michael Choukas (Brattleboro, Vermont: Ste-
phen Daye Press, 1934).

mausoleum embellishes Ravenna—reached the peninsula, an icon of the Virgin became upset and warned Mary's newly arrived rival to leave because the area was under the Virgin's exclusive dominion. In the middle of the tenth century the emperor issued a Bull forbidding entry to women, female animals, eunuchs, children, and beardless men. It was in this document that Athos was first referred to as "Hagion Oros"—the Holy Mountain. The order also forbade the dedication of any churches to female saints; however, at least two such churches exist on Athos—St. Barbara and St. Katherine—and a "skete" is named in honor of St. Anne. Since the tenth century, most provisions of the Bull have been rigorously—if not always effectively—enforced.

William Martin Leake, who visited Athos in 1806, claimed in his *Travels in Northern Greece* to "have heard the sailors of the Aegaean relate stories of women who have been punished with immediate death for having had the audacity to land upon it." But one woman spent *A Month Among the Men*, as she entitled her account, and lived to tell the tale. In that book a French adventuress named Maryse Choisy, telling of preparations for her 1929 visit, relates how she had her breasts trimmed and outfitted herself in Istanbul with a certain "rubber accessory," but one "not too big," she hastens to add. "If God had not wanted me to go," she maintains, "I would never have found a rubber thingumabob to complete my disguise." Other females managed to enter Athos by force rather than by guile: in December 1948, during the postwar communist insurgency in Greece, a guerilla band which included twenty-five armed women occupied Karyes for a few hours. The sociologist Choukas mentions in his book an account published in Greek called *The Holy Mountain—The Saints Unmasked* which refers to "floating prostitution boats" that ply the Athos waters to service the monks.

At one time cats were imported into the settlement and allowed to breed to control mice and snakes, but more

characteristic of Athos was the November 1932 order of
the Holy Synod—the community's governing body—de-
creeing that all hens on the peninsula be executed. One
anomaly, however, is the existence in the courtyard of
Chilandari monastery of a vine—called St. Simeon's—
said to cure sterility. Perhaps the plant is maintained for
the benefit of visitors from "the world," but the monks
might occasionally discreetly make use of its powers,
possibly to get an idea of what they are missing by remaining at Athos.

While it may be amusing to discuss the absence of
women, it is less so to experience it. The choice of that
restricted way of life by the monks is symptomatic of a
more fundamental attitude which dominates the Holy
Mountain: they wish to reject not only women but also
the entire world, including their fellowmen. The retreat,
moreover, is not only spacial and physical—as typified by
the hermit life—but also spiritual. Mysticism being the
hermit life of the soul, Athos, as might be expected, has
always attracted mystical men and movements. The Holy
Mountain is a kind of "magic mountain," a sanitarium for
the soul rather than the body; the ethereal world of spir-
ituality that pervades the place was described, at least
metaphorically, in a curious passage in *The Book of Sir
John Maundeville, A.D. 1322-1356,* the earliest known
account of a traveler to Athos:

> And there is another hille, that is clept Athos. . . .
> And abouen at the cop of that hille is the eyr so cleer
> that men may fynde no wynd there, and therefore
> may no best [beast] lyue there, so is the eyr drye. And
> men seye in this contrees that philosophres somtyme
> wenten upon theise hilles and helden to here nose a
> spounge moysted with water for to have eyr, for the
> eyr aboue was so drye. And abouen in the dust and
> in the powder of the hilles thei wroot lettres and
> figures with hire fyngres. And at the yeres ends thei
> comen ayen and founden the same lettres and figures

the whiche thei hadde writen the yeer before with-
outen ony defaute. And therfore it semeth wel that
theise hilles passen the clowdes and joynen to the
pure eyr.

It was in this rarefied atmosphere that the strange
medieval movement known as Hesychastism flourished.
The Hesychasts—or Quietists, as they were also called, in
reference to the state of interior quiet they sought to obtain by contemplation—claimed that the mysterious light
seen by the disciples at Christ's Transfiguration on Mount
Tabor was a part of the divine essence and couid thus be
seen by a holy man after contemplating his navel, supposedly the seat of the soul. In *The Decline and Fall of the
Roman Empire*, Gibbon describes the technique employed by an eleventh-century Athonite monk:

When thou art alone in thy cell, shut thy door, and
seat thyself in a corner; raise thy mind above all
things vain and transitory; recline thy beard and chin
on thy breast; turn thine eyes and thy thought towards the middle of the belly, the region of the navel
and search the place of the heart, the seat of the soul.
At first all will be dark and comfortless, but if thou
persevere day and night, thou wilt feel an ineffable
joy; and no sooner has the soul discovered the place
of the heart than it is involved in a mystical ethereal
light.

This practice was denounced by a monk named Barlaam, who labeled the Hesychasts "omphaloscopoi," or
"navel-gazers." He charged that the rite implied two sub-
stances in the Godhead, one visible and one invisible.
Barlaam was a moderate at Athos—hardly a difficult position to attain, for most of the other leaders there were
extremists of one sort or another. As leader of a delegation
sent in 1339 by Andronicus III to Pope Benedict XII at
Avignon to discuss unification of the Orthodox and Ro-

man wings, Barlaam attacked both the Thomists of the Latin church and the mystics of the Eastern church. In other words, Barlaam was an early representative of the Renaissance, while his Athos rival, Gregory Palmas, represented the Middle Ages. Palmas arrived at Athos at about age twenty and attached himself to Grand Lavra. He later left the Holy Mountain for a time, but he returned about 1331 as a spokesman for the Hesychasts. He and Barlaam clashed bitterly over the Hesychast doctrine. For a number of years the controversy divided the Orthodox church into opposing camps. In the end it required a special convocation to settle the dispute. The doctrine was finally endorsed at the Constantinople Council of 1351, whereupon the defeated Barlaam left for Italy where he joined the Roman church and became a teacher of Greek to the poet Petrarch. Perhaps that result was inevitable: the freshening breezes of the Renaissance and its humanism never reached into the hermetic hermit world of Athos to pollute the "pure eyr" of Quietist mysticism.

Staring at one's navel for illumination—of the soul or simply of the belly—may strike those of us accustomed to the outside world as somewhat eccentric, but even that curious activity seems relatively normal when compared with the medieval Orthodox practice of becoming a "fool in Christ." The fool would renounce not only his possessions and the world but also his mind. As a madman, he could better criticize society for its sins without being punished. Travelers to Athos have encountered no "fools" there, but visitors have often commented on how the monks lack intelligence and learning. As early as the sixteenth century, Pierre Belon, a French naturalist who traveled in the Mediterranean between 1546 and 1549 under the patronage of François I, complained that it was impossible to find more than three or four literate monks in the monasteries of Athos.

Belon was a keen observer and a prolific writer. On his return from the Levant he published a book in 1551 on fish which was perhaps the first work on comparative anatomy and embryology, for in it Belon compares the anatomical structure of various fish and he includes a sketch of a porpoise embryo. The Belon oyster—that tasty shellfish—memorializes the Frenchman's pioneering efforts. Among Belon's works on natural history were those dealing with such subjects as trees, animals, and birds; in the latter work he compares the bones in birds' wings to those in a man's arm—an unusual perception for the time. In that bird book, entitled *Portraicts d'Oiseaux*, appeared a "Portraict de la Montaign d'Athos." This drawing of Athos, reproduced in Paul A. Mylonas's book of old engravings of Athos, shows a lumpy-looking peninsula with neat groves of trees forming enclaves that shelter monasteries, while overhead birds soar and a chubby white cloud scuds across the sky. In 1556 Henri II awarded Belon a pension and gave him a villa in the Bois de Boulogne. Eight years later, at about age forty-seven, Belon was murdered by robbers one evening while gathering herbs in the Bois.

The uneducated nature of the Athos monks was also noticed by Richard Pococke, who visited the Holy Mountain in 1737. "They have no manner of learning among them," and "lead very idle unprofitable lives," Pococke wrote, while his countryman, William Martin Leake, noted during his 1806 visit that at Iviron's library "none of the Latin books have been touched, because nobody can read them: indeed, the whole library is nearly useless, such is the extreme ignorance of the monks."

Other visitors have accused the monks of sins worse than ignorance: venality or—even more damning for an Athonite—of being overly worldly. Many monastery libraries have been depleted over the years by the sale of ancient books off their shelves. Monks also used the old manuscripts in casual, abusive ways—pieces of parchment served as fishing bait, and pages were employed to wrap objects. During the occupation of Athos in the 1820s, monks sold manuscript pages by the pound to

Turkish soldiers for use as souvenirs or, less happily, to make cartridge wads.

Other more productive commercial activities take place on the Holy Mountain. Chilandari monastery owns beehives, and in the summer the monks tend over fifteen thousand skeps. Guests at Chilandari sometimes enjoy the honey in the form of a "glyco," or sweet, traditionally offered to welcome arriving visitors, while the wax is used for church candles. Karyes shops carry monk-made wood carvings of both religious and secular objects which are sold on the spot and by mail order, mainly to America.

Back in the mid-eleventh century the sharp business practices and increasing wealth of the monastic community impelled the emperor to issue a decree limiting the commercial and cattle-raising activities of the monks. The order, however, had little effect; and in the following century Eustathius, archbishop of Salonika, condemned the corrupt practices of monks whom he accused of pretending to see visions to obtain offerings from the devout. Richard Pococke, the eighteenth-century English visitor mentioned above, claimed that the monasteries "fend out priefts to collect charity, and the perfon who returns with the greateft fum of money is commonly made goumenos or abbot, till another brings in a greater."

Arnold Toynbee relates* a telling story about the commercial arrangements enjoyed by inhabitants of Athos, a tale which seems to belie the opinion of some visitors that the monks are "ignorant." Chatting with the holy occupants at an unnamed Athos monastery where he spent a night in June 1912, Toynbee learned that his hosts slept during the day, reserving the night for services. When the visitor asked how they managed that arrangement, a monk replied that the monastery owned "fine estates . . .

---

*See *A Study of History*, Volume IX, pp. 307–308, in a footnote to a passage on "The Day-and-Night Cycle" of life. Toynbee mentions as exceptions to the normal practice of sleeping at night such professions as burglar, fish-spearer, baker, journalist, and monk.

with peasants on them to work them for us." Toynbee
now asked how the peasants fared. "O, the peasants live
like dogs," replied the monk, "but you can see for yourself
what an admirable arrangement ours is. As the peasants
work for us and fetch and carry for us, instead of our
having to do any of this for ourselves, we can afford to
sleep in the day-time and so keep ourselves fresh for
praying at night." The advantage of this schedule, the
monk pointed out, was that at night the volume of prayers
reaching God is minimal, thus allowing Him to give them
better attention, for during the day, continued Toynbee's
host, there are too many people "in the running to gain a
hearing for their prayers."

Toynbee's encounter afforded a rare chance to learn
from the monks themselves something about how they
view their existence. There is no shortage of outside observations or opinions about the inhabitants of Athos, but
because of the language barrier—few of them speak anything other than Greek—and because the monks are rather
wary of visitors from "the world," it's difficult to discover
how they really see themselves. I came across one source
of their self-image in an edition of three "boosterism"-
type picture albums published by the monks in 1928 and
apparently formerly sold at Athos. In Volume A, on monasteries, one Patriarch Parthenios Iviritis described Athos
as "the unic ornament of the whole world . . . the Paradise of the world and the Ark of National traditions
[which] concentrates now the attention of the entire mankind." The monks are fond of calling Athos "the ark of the
Byzantine civilization," but it is an ark no longer afloat:
the Byzantine Empire disappeared, after 1,123 years of
existence, five centuries ago when Janissaries of Ottoman
Sultan Mohammed II entered Constantinople on May 29,
1453. Volume B, on monks, describes them as "the holy
bees of religion" who devote themselves "to the cruel and
painful ascetic life" and are "models of self sacrifice and
self denial for the sake of the highest ideals of mankind
and they preserve virtue unchanged through the ages."

Stiffly posed figures at Iviron are described as "learned monks . . . studying in this library," while other photo captions refer to "a devout monk in his poor cell, making with artful effort head covers for the monks," and to a quartet of "simple dieted monks" shown fishing. Volume C, on relics, offers photographs of old manuscripts, gold coins, a Vatopedi gold chalice—a "unic and of ineffable value imperial drinking glass"—crucifixes, and reliquaries, such as a "big piece of the Holy and Life giving Cross, in the precious box" at Vatopedi.

My own experience at Athos was that the monks were neither overly worldly, as some visitors have seen them, nor devotees of a "cruel and painful ascetic life," as they saw themselves in the picture album mentioned above. They did strike me as simple minded in the sense that their minds were possessed by a single concept—religion—rather than by a complex of ideas. And I was struck by their absolute lack of curiosity about the outside world. By way of contrast, my guide on Easter Island, who had never left the island, was most inquisitive about the world beyond that little sea-locked dot of land in the Pacific. And even the isolated, uneducated jungle-imprisoned natives of the remote Amazon village of Benjamin Constant asked me a question or two about the wide world beyond. But from the residents of Athos there were no such inquiries.

The monks, however, for the most part accepted outside visitors in a reasonably hospitable manner; and never did they ask for a donation, but we always offered one, which was gratefully and graciously received. At most of the monasteries we visited, the monks patiently, and in some cases proudly, showed us the important manuscripts, valuables, and relics—a task they must have performed thousands of times—and they readily accepted our presence at their religious services.

Our visit fortunately took place in May, a time of year when only about five or ten people spent the night at each of the main monasteries. Later in the summer, during "high season," as many as fifty visitors per monastery would impose on the hospitality of the monks. That was back in 1973, but those days are now over. Too many casual curiosity seekers, who taxed the hospitality and patience of the monks, overran Athos every summer; and some of those representatives of "the world" occasionally pilfered objects from the monasteries. In 1977 the Greek government decided to restrict the total number of visitors to ten a day and to limit their stay to four days. Moreover, visitors were required to show a "provable" religious and scientific interest in Athos. (As sight-seeing ships with women aboard had fallen into the practice of drawing too close to Mount Athos, the government also found it necessary to decree that boats carrying females had to remain at least five hundred yards away from the coast of the holy peninsula.)

Our reception at the monasteries ranged from indifferent to warm. When we arrived at Dionysiou our hosts served us water, ouzo, coffee, and a "glyco"—orange slices in jam. That monastery was not only the most hospitable but also the most civilized: we enjoyed there such amenities as flush toilets and toilet paper. Moreover, the food at Dionysiou was the best we found at Athos. Dinner was a fish dish with a tangy sauce, good bread, and a decent dry wine. But what the meal provided in taste it lacked in atmosphere, for on the refectory walls were pictured The Last Supper, which recalled intimations of mortality, and a graphic mural showing demons pulling people down toward the waiting fangs of a dragon. To add to the visual reminders of one's vulnerability was the ominous-sounding voice of a monk who, in an endless monotone, read a long liturgy during the meal—the only talk permitted while dining.

More typical of the food at Athos was the tasteless dinner of cold pea beans, salty and wrinkly olives, and bread and water served at Grand Lavra. It was at that monastery, however, that John Covel, the 1677 visitor, found "the best monkish fare that could be gotten," including "excellent fish (severall ways), oyl, salet, beanes, hortechokes . . . good wine (a sort of small claret) and we always drank most plentifully." Twenty-nine years later, however, William Martin Leake blamed the poor diet at Athos for the "cutaneous disorders and ruptures [which] are very common among the monks."

These days it is the health of the entire community rather than simply the well-being of individual monks that is worrisome. The monastic settlement is gradually wasting away. During the fifteenth and sixteenth centuries, the forty active monasteries housed forty thousand monks. In 1963, when Athos celebrated its millennium, some two thousand monks remained on the peninsula; by 1973, the year of my visit, the number had dwindled to around fifteen hundred, the youngest of them, with few exceptions, in their fifties. Sacheverell Sitwell has suggested that the population of the Holy Mountain is reproduced "by ritual process near to parthenogenesis." Whatever the process it no longer works fast enough to give Athos a future, for you can see there a living—and dying—example of "the waning of the middle ages."

It is a rare and poignant thing to see tangible, definitive signs of the end of an era or of a species or race. One such unusual ending occurred in June 1844 when fourteen men went to Eldey, a volcanic speck some ten miles off the coast of Iceland, to hunt the great auk. On landing at the island, the men managed to find two of the birds, which they slaughtered, and one auk egg, which they smashed. That was the very end of the line for that species, for no live auk has ever again been found: a race of living things became extinct just then and there. The process of extinction at Athos is slower but, I think, no less sure.

Some years ago I saw displayed in connection with an exhibit at the British Museum a remarkable article entitled "The Last Man" published in the Hobart, Tasmania, *Town Mercury* on December 28, 1864. The story begins: "At the last ball at Government-house, Hobart Town, there appeared the last male aboriginal inhabitant of Tasmania. He was accompanied by three aboriginal women . . . not of such an age or such an appearance as to justify the expectation of any future addition to their number." This sort of extinction—that of the Tasmanians and, prospectively, that of the Athonites—strikes close to home, too close, in fact, for you realize that your group, too, is subject to disappearance from the face of the earth and the body of the universe. As Ernest Becker so starkly—and, sad to say, not wrongly—suggested in *The Denial of Death*, "the Creator may not care any more for the destiny of man or the self-perpetuation of individual men than He seems to have cared for the dinosaurs or the Tasmanians."

Such, I think, is the pathos of Athos. You find there "the tonality of death," as E.M. Cioran phrased it in a passage analyzing why hermits retreat from the world. That death tone, the end-of-an-era feeling as described in the Hobart *Town Mercury*, is especially vivid at Athos. There, it is a civilization—rather than a race—which is vanishing before your eyes. It is perhaps that "momento mori"—even more than the temptations of Athos as an alternative to the life of the world—which leads you to take the journey within as you travel around the Holy Mountain. For those of us mired in "the world," an Athos-type way of life is beyond possibility: like the Athens painter—that real life Zorba—we met at Stavronikita at the beginning of the journey, we who have lived in the world are too spoiled by it to become Athonites in attitude, let along *in toto*. It is, then, less the living Athos that haunts us as it is the dying one: the decay and disappearance of an entire community a millennium old reminds us of our own mortality—and of every man's.

Shortly after describing how Xerxes built his canal across Athos, Herodotus relates how the king began to weep while gazing at his fleet and at his men massed for battle on the plains by the Hellespont. Asked why he cries, Xerxes replies, "There came upon me a sudden pity, when I thought of the shortness of man's life, and considered that of all this host, so numerous as it is, not one will be alive when a hundred years are gone by." So it is at the Holy Mountain for both monks and visitors alike, and such is the awareness reached at the end of the journey within which one travels during the course of a visit to that Greek peninsula, so remote and isolated in space and time, known as Mount Athos. May Zorba's blackbird caw his call to us all—"Kyrie eleison."